JAZZY JUMBO PUZZLE BOOK

400 BRAIN GAMES FOR EVERY DAY

Andrews McMeel
PUBLISHING®

Play these other great puzzle books by USA TODAY:

USA TODAY Sudoku Super Challenge

USA TODAY Crossword Super Challenge

USA TODAY Logic Super Challenge

USA TODAY Jumbo Puzzle Book
Super Challenge

USA TODAY Sudoku Super Challenge 2

USA TODAY Crossword Super Challenge 2

USA TODAY Logic Super Challenge 2

USA TODAY Jumbo Puzzle Book
Super Challenge 2

USA TODAY Crossword Super Challenge 3

USA TODAY Jumbo Puzzle Book
Super Challenge 3

USA TODAY Logic Super Challenge 3

USA TODAY Sudoku Super Challenge 3

USA TODAY Sudoku and Variants
Super Challenge

USA TODAY Word Fill-In Super Challenge

USA TODAY Teatime Crosswords

USA TODAY Sunshine Sudoku

USA TODAY Lazy Day Logic

Play more at puzzles.usatoday.com or by downloading our FREE apps!

(Get them on Google Play or iTunes or just scan the
QR codes below with your smartphone camera.)

For hours of mind-pumping brain games, we offer this eclectic mix of word and number puzzles: traditional crosswords, logic, sudoku, Word Roundup, and Hidato. This hefty tome includes enough puzzles to work one per day for a year's worth of brain fitness. We can't promise better brain function, but you will enjoy hours of fun and entertainment.

Happy puzzling!

CONTENTS

LAST ACT

By Mark McClain

ACROSS

1 Anticipate
6 Dull sound
10 Includes
13 Scold
14 Italian salami city
16 Noah's boat
17 Instance of excessive press coverage
19 Flowery necklace
20 Pooh's gloomy companion
21 Small globs
22 Short-lived craze
23 Castle defense
25 Requests for help
27 "What's Happening!!" protagonist
30 Letters on forever stamps
31 Recruit
34 Hayley Williams genre
35 State where Juneteenth originated
38 Yummy
39 "Fernando" group
41 Bus place
43 Bus place
44 Novelists and schemers devise them
46 Indian metropolis
48 Observance before a holiday
49 Group of seven
51 ___ wrestling
52 Exit sign color
53 Follow as a result
55 Morning TV host Kelly
57 Color akin to beige
59 "The Accidental Tourist" author Tyler
61 Thickened area of skin
65 Yes, to Yves
66 Intermediate socioeconomic group
68 Caterer's coffee dispenser
69 Prefix suggesting a bargain
70 Not available
71 Disreputable newspaper
72 Sharp blow
73 Tool buildings

DOWN

1 Highest point
2 "This is fun!"
3 "Shrill" star Bryant
4 "Bad apple," for example
5 Remove by ripping
6 ___ Fridays
7 Ranch bunch
8 Take the top off of
9 Stunt stand-in
10 Maggie or Lexie, to Meredith Grey
11 Carpet installer's calculation
12 Slide out of control
15 Agree
18 Came to a halt
24 Made excessive demands on
26 "Sadly . . ."
27 Gathers
28 Leisurely walk
29 Posting with a "required skills" section
32 Kitchen appliance
33 Used a keyboard
36 King Kong, e.g.
37 Clean energy type
40 Mail-directing abbr.
42 Twice plus one
45 Bagel option
47 Noticeable effects
50 Simple tops
54 Provide funding for
56 He has 99 names
57 Guided excursion
58 Mystical energy field
60 Poet ___ St. Vincent Millay
62 Mendota or Monona, in Madison
63 Like some eBay items
64 Nine-digit IDs
67 "I get that a ___"

TEST GROUP

By Gail Grabowski

ACROSS

1 Play loudly
6 Springing movement
10 Part of a deck
14 Presentation stand
15 Operatic solo
16 Ingredient in some bar soaps
17 Cause a rift between
19 Vague amount
20 Pulled up a chair
21 Fuss's rhyming partner
22 Ab strengthener
24 TV correspondent Marsh
25 Supermarket section with a slicer
26 Not sharp
28 The "P" in a PG rating
32 Mari Copeny's city
33 Brought into the world
34 ___ Alto, California
35 Letter before kappa
36 Attaches, in a way
37 Singer Redding
38 Basic part of speech
39 Boring routines
40 Holey kitchen utensil
41 Sovereign rulers
43 Mystery or romance
44 Defeat decisively
45 Lightbulb unit
46 Image problem
49 Bit of chocolate
50 Fill with wonder
53 Continent with 11 time zones
54 Gas stove flame
57 Knitting material
58 Much-admired person
59 Regions
60 Risked a ticket
61 Girls Who ___
62 Downright mean

DOWN

1 Cradles and cribs
2 Voice actress ___ Jill Miller
3 "Be that ___ may . . ."
4 MLK's title (Abbr.)
5 Periodic table listing
6 Go unrenewed
7 Historical periods
8 Go public with
9 Guides for dressmakers
10 "Here's a perfect example . . ."
11 Much of the time
12 Tomato often used for tomato paste
13 Thought-provoking
18 Family reunion attendee
23 ___ Miss
24 Get groceries, for example
25 Has the courage
26 Produce flowers
27 Illuminated
28 Puts on an unhappy face
29 ___ tots
30 Still in the running
31 Draw the short straw, say
32 "Works for me"
33 ___ out (say suddenly)
36 Team photo, e.g.
40 Fixed course of action
42 Eggs on sushi
43 Trot or pace, for a horse
45 In one piece
46 Small bodies of water
47 Letters of urgency
48 In ___ straits
49 Lump of dirt
50 Quite some time
51 "I can't hear you"
52 Website that becomes a name if you add a B at the beginning
55 Wedding phrase
56 Investment initials

I HAVE AN IDEA!

By Evan Kalish

ACROSS

1 Loud crowd sound
5 Insect in a hive
8 Actress Sedgwick
12 Ye ___ Shoppe
13 Verbally instructed
14 Another name for the Oceti Sakowin
15 Nowhere close to drifting off
17 Effect's precursor
18 Change over time
19 "Wait Wait . . . Don't Tell Me!" airer
21 Hair goop
22 Lion's lair
23 Rules and ___
26 Prefix for "mobile"
28 Protective car features
31 Defamation in print
34 Small complaints to "pick"
35 PED ___
37 "___ Unbound" (Aisha Saeed novel)
38 Book-loving Disney heroine
39 Faucet annoyance
40 Ride some waves
41 Malevolent
42 Seasons, in a way
43 Cherished child, e.g.
46 A leap one has 366 days
47 "Say more!"
48 Olokun's domain
51 Lacking sufficient lighting
53 Airport screening org.
55 Five-cent piece
57 Wear away over time
59 Trip that's an anagram of "reloading"
62 Apple throwaways
63 Lodging options
64 Bhutan's continent
65 Was sure of
66 Letters before an alias
67 Exclamation on a fun ride

DOWN

1 Participated in crew
2 Pizza fruit
3 Item that doesn't come standard
4 Actor's demo video
5 Constricting snake
6 Deer family member
7 Genesis location
8 Korean carmaker
9 Encouraging phrase
10 Bit of deceit
11 Skating jump
13 Jacket fabric
14 Clean with hard rubbing
16 Singer Lavigne
20 Unpack grammatically
24 Swiss city or lake
25 Traveling in a ship
27 Filing deadline
28 Many a phone pic
29 "That should suffice"
30 Foul mood
31 ___ Vegas, New Mexico
32 "OK, no longer in bed!"
33 "Whip It" director Drew
36 Navigation aid
38 Beverages on tap
42 Poet Sanchez
44 Romantic outings
45 1619 Project journalist Nikole Hannah-___
48 Smidgen
49 "___, meenie . . ."
50 Unwelcome pool growth
51 52-card unit
52 Metal in steel
54 Word aptly hidden in Marian Anderson's name
56 Paw part
58 Drops on morning grass
60 Printer cartridge stuff
61 Genetic strands

DO ME A SOLID

By Zhouqin Burnikel

ACROSS

1 Unflattering press
6 Like an overcast sky
10 Chess greats, for short
13 Submit tax documents online
14 Neighbor of West Virginia
15 Italy's outline resembles one
16 Popular jiaozi filling
18 ___ paratha
19 General Motors safety service
20 Unnamed person
22 Like ___ of bricks
24 English muffin alternative
25 SoCal area where the Chicano Blowouts took place
29 "Too bad"
32 Ballet skirts
33 Twitter post
34 Grand ___ Opry
37 Seafood in California rolls
38 Second-row chess pieces
39 Name that's a number minus a letter
40 Sombrero, e.g.
41 Medical lab workers
42 Blow some cash
43 Bet requiring precision
45 Criticizes harshly
46 Break off
48 Cautionary ___
50 Frida Kahlo or Georgia O'Keeffe
53 Title that means "enlightened one"
57 ___ buco
58 Flag-carrying team
61 Horse strap
62 Garbage can emanation
63 Chillingly strange
64 Summer time zone for Ga.
65 Deli counter call
66 Great bargain

DOWN

1 Ask earnestly
2 ___-Caribbean
3 "Let's Talk About Love" singer Celine
4 "In addition . . ."
5 Vacation vehicles, often
6 Leave amateur status behind
7 Greek letter that sounds like a verb
8 Haughty manners
9 Video game composer Shimomura
10 MLB fielding awards
11 Deer with a dewlap
12 Bar seat
15 Trite
17 Statistician's stuff
21 Help with a heist, e.g.
23 "Another problem?!"
25 Carve in stone, say
26 Distinctive vibe
27 Trip for a country's leader
28 Butter container
30 Chickens' mothers
31 "How to Get Away With Murder" student
33 Mediator's asset
35 Allowed to borrow
36 Finishes
38 Bench press muscle, for short
39 Place for a full-body scrub
41 Like the taste of umeboshi
42 Large hammers
44 Gas used in arc lamps
45 Vague memory
46 Reproductive unit of some plants
47 Made less onerous
49 Cancel a launch
51 Anna Schwartz's subj.
52 Was borne
54 "My Boo," e.g.
55 Long-eared hopper
56 Jessye Norman delivery
59 Brine-cured salmon
60 Costa ___ Sol

TWO-TIMERS

By Caitlin Reid

ACROSS

1 Performs in character
5 Shape of a rainbow
8 Losing streak
13 U group
14 Snoozefest
16 Region of East Asia
17 Exclusive seating section
19 Extremely nice person
20 Chops into cubes
21 Shoulder ___
23 "___ me every time!"
24 Apt anagram of 1-Across
26 Succumb to heat
28 "Gimme five!"
31 Statement before hitting the hay
35 Jamie ___ Curtis
36 School fundraising grp.
37 "I don't believe it!"
39 Classic case
43 Warning signals
44 Eden exile
45 Use a bench
46 Anagram of "winter's O"
48 Burger side
50 Account owner
51 ___ reversal
53 Places for 29-Down
56 Beam of light
58 New Mexico river
61 Small openings
63 Like many nonprofits
66 Prefix for "physicist"
67 Sportscaster Andrews
68 Animal's male parent
69 Hardly tidy
70 Prefix for "affected"
71 Eyelid bump

DOWN

1 CIO partner
2 "Dang it!"
3 Cab
4 Exterior finish on some houses
5 Deep, dark pit
6 Burglarize
7 Something gathered from a field
8 Genre that came before rocksteady
9 Like goals sought over years and years
10 Goad
11 Be introduced to
12 Pen ___ (friends to write to)
15 School tests
18 Gather from a field
22 Descriptor for some special editions
25 Puente, el Rey del Timbal
27 Headey who played Cersei Lannister
28 Beauty retailer
29 Skin treatments
30 Resident of Plano or Llano
32 Manufacturer
33 Big name in cola
34 New Haven student
36 Wall decoration
38 "___ just say . . ."
40 Pants
41 Some German cars
42 ". . . said no one ___"
47 Full of rage
48 Bodybuilder's gesture
49 Break
52 Unwraps
53 Email filter target
54 Get ready for a photo
55 The "A" in MFA
57 It has three feet
59 Fail to mention
60 Agile
62 Nondairy milk source
64 Top number on a grandfather clock
65 Golfing peg

INK IN

By Brooke Husic & Evan Kalish

ACROSS

1 Title for a German woman
5 Turquoise relative
9 Ages ___
12 Droop
13 Support financially
14 Address starting with "http"
15 Collared shirts
16 Errs
17 Bigelow beverage
18 Nikita Gill's "People ___ Homes"
19 Buss up shut, e.g.
20 Kitchen professional
21 Canadian author of speculative fiction such as "The Handmaid's Tale"
24 Bit of ink
25 Balance-facilitating organ
26 2017 reboot starring Justina Machado
33 Rental car option
35 Poisonous substance
36 "The Big Sick" actress Kazan
37 UV-blocking molecule
38 Exterior of a ship or a seed
39 HP competitor
40 Part of the symbol for Sagittarius
41 French article
42 Some health professionals
43 Dorm community-builders
44 Yin's counterpart
46 Abbr. for a corporation
47 Salad with eggs and avocado
48 Law
52 Promotes insufficiently
56 Cambodia's continent
57 Scared
58 Quantity of paper
59 Fabric shelter
60 Bitter beers
61 Donate
62 Chapters of history

DOWN

1 Fauna's counterpart
2 Measuring tool
3 Margaret Peterson Haddix's "___ the Hidden"
4 Home to many Haudenosaunee
5 Get ___ in the door
6 Numerical target
7 Ill-suited
8 Some Instagram posts
9 Officially approved
10 Desire for more and more
11 "When I Am Older" singer in "Frozen II"
12 Musubi meat
16 Fridays for Future activist
20 Nail polish layer
22 Super cool
23 Withdraw gradually
26 Bad smells
27 Prefix for "technology"
28 Old's opposite
29 Wheel bar
30 Up to, informally
31 Sauce that may include chocolate
32 Electric ___ (shocking fishes)
33 Rise dramatically
34 Musician Furman
39 Employ voice-to-text software
42 Palindromic name
45 Stabilizing muscles
46 "Hello, ___" (Adele lyric)
47 Corp. heads
48 Montenegrin, e.g.
49 Lead-in to "friendly"
50 Mother of Solange and Beyonce
51 Food, informally
52 Letters on a Crystal Dunn jersey
53 Org. with icing penalties
54 Female deer or kangaroo
55 Graduation garland

FRONT WHEELS

By Susan Smolinsky &
Zhouqin Burnikel

ACROSS

1 Takes a bow, say
6 Blunder
10 Suffix for "Oktober"
14 "Come See ___ Me"
(Supremes hit)
15 "A League of Their Own"
actress Petty
16 Lightbulb, in a cartoon
17 Scorpio and Pisces, in
astrology
19 Movie
20 Ingredient in soap
21 Bowls over
22 Some livestock
24 Favoritism
25 Costume designer ___ E. Carter
26 Pastry chef's specialty
29 Alligator relatives
32 Promotes aggressively
33 Camping shelter
34 ___ versa
36 Fat
37 Self-promotes aggressively
38 They might get inflated
39 Alone
40 Get shellacked
41 Outdo
42 Bracket stat
44 What chicks and ducks and
geese better do, in song
45 Commands to attack
46 Lavish party
47 App on which "Old Town
Road" first became popular
50 ___ market
51 Non-friend
54 Black-and-white cookie
55 Marching band
accompaniment
58 Suffix for an attendee
59 ___ code
60 Performed by skaters
61 Activist Braden
62 Phone transmission
63 Hockey star Ted

DOWN

1 Cry loudly
2 Website with auctions
3 Musical symbol
4 ___ date
5 Stretches to the limit
6 Goes by jet
7 They can be turned into
lumber
8 Vase with a base
9 Breakfast sandwich bases
10 Candy bar named for a Big
Apple thoroughfare
11 Manuscript modification
12 Put on 2-Down
13 Domesticated
18 Goodie bag contents
23 Cash dispenser
24 Large retailer
25 Cooking appliance
26 V close pals
27 Parcel out
28 Eucalyptus eater

29 Bring to an end
30 West African river
31 Thoroughly clean
33 Horse gaits
35 Annual athletic award
37 Pet celebrated on Oct. 27
41 Eight-sided figure
43 2011 animated movie set in
Brazil
44 Clairvoyant
46 Root-beer-and-ice-cream
treat
47 Draped Roman garment
48 The 26th element
49 Razor-sharp
50 Show off muscles
51 Fall flat
52 Black-and-white whale
53 Paradise in Genesis
56 Miner's find
57 Game with 108 cards

PAY UP

By Lynn Lempel

ACROSS

1 Brink
6 TV star Roman
10 "Thank goodness!"
14 Wield
15 Lion's sound
16 Prefix for "dynamic"
17 Reason to get a new ID card
19 "Monsoon Wedding" director Mira
20 "I've heard enough!"
21 Bakery appliance
22 Dwelled
23 Tiger marking
26 Wood for old piano keys
28 Some monthly mail
32 Puts into piles, say
35 Mention as a reference
36 Squeak remover
37 Job title abbr.
38 Number with a dollar sign
40 Toothed tool
41 Mind-reading letters
42 Arbor Day planting
43 Portended
44 Unit counted for graduation
48 Get really excited or mad
49 Evergreen plants with stiff, spiky leaves
52 Device for detecting underwater objects
54 "Oh, got it now"
56 Sign before Virgo
58 Notable time periods
59 Typo-catching feature
62 Angry monologue
63 Suffix suggesting smallness
64 Major artery
65 Nonkosher sandwiches
66 Job title abbr.
67 Rawls or King of golf

DOWN

1 Express strong emotions
2 Physicals, e.g.
3 Send as payment
4 Test for an MBA applicant
5 ". . . and so forth" (Abbr.)
6 Take a trip
7 First-class
8 Like a compass needle
9 Wrath
10 Grilled sandwich with Italian bread
11 Big burden to bear
12 Lake west of Buffalo
13 Set of blanks on "Wheel of Fortune"
18 People whose flag features a black circle divided into quadrants with a black dot in each
22 Spot for an earring
24 Dead-end routines
25 "___ no use!"
27 Unit of computer memory
29 More frosty
30 Enjoy
31 Flexible Flyer vehicle
32 Builder's detail, for short
33 ". . . approximately"
34 Loathsome
38 Make ready
39 Slips from cashiers
40 Campus mil. group
42 Ruler of old Russia
43 Big name in pens
45 Ridicules
46 Fabric with small holes
47 Face-off
50 Fully attentive
51 Splinter groups
52 Person from Belgrade or Kragujevac
53 Taken by mouth
55 Adjusts using a dial, perhaps
57 Acceptable
59 Salt source
60 Hailed vehicle
61 Tool for tilling

IN THE ORCHESTRA

By Gail Grabowski

ACROSS

1 Be in charge of
5 Pulled apart
9 World-weary sounds
14 Water balloons, say
15 Spilled salt, to some
16 Fields of expertise
17 Completely engrossed
18 Posh affair
19 Coffee concoction
20 High-ranking officers
23 "Chocolat" actress Olin
24 Was in charge of
25 Stat for a student
28 "To be fair . . ."
32 Complain
33 Nocturnal flying predator
36 Charlie's Angels, for example
37 Make impure
38 Easterlies, e.g.
42 Like the Pantheon
43 Stretch ___
44 Word before "bar" or "pride"
45 Very much
46 Revenue source for magazines
49 Female fowl
50 Part of FWIW
51 Two truths and ___
54 Used one's influence to gain an advantage
60 "All done!"
62 Art ___
63 Site of a hamster wheel
64 Last Greek letter
65 Small flying insect
66 Victor's shout
67 Flag holders
68 Literary governess Jane
69 License prerequisite, perhaps

DOWN

1 "No ___, no foul"
2 Something checked on a phone
3 More than enough
4 Very fond
5 Ancient 42-Across attire
6 "Rock the Casbah" actor Sharif
7 Depend
8 Make possible
9 According to some food theorists, chicken soup is one
10 401(k) alternatives
11 Leaves
12 Beret or bowler
13 U-turn from NNW
21 Kilt pattern
22 Hummingbird feeder color
26 Bamboo eater
27 Fidgety
29 The Grand Canyon State, on scoreboards
30 Nothing at all
31 Works hard
32 Singer Ella
33 The "O" in O Magazine
34 Composed prose
35 Iced tea garnish
37 ___ garage
39 Florist's delivery vehicle, often
40 Chill in the air
41 ABC show for early risers, for short
46 Verizon ISP
47 ___ up (unearth)
48 Bring forth
50 Kennel pests
52 Very impressed
53 Some frozen waffles
55 Strongly encourage
56 Declare false
57 ___ tissue
58 Lug
59 Text status
60 Do better than
61 Medical grp. with copays

THE SOUND OF MUSIC

By Patrick Blindauer

ACROSS

1 Holders of fodder
6 Word of greeting
9 Lip-soothing stuff
13 Distributor of the arcade game Dig Dug
14 Lymph ___
15 "Understood"
16 Museum display
18 Jobs for those who jam
19 "See you later, alligator!"
20 Turn on the spot
21 Destroy like the Hulk
22 Not in peril
23 Brainstorming goal
25 Pariah
30 "Don't worry about me"
31 Food for woodpeckers
32 Name of a Stooge
33 Bit of bank business
34 Alternative to Liz
36 One of 26.2 in a marathon
37 Night ___
38 WhatsApp message
39 Not particularly good or bad
40 Ocean swimmer
44 Translation of "vino"
45 "___ Well That Ends Well"
46 Out of bed
49 Actress O'Connor
51 Org. with dunks
54 Biblical garden
55 Sofkey ingredient
57 Unit of lightning
58 "Don't ___ on My Parade"
59 Unit of gem weight
60 Partner in a pact
61 Hoppy happy hour order
62 Wipe away

DOWN

1 Tearful-sounding car
2 "It was nothing"
3 Past the due date
4 Rocky resource in Catan
5 Half-dozen purchase
6 Handbag type
7 Book printings
8 "Are we there ___?"
9 Whopper counterpart
10 Europe neighbor
11 Lower limbs
12 Breathable fabric
14 Skin care brand
17 LP player
21 Hardens
22 Momentarily
24 Call of ___ (video game series)
25 Word before "talk" or "print"
26 Foamy drink
27 Like some rural Pennsylvanians
28 Unaccompanied
29 Casual top
30 Its capital is Des Moines
33 The "L" in LACMA
34 Fava, e.g.
35 Like some hard drives
36 Green growth on stones
38 Birthday sharer
39 "___ is golden"
41 Number of questions in a guessing game
42 Quickly entered the room
43 Parasitic insect
46 McEntire in the Country Music Hall of Fame
47 Object of adoration
48 Have available for purchase
50 Falco who played Carmela Soprano
51 Romance writer Roberts
52 Upper undergarments
53 Poker bet
55 Financial planning initials
56 "The Price Is Right" prize

BACK GARDEN

By Zhouqin Burnikel

ACROSS

1 Airport queue vehicle
4 Cool and collected
8 Island home to the world's biggest nightclub
13 Tributary of the Colorado River
15 Antioxidant-rich fruit
16 Party all night, perhaps
17 "No thanks"
18 Helsinki citizen
19 Courtroom excuse
20 Glass vessels with stoppers
23 Seasonal mall worker
25 Quarterback Manning
26 Used a papasan
27 "That's that"
32 Yum cha beverage
33 Google Play purchases
34 Christmas song word
37 "___ several seats"
39 Takes a tumble
42 Tip jar inserts
44 ___ folder (social media stockpile)
46 Viscous substance
48 Actress Lindley
49 Distance learning outcome, perhaps
53 Comment further
56 Light brown color
57 Raced in a sledding event
58 Aerial shipping method
63 Bruce Wayne lives in one
64 Participate on Election Day
65 Super
68 Occupied
69 Consumer advocate Brockovich
70 Stuffing herb
71 Carried around
72 Take a break
73 Curtain holder

DOWN

1 Sci-fi film FX, often
2 Purpose
3 Relief pitcher's nightmare
4 Barista's workplace
5 Hyaluronic ___ (skin care ingredient)
6 Narrow way
7 Chopped into small pieces
8 Like Nowruz
9 Conveyor part
10 Climbing vines
11 Serengeti equine
12 Elite party attendees
14 Dog breed from Honshu
21 Nothing
22 Tavern offering
23 "Only a ___ deals in absolutes" ("Star Wars" quote)
24 Lineup of the best players
28 Choose
29 Host of Tiny Desk Concerts
30 Endorse digitally
31 Bathroom, in Leeds
35 Marathoner's snack
36 Flood-blocking structure
38 Rock genre
40 "Selah and the Spades" director Tayarisha
41 Lawn repair material
43 Lawn repair material
45 Came through the door
47 FIFA Player of the Century co-winner
50 Young fellow
51 "___ Loved a Man" (Aretha Franklin hit)
52 Sikhism's 10
53 Own up to
54 Pipe-clearing brand
55 Coffee break snack
59 Tip of an airplane
60 Passed-down stories
61 Ailment suffix
62 Ductwork opening
66 Braggart's display
67 Word before "Robin" or "Lobster"

SALTY LANGUAGE

By Tracy Gray

ACROSS

1 Adjective describing the universe
5 Overtake
9 Make a watercolor
14 Not up to much
15 Cinco + tres
16 ___ but goodie
17 Not too long from now
18 Follow closely
19 Bits of superstition
20 TikTok, e.g.
21 Dining room cabinet
23 Music device
25 Grooves in the ground
26 "Send me!"
29 Mishandle
32 "___ (You Can See Forever)" (Streisand song)
36 Word after "canola" or "castor"
38 Prescription amount
39 ___ Records (Sony Music label)
40 Home care assistant
41 Nosh on nachos, say
42 "SpongeBob SquarePants" exclamation
46 Safari sighting
48 Pocketed illegally
49 Cranberry and crimson, e.g.
51 Made-to-order
55 File paperwork for house damages, say
60 2019 event for Pinterest, for short
61 Crunchyroll offering
62 Boxing enclosure
63 Archer Stutzman
64 Place to get a milkshake
65 Roti flour
66 Spooky-sounding Pennsylvania city
67 Big Dipper's seven
68 Look intently
69 Salt, in chemistry class

DOWN

1 Some passport stamps
2 Take in
3 Bunny ___ (gentle ski trail)
4 J's point value in Words With Friends
5 Road crew's concern
6 Fruit in Amazonian cuisine
7 Leg part
8 Sun-related
9 Floating basketball hoop, e.g.
10 "You're so close!"
11 Fateful March day for Caesar
12 The whole ___ yards
13 School challenge
21 Building block of life
22 Country west of Haiti
24 It may be dirty or sticky
27 Attire
28 Whales with strong teeth
30 Corkscrew shape
31 Stash away
32 Poem type
33 Biblical boat maker
34 ___ Spumante (Italian wine)
35 Missile thrown at a board
37 French article
40 Tennis stat
42 Concert starters
43 "Today" host Kotb
44 "Close, but ___"
45 Grad
47 Pre-foundation layer
50 Leftover food morsel
52 Bejeweled crown
53 Vision-related
54 Place to stay
55 Inflates
56 Kilogram, for example
57 "Wine Country" star Fey
58 Low-calorie, in adspeak
59 Anagram of "neat"
63 "___ in Black"

OK THEN

By Evan Kalish

ACROSS
1 Phone programs
5 "Hollaback Girl" singer Stefani
9 Former member, for short
13 Island where many Chamorros live
14 Tripoli's country
16 Best friend of Carmen, Bridget and Tibby
17 Gymnast nicknamed the "Sparrow from Minsk"
19 Villain's secret hideaway
20 Thoroughly read
21 Resists
23 Six-point plays (Abbr.)
24 Enjoy a meal
25 Part of a play
28 "what I mean when I say I'm sharpening my ___" (Ewing poem)
34 Absolutely rocks an outfit, e.g.
36 Siete minus cuatro
37 Animated explorer
38 No longer wild
39 Blow like a volcano
40 Lambs' mothers
41 TV host Kelly
42 Inform
43 "DO NOT ___" (chalkboard plea)
44 Persian poet/astronomer/ mathematician
47 Stanley Cup org.
48 Homophone of one vegetable; anagram of another
49 Physique, for short
51 Decorative pattern
54 Plucked instruments
57 Yaki ___ (noodle dish)
58 Risky football play
62 Do some karaoke
63 Drink often topped with foam art
64 Berry popular in Brazil
65 Typists hit them
66 Free passes in tournaments
67 Payment to a landlord

DOWN
1 A while ___
2 Orange juice option
3 Summon via beeper
4 Like some phones
5 Alternative to matte
6 Down to the ___
7 Recede
8 Big Apple college
9 Like some restrooms
10 "The Half of It" star Lewis
11 Word after "storage" or "AC"
12 The Red Planet
15 In the beginning
18 "Great job!"
22 Pen fluid
24 One way to breathe
25 Prefix for "turf"
26 Assertion
27 Florida city on a bay
29 Feature of Rogue's hair
30 Sincerely
31 Person from Des Moines, e.g.
32 Just-picked
33 "Self-Portrait with ___" (Amrita Sher-gil painting)
35 Young animals
39 Gasoline additive
43 Show feelings
45 Small barrel
46 Tolerates
50 Capital of Senegal
51 Dawn's opposite
52 "Nurse Jackie" star Falco
53 Japanese electronics giant
54 Location
55 Jollof grain
56 Digitized document
59 Capture
60 Pig's place
61 Collection of sewing items

PACKING ON THE PDA

By Zhouqin Burnikel

ACROSS

1 Baby donkey
5 Signs of surgery
10 Narrow-waisted insect
14 "The Good Dinosaur" dinosaur
15 Fortuneteller's deck
16 "Oh, what a shame!"
17 Skeletons in the closet
20 Chicago White ___
21 "It's probable that . . ."
22 Industrial tub
23 Mecca resident, e.g.
25 Scarlet Witch actress Elizabeth
27 Sentence subject, often
29 Platypus feature
30 "Hey, you're here!"
33 Lightweight two-wheeler
35 Image that might be tapped
39 Dr. Martens products
41 Cha chaan teng drink
42 Garden shed item
43 Rainer Maria genre
44 Province north of Montana
47 Bonnie, to Christy Plunkett
48 "You betcha!"
49 Feb. 29, 2024 occurrence
50 Big-time player
51 Not look forward to
53 Competed in a super-G race
55 Insurance filings
57 Brokerage purchased by Morgan Stanley in 2020
60 Ladder part
61 Bandleader's shout
65 Shoe brand once owned by Reebok
66 Foot curve
67 Wear away
68 Immoral acts
69 Source of the pink in pickled turnips
70 Kept under wraps
71 Envelope-pushing

DOWN

1 Crazes that fizzle out quickly
2 Cookies in sleeves
3 Actress Davalos
4 ___ off (prune)
5 Athlete's place
6 Get well soon ___
7 Torah containers
8 Parks who wrote, "The only tired I was, was tired of giving in"
9 Estrogen, for example
10 "This means ___!"
11 Tylenol alternative
12 Evil personified
13 Attention-getting whisper
18 Flightless bird of old
19 Mobile phone
24 Foot or yard
26 Make a mistake
28 "I'm impressed!"
29 Goatees, e.g.
30 Do as you're told
31 Frequent GPS destination
32 Powwow performance
34 Little chirp
36 Presidential retreat
37 Dirty laundry might give one off
38 Orange Pixar fish
40 Oregon's capital
42 "Just tell me already!"
45 Pet shop purchases
46 Chill for a bit
52 "That's correct!"
54 Dry-___ board
55 Sideways-walking creature
56 Tempt
58 Toaster oven sound
59 Word before "money" or "chair"
62 Roth ___
63 One in a stroller
64 Altar statement

RUNNING STARTS

By Brooke Husic

ACROSS

1 "Funny tweet!"
4 Music releases such as "See. SZA.Run" and "S"
7 ___ crackers
13 Spanish for "gold"
14 Show the way
16 Flash photography effect
17 ___ Grande
18 Outskirts
19 "Nevertheless . . ."
20 Shortcomings
23 Make into law
24 Hydrogen's atomic number
25 Game with a "freeze" variant
28 Satirical news source
32 Quench
33 Nickname for Fenty Beauty's founder
34 "The Sisterhood of the Traveling Pants" screenwriter Delia
36 "Ah, the comfort of my own bed!"
41 Bird that might be orange and black
42 Even once
43 Requests
44 Uses a statistical model, perhaps
48 Garden tool
49 "Me day" destination
51 Lilith Fair musician (and homo-phone of a word in this clue)
53 "Spirited Away" production company
57 Profession
60 See 54-Down
61 Place for chapstick
62 WNBA venues
63 Wound remnant
64 Prefix for "friendly"
65 Phone-related request to a friend
66 Character in "Little Women" or "The 39 Clues"
67 Pale shade of brown

DOWN

1 "The Master's Tools Will Never Dismantle the Master's House" author Audre
2 Situate
3 Shower sponge
4 Voting-related
5 Mani partner
6 Herb in some pasta dishes
7 Wood texture
8 Tony winner ___ Elise Goldsberry
9 Totals up
10 Conversation opener
11 Anagram of "yea"
12 Got together with
15 Foxes' home
21 Milk tea ingredient
22 Pro's opposite
25 Milk tea flavor
26 Molecule part
27 Chromosome part
29 Friendly
30 Fury
31 Fuel replenishment ship

32 "I'm trying to listen!"
34 ___ out (barely got)
35 Outskirts
36 Singer Cyrus
37 ". . . ish"
38 Straight-legged gymnastics position
39 The "L" in UCLA
40 "What ___ Been Looking For"
44 DivaCup alternative
45 Tai ___ (martial art)
46 Pill form
47 ___ gel packets
49 Water vapor
50 Pocketbook
52 Make fun of
53 Dispatched
54 With 60-Across, "That's right"
55 Dolphin relative
56 Largest island in Micronesia
57 Feline
58 "Dog Days ___ Over" (Florence and the Machine song)
59 Latin for "king"

TOPIC-HEAVY

By Patrick Jordan

ACROSS

1 Corrosive substance
5 Casual discussion
9 Storm-tracking tool
14 Morrison who wrote, "No man should live without absorbing the sins of his kind"
15 Sharpen
16 Sharp
17 Velvety growth
18 Vowel after theta
19 Excessive want
20 Collectible magazine
23 Surprise, and then some
24 Beverage brand with an ursine mascot
25 Bit of protective gear
28 Daddy deer
30 Regulations involving deductions
33 Faucet
36 Site that takes bids
38 "Birds of Prey" actress Perez
39 Stuff that's neither plant nor animal
43 Curly-haired "Tomorrow" singer
44 Enjoy a game
45 Author Linda ___ Park
46 They're set and broken
49 Grp. that fights for rights
51 Sharp nickname on "Billions"
52 Woeful remark
54 No ifs, ___ or buts
57 Person living under a monarchy
61 Looked intently
64 Metropolis reporter Lane
65 Footwear company
66 Leading the other racers
67 Two fewer than thrice
68 Irritate
69 Musical groups
70 Disorderly situation
71 Make a cut in

DOWN

1 Money dispensers
2 Houses for chickens
3 Close-up map section
4 Track-and-field event
5 ___ seeds
6 Troublemaker
7 Amusing stunt
8 Crockery for serving oolong
9 Pasta sauce brand
10 Land area unit
11 Slated to give birth
12 Quieted a growling stomach
13 Ketchup color
21 1 or 2, but not 1.2
22 Home to Nemo and Dory
25 Some internet content
26 French goodbye
27 Surname on tractors
29 Org. for lawyers
31 Radiography site
32 Camp bed
33 Prom queen's headpiece
34 Addition to a building
35 City on Puerto Rico's southern coast
37 Chihuahua's bark
40 2016 Olympics city, for short
41 Time-honored works
42 ___ and cheese
47 When vampires sleep
48 Zigzagging ski event
50 Removes a blockage from
53 How a solo is played
55 "Speak of the ___!"
56 Octavia E. Butler's genre
57 Be a bookworm
58 Wagering factor
59 Finds a purpose for
60 27th U.S. president
61 Talk interminably
62 Vindicated shout
63 School of Buddhism

IT'S A TIE

By Gail Grabowski

ACROSS

1 Specialized, committee-wise
6 Missing, for short
10 Part of a wooden crate
14 Cash, slangily
15 Thinnest U.S. coin
16 Voicemail prompt
17 Spike in the electrical current
19 Learn by ___
20 Some SAT takers (Abbr.)
21 "Teen Spirit" star Fanning
22 Unlawful acts
24 "Turn the ___ Around" (Vicki Sue Robinson song)
25 Deliberately avoid
26 Soak up
29 Umbrellas and such
33 Relatives of ravens
34 Strong determination
35 Agricultural measure
36 Sushi staple
37 Penalized monetarily
38 ___-back (easygoing)
39 "Come ___!" (welcoming words)
40 Doesn't continue
41 Brief attempt
42 Train track foundations
44 Ignite
45 Provider of support
46 Engagement gift
47 Causes a stinging pain
50 Zebra's hair
51 "The Price Is Right" channel
54 Rain hard
55 Disreputable member of the family
58 Palo ___, California
59 Provider of support
60 Submarine tracking device
61 Put under a seat, say
62 Proof of homeownership
63 Sweepstakes submission

DOWN

1 Concert equipment
2 Bouncer's post
3 "___ it going?"
4 Word in a futbol chant
5 Professional pursuits
6 Chaperone, typically
7 Electricity carrier
8 Gasp in a text
9 Novelist who created Jack Reacher
10 Give false hope to
11 Weaving device
12 Initial poker stake
13 Driving range props
18 Big chunk
23 Be on the ballot
24 Archer's equipment
25 Events that might be held in garages
26 Memorizer of lines
27 41-Down singer Mars
28 Supreme Court justice Sotomayor
29 Watermelon coverings
30 Greeting in an inbox
31 Font similar to Helvetica
32 Color again
34 Like a good day for flying a kite
37 "This one stings"
41 2018 hit featuring Cardi B
43 Lunch menu letters
44 Garden hose problem
46 Competed in the Indy 500
47 Places to be pampered
48 Shed feathers
49 Prefix meaning "self"
50 "Mistakes were ___"
51 Penny
52 Member of a fairy tale trio
53 Agile
56 Fabricated statement
57 Word of endearment

UNITED FRONT

By Zhouqin Burnikel

ACROSS

1 "That doesn't ___ right"
5 $1,000,000, for short
8 Train for a boxing match
12 Spitballs, e.g.
13 Pleasant
14 Piece of garlic
15 Ballet garment
16 Wallet singles
17 Felt out of sorts
18 Moods
21 Listing of notables
24 ___ out a win
25 Tech hidden in "Cosmic Girls"
26 "The Big Short" actress Marisa
27 Long-winded diatribe
29 Red salad bar veggie
30 ___ Taylor (fashion brand)
31 Name that's another name in reverse
33 That woman
35 Video game series in which a hooded Mickey Mouse asks, "Say, fellas, did somebody mention the Door to Darkness?"
40 Place for a nap
41 Godmother, often
42 Leave slack-jawed
44 Noodle often eaten with a dipping sauce
47 Sets down
49 Renewable energy option
51 Timeline segment
52 Olivia Benson's profession
53 Muscle strengthened by dips
55 Totally uncalled for
58 Geographic reference book
59 Fragrant necklaces
60 Gravy imperfection
64 Makes a blunder
65 Narrow road
66 Storybook monster
67 Makes a blunder
68 The "O" in WHO (Abbr.)
69 Flimsy

DOWN

1 Plopped down
2 Large feathered runner
3 CPR administerer, often
4 Fluffy chocolate dessert
5 Dairy Queen Blizzard flavor
6 Slush Puppie alternative
7 Decrease
8 ___ pickings
9 Monitor closely
10 Exact retribution for
11 Website with threads
13 "To All the Boys I've Loved Before" actor Centineo
14 Sidewalk seating site
19 Pang
20 "Alrighty"
21 Org. for Simona Halep
22 Sound the horn
23 Prefix for "potent"
28 CoverGirl competitor
29 "It's freezing out here!"
32 Small stock purchase
34 Has sushi delivered, say
36 Timberwolves' org.
37 Working hard for the money
38 Fairy ___
39 Make a trade
43 Hosp. areas
44 Waste material
45 Sojourner Truth, for one
46 University in Waco
48 "Showtime at the ___"
50 Rainforest predator
52 Use swear words
54 "All ___" (legal drama)
56 Bumbling sorts
57 Goose bumps cause
61 "This is terrible"
62 Hosp. scan
63 Livestock enclosure

NATIONAL INTERESTS

By Mark McClain

ACROSS

1 Root vegetable used to make poi
5 Tegan's twin
9 Word hidden in "instrument"
14 Actress Bhatt
15 Female sheep
16 Take a break
17 The "T" in STEM
18 Conversate
19 Cove, e.g.
20 Mickey Guyton, for example
23 Not current
24 Thumbs-down vote
25 Love to bits
28 Birthstone whose first letter is the same as that of its month
30 Sandwich akin to a fluffernutter
33 Assumed name
34 Stretch of time
35 Length times width, for a rectangle
36 Alabama A&M, for example
39 Dinghy thingies
40 Tree with cones
41 Solving lifelines
42 Fast-food morsel
43 ___ out (allocate)
44 "A Ballerina's Tale" star Copeland
45 Barbie's beau
46 Device for cooling
47 Professional with a civil engineering degree, perhaps
54 Animal with a dromedary species
55 "___ relate"
56 App symbol
58 Plentiful
59 First word of some fairy tales
60 "___ shalt not . . ."
61 Disgusting
62 Require
63 Toilet paper label word

DOWN

1 Bit of body art, for short
2 Brother of Izzy and Max in "The Mortal Instruments"
3 Puerto ___
4 Iolani Palace island
5 Go with your third choice, say
6 Oscar or Emmy
7 Depend
8 Inquires
9 ___ cord
10 Like a grapefruit
11 Regulation
12 App buyer
13 Had a conference
21 Like Thor
22 Silly beyond belief
25 Rite site
26 Personal log
27 Porridge base
28 Express a view
29 Cover with concrete
30 Word processing command
31 TV legend White
32 Noisy birds
33 Beginning on
34 Peevish mood
35 With no alterations
37 Turn over
38 Beast with a horn or two
43 String of songs
44 ___ milk
45 Got down to pray, maybe
46 Metaphorical perch for an undecided person
47 The Dalai ___
48 Units of current, for short
49 Class covering supply and demand, for short
50 Wind direction indicator
51 Olive seeds
52 Repeat
53 Housetop
54 Fruit cocktail container
57 Pecan tree seed

LAND HOLDINGS

By Evan Kalish

ACROSS

1 Blocks of sticky notes
5 Mark from an old injury
9 Soothing lotion additive
13 Prayer leaders
15 "Cheerio!"
16 Have staying power
17 Surname in "Evita"
18 ". . . and we need it now!"
19 Preschool basics
20 Teacher's bonus offering
23 Manta, for example
24 History book sections
25 West African country
27 Selected
30 Just a ___ throw away
32 Genre for Missy Elliott
33 Manta, for example
37 Throat-clearing sound
39 Carly ___ Jepsen
40 Door-shutting sound
41 Pie variety
46 Prefix meaning "three"
47 Attention-grabbing
48 ___ potatoes
50 Judicial worker
51 Nuisance
52 Tightly wrapping snake
53 TV production teams
59 "Stranger Than Fiction" actress Thompson
61 ___ awake
62 Allowed
63 "You said it!"
64 "Sorry to say . . ."
65 Bird that might be "bald"
66 Ship fixture
67 They might be topped with marshmallows
68 Unwelcome sight on fruit

DOWN

1 Plumbing fixture
2 Mastercard competitor, for short
3 Item thrown at a bull's-eye
4 Treats cooked over a campfire
5 Bright spots in the night sky
6 Phone protector
7 Not too much
8 Soccer great Megan
9 Pie ___ mode
10 Blood test findings, e.g.
11 Cinematic award
12 Online platform for craftspeople
14 Traps
21 Yuletide candy shape
22 "Let's Stay Together" singer Turner
26 Comprehends
27 Shape of some Maryland decals
28 "Funny!"
29 Features of torches and campfires
30 Fear-inducing
31 Balsa or banyan
34 Feature of many a stone bridge
35 Not easily found
36 Give off
38 Like roosters, but not hens
42 Drug agent, for short
43 "Got questions? Let 'er rip!"
44 Region
45 Arm-wrestling asset
49 Video watched live
50 Punctuation mark seen in "I, Too"
51 Freedom of the ___ (First Amendment right)
52 Narrow laser light
54 Actress Kunis
55 Dutch cheese
56 Frozen breakfast brand
57 The Great ___ of China
58 Winter vehicle
60 51-Across at a picnic

SYRUP COLLECTION

By Zhouqin Burnikel

ACROSS

- **1** Colorado River feeder
- **5** Hushed "Hey, you!"
- **9** Sound of an air kiss
- **13** Birds on Australian 50-cent coins
- **14** Protruding navel
- **16** ___ over (study closely)
- **17** Something pop culture has
- **19** Far from rosy
- **20** Toy holder
- **21** They know what they're doing
- **23** Flo Milli genre
- **24** "Real shame!"
- **27** Marathoner's number tag
- **30** Slip up
- **31** Tabloid show since 1991
- **33** B-school subject
- **35** Softest of minerals
- **38** Swarming pests
- **40** Pool divisions
- **42** Buddy
- **43** Throat ailment
- **44** Stretch of land
- **45** Cotton ___
- **47** See 50-Across
- **48** World Showcase theme park
- **50** With 47-Across, marine animal of the class Asteroidea
- **52** Blimp's domain
- **53** Highly divergent
- **57** Refinable resource
- **59** Interstate sign word
- **60** Get ready to play a hole
- **63** Fabric-eating insect
- **65** Lump in the throat
- **68** Largest continent
- **69** Part of a skin care routine
- **70** Agenda entry
- **71** "Phooey!"
- **72** Coin with a torch on it
- **73** Bird extinct since the 17th century

DOWN

- **1** Amethyst, e.g.
- **2** Apple computer
- **3** Like a well-kept lawn
- **4** Good quality
- **5** Toaster Strudel alternative
- **6** "How's it goin'?"
- **7** Staircase components
- **8** Weapon for Wonder Woman
- **9** Fuel efficiency stat
- **10** Fretful types
- **11** "Pretty Little Liars" character Montgomery
- **12** ___ hearts (nutritious seeds)
- **15** Marry without a big ceremony
- **18** Arthur ___ Courage Award
- **22** Competes on "The Voice"
- **25** Hidden hazards
- **26** Music festival setups
- **27** Judo skill signifier
- **28** "See if ___!"
- **29** "Enjoy your meal!"
- **32** What carne asada is made from
- **34** Classic wafer brand
- **36** Annalise Keating teaches it
- **37** Bracelet fastener
- **39** Like many Senior Olympics participants
- **41** Took without permission
- **46** "No idea"
- **49** State where Fritos originated
- **51** Vicinity
- **54** ___ with (supported)
- **55** Arcade game pioneer
- **56** Lukewarm
- **57** Philosopher Khayyam
- **58** Parks who learned from Septima Clark
- **61** As many as
- **62** Made a desperate request
- **64** ___-been
- **66** Tight-lipped
- **67** Music genre with D.C. roots

STATE NAMES

By Brooke Husic & Evan Kalish

ACROSS

1 Gets older
5 Fountain beverages
10 Challenging
14 Word before "classic" or "following"
15 Employ
16 "Paradise Lost" garden
17 ___ Land (Hollywood nickname)
18 Scuffle
19 Regretted
20 Pioneer in stream-of-consciousness narration
23 Regarding
24 Little pieces
25 Wraps up
28 Element after fluorine
30 With 33-Across, painter with a museum in Santa Fe
33 See 30-Across
37 Tree on Connecticut's state quarter
38 Clear fountain beverages
40 "___ It Go" (Menzel hit)
41 DVD players' forerunners
43 Core muscles
44 Part of TTFN
45 Fictional teen pop star who sang "The Best of Both Worlds"
50 Vegan milk option
51 Piece of boating equipment
52 Producer and star of "Little Fires Everywhere"
61 Share a border with
62 Alternate name
63 Unchallenging
64 Bowling alley reservation
65 Attempt again
66 Kitchen floor choice
67 Follower of "eagle-" or "hawk-"
68 Mentally grasp
69 Schedule space

DOWN

1 Knee stabilizer, for short
2 Fruit in Bahamian duff
3 Tracee ___ Ross
4 Appetizer
5 Prefix for "pro" or "precious"
6 Zodiac animals before tigers
7 Sandwich seller
8 Zone
9 Crockpot creation
10 Protagonist, perhaps
11 Grown-up
12 Coral structures
13 Best-selling role-playing game, for short
21 Buddhist temple instruments
22 Double-reed instruments
26 Guac or queso
27 ___ Lawrence College
28 "Au contraire!"
29 ___ out a living (get by)
30 National Park Service URL part
31 "___ one teach one"
32 Bhindi kadhi veggie
34 ___ de queso (Puerto Rican dessert)
35 Spanakopita cheese
36 Train station fig.
39 Deep Blue's company
42 Laughed heartily, maybe
44 Sales goals
46 Congressional "no"
47 Embroiled in a conflict
48 Loud
49 Earth tone
52 Leafy green
53 56-Down with bidding
54 Ancient letter
55 Pub drinks
56 Location on the web
57 Rabbit relative
58 Long part of a lemur
59 Capital home to Vigeland Sculpture Park
60 Russian "no"

MATERIAL MATTERS

By Gail Grabowski

ACROSS

1 Place for a book title
6 Like a lemon
10 Give the band a hand
14 Select from a menu
15 Brand hidden in "focal point"
16 Saintly glow
17 Was totally comfortable
19 "Help ___ the way"
20 Subject for a primatologist
21 Smokestack buildup
22 Hoisted
24 "Aww!"
25 USGA sport
26 Sooner than
29 Simmer down
32 Exhilarate
33 Box-office failure
34 The Big Easy acronym
36 Be adjacent to
37 Pane material
38 Habitual grump
39 Forbidden activity
40 React to yeast
41 "Akata Witch" study
42 Goes here and there
44 10-Down creators
45 Winter garment
46 Innermost part
47 Cause of a 1773 Boston "party"
50 "Speedbumps: Flooring It Through Hollywood" memoirist Teri
51 Indy circuit
54 Neighbor of Pakistan
55 Jukebox musical divided into four seasons
58 Cooking fat
59 Skip over
60 Social customs
61 Arthur Ashe Courage Award, for one
62 Blossoms-to-be
63 Live and breathe

DOWN

1 Place for a snooze
2 Get ready
3 Not occupied
4 Pay stub figure
5 Sign of a correction
6 Sierra Nevada lake
7 Frequently
8 Tach reading
9 Figure skating jumps
10 Very light dessert
11 At long ___ (finally)
12 Gel-producing plant
13 Koi habitat
18 Open-topped bag
23 Sick
24 Carnival confection
25 Animal in a gaggle
26 Lima ___
27 Macaroni shape
28 Regional wildlife
29 Field trip group
30 Make a fake version of
31 Innate ability
33 Drop hints that you're single, say
35 Sesame Street basics
37 "Nice work!"
41 Infatuated words
43 Physician, for short
44 Cause to yawn
46 Performing groups
47 Backsplash piece
48 Historical periods
49 Group you're almost eligible for if your age is this clue number
50 Power network
51 "Shark Tank" investor Greiner
52 "The ___ have it!"
53 Subtle "Hey!"
56 Earthbound Australian bird
57 Fight in the ring

STAR SEARCH

By Stella Zawistowski

ACROSS

1 ___ Brothers ("Sucker" pop group)
6 Use crayons
11 Soaked
14 Having a slim lead
15 Partner of beyond
16 Big stock event (Abbr.)
17 Label for new items in a store
19 Fruit in a Newton
20 Escorted
21 Anais Nin specialty
23 Lend a hand
25 Smokey the Bear ad, e.g.
26 Ferrari model whose name translates to "redhead"
32 Grown-up acorns
36 Pig Latin "nope"
37 Series of items
39 Ocelot, for example
40 Place for learning
43 In general
45 Ump's relative
46 Takes to court
48 Blender setting
49 Grad
51 Make a modest beginning
54 Tiny amount
56 For each
57 Fish with a nasty bite
61 Identifying neckwear
67 Poetic tribute
68 Quota for a rep
70 "___ Liaisons dangereuses"
71 Get out of
72 Post-workout "hot spot"
73 Have a snack
74 "Little Woods" actress Thompson
75 ___ Regency (hotel brand)

DOWN

1 "___ on That Beat (TZ Anthem)"
2 Magnum ___
3 Have a snack
4 Pre-deal bet
5 Cook over high heat
6 Tabata training, e.g.
7 ___-Wan Kenobi
8 Zero, in tennis
9 Bridge with a road under it
10 Additional tries
11 Coffee shop amenity, often
12 Really remarkable
13 Ancient Roman costume
18 Front's opposite
22 Concept in Chinese philosophy
24 Tech hidden in "forward slash"
26 "RuPaul's Drag Race" headpiece
27 Outshine the rest
28 Hot mess
29 Tiny amount
30 Yes votes
31 Singer found at the ends of five country names
33 Honda's luxury brand
34 Superman's birth name
35 Alloy that might be stainless
38 Dances like Eleanor Powell
41 Necessary item
42 Up to now
44 Dark 'n' stormy booze
47 Maple tree ooze
50 Deg. with an ethics component
52 Body of water in "The Prince of Egypt"
53 Gait between a walk and a canter
55 Small section of a map
57 ___ vaulting
58 Notion
59 Musical "don't play" symbol
60 "Woe is me!"
62 Deep cut
63 Cafeteria carrier
64 Contents of el mar
65 Mannerly fellow, for short
66 Bit of sports data
69 Journal overseers (Abbr.)

FROZEN FOUR

By Zhouqin Burnikel

ACROSS
1 Lend a hand
5 Like mint-condition memorabilia, often
9 Letter after alpha
13 Out-loud exam
14 Bell Labs operating system
15 "You're So Vain" singer Carly
16 Make allowance for
19 Lines of stitching
20 "Evita" narrator
21 Get the idea
22 Poolroom powder
24 Light brown
25 Tabloid news site
28 Dish whose ingredients include nostalgia
34 Trickle slowly
36 Great distress
37 Upper-echelon
38 Wing it onstage
40 Lil ___ X
42 India's capital territory
43 Bus passenger
44 Bit of slalom gear
46 "Just Give Me a Reason," e.g.
47 Absolutely terrified
51 Nose around
52 Try to win the affections of
53 Suffix for "evil"
55 Pi Day mo.
58 ___-Caps (candy)
59 Salary bump
62 Is innovative
67 ___ defense (courtroom strategy)
68 Sound reverberation
69 Record to watch later
70 "___ of Anarchy"
71 Tree part
72 Eyelid problem

DOWN
1 All the rage
2 Significant time periods
3 Canoeing site
4 Fold in some shorts
5 Becomes depleted
6 Hardworking insect
7 Brazilian city, for short
8 Precise, in Spanish
9 "About the Author" blurb
10 Flightless birds
11 Muscle quality
12 Up the ___
15 Like many candles
17 Apple product line
18 Blacken on the grill
23 "Let's go!"
25 Old Russian autocrats
26 Field doc
27 The Legend of ___ (Nintendo franchise)
29 Spring Festival meal
30 Went on the lam
31 Prepare for a Turkish wrestling match
32 One or the ___
33 God
35 Place for ships to dock
39 Cold one
41 Icy road worry
45 "It slipped my mind"
48 Mafia bosses
49 Opposite of later
50 Cause of a cold sweat
54 Really funny people
55 Degrees for execs
56 Sarah Lee Guthrie's father
57 Equestrian's strap
60 Formal garment
61 Covetous emotion
63 Muscles worked by side planks
64 ___-warrior (environmental activist)
65 "Don't know 'em"
66 Female deer

OPENING BARS

By Matthew Stock

ACROSS

1 Guiding principle
6 Alphabetically consecutive name
9 WWF logo animal
14 Role (or, when backward, actress) in "The Color Purple"
15 Alley-___
16 Chain that "has the meats"
17 Like the smell of rotten eggs
18 "It's so obvious"
19 Track-and-field events
20 Popular brown pupper
23 ___ Campus (women-centric publication)
24 [Their error, not mine]
25 ___ Angeles
26 Part that might be pierced
29 Additionally
31 Bit of beach architecture
34 Dallas suburb
36 Part of a litter
37 Saguaros and prickly pears
40 Little taste of a drink
42 Most minimal
43 Elevate
45 Cantina dip
47 Intergalactic sci-fi subgenre
49 Hard-to-beat Wii Sports character
53 "Gangnam Style" artist
54 Rake relative
55 "Better Call Saul" channel
57 Itty-bitty
58 Kitchen item for washing greens
61 Work ___ (industrious trait)
64 Fish found in a pond
65 Acquires
66 On the ___ of disaster
67 One administering CPR, perhaps
68 Photographer Leibovitz
69 Units of computer storage
70 Actress Ruby
71 Wild party

DOWN

1 ___ Slide (line dance)
2 "The Marvelous Mrs. Maisel" actress Brosnahan
3 Slipups
4 Large-scale
5 Extinct birds
6 Recycling bin objects
7 Promote
8 Didn't overturn
9 Does an aquatic kiting activity
10 Word before "Spring" or "League"
11 "The Good Place" network
12 Hair-coloring substance
13 Burro, e.g.
21 Kudrow who played Phoebe on "Friends"
22 Tuft of hair
26 "At Last" singer James
27 Hoppy bar orders
28 It's often paid on the first of the month
30 Relating to the eye
32 Sound
33 Soup dumpling emanation
35 Timesaving techniques
37 Synonym for 66-Across
38 Snapchat and TikTok, for two
39 Sculpting medium
41 Palme d'Or winner for Bong Joon-ho
44 54-Across or 58-Across, for example
46 Lava ___
48 Reached the top of one's game
50 Patio covering
51 Itty-bitty
52 More succinct
56 Tobacconist's product
58 Trig ratio
59 Rounded roof
60 Mama's mama
61 ___ and flow
62 Strive
63 Chart-topper, e.g.

RUN BEHIND

By Hannah Slovut

ACROSS

1 Group of three
5 Accompanying
9 Bunny movement
12 Steal a fry, say
13 Cream-filled chocolate snack
14 ___ pit (campsite cooker)
15 Wide-ranging
16 Unit in an online cart
17 Sign on a store's door during business hours
18 Post-sprain support
20 "Once ___ a time . . ."
21 Location for some science classes
22 Cold feature of a dog
24 Acorn or pecan
27 Subject of some ADA regulations
30 Stuff a cow chews
31 Eve's partner
33 British bathrooms
35 Bleated like a sheep
39 Someone skilled at networking
42 Impatient
43 A gold one might be given for a job well done
44 Domesticate
45 A cat or a dog might be one
47 Astonish
49 Slender bar
50 Incites
54 Tell a tall tale
56 Prefix for "skirt" or "golf"
57 Match-three puzzle game with sugary pieces
63 Yemen neighbor
64 Leg part
65 Seoul's peninsula
66 Held on to
67 Setting for 31-Across
68 Outer limits
69 Psychic ability
70 Parenting pair, perhaps
71 Onion relative

DOWN

1 Shredded
2 Chess piece
3 Poker declaration
4 "This can't be good"
5 Fan sound
6 Greek vowel
7 "The 100" and "Batwoman" channel
8 Class with cooking and sewing, informally
9 Animal whose full name means "river horse"
10 Cream-filled chocolate snacks
11 Short pasta
12 Degree held by many CEOs
14 Crafts made from nontraditional materials
19 Hoops, for short
23 Toothpaste container
24 New Horizons grp.
25 Japanese noodle
26 Diplomacy
28 Large crowds of people
29 Annoyed looks
32 It might lead to an editorial correction
34 Bit of numerical info
36 Off in the distance
37 Red "Sesame Street" character
38 Turned another color
40 Nays' opposites
41 "Yours ___" (letter signoff)
46 How some shirts are worn
48 Coin worth less than a dime
50 Evidence of flames
51 Multiplied by
52 Like some phone users' purchases
53 Black-and-white bear
55 Slowly cause to deteriorate
58 Must have
59 Bears' homes
60 Strong desire
61 Look for
62 Possesses

SHARE OPTIONS

By Zhouqin Burnikel

ACROSS

1 Airport rental
4 Initial stage
9 Knock out of the air, perhaps
13 "Chernobyl" channel
14 "Touched by an Angel" actress Reese
15 Place for a keystone
16 "My deepest gratitude!"
19 Hunts for food
20 Stare openmouthed
21 Total number of I and Q tiles combined, in Scrabble
22 Emphasize
24 "What ___ can I do?"
26 Ford Field football team
32 Landscaper's roll
35 "That's right!"
36 Set to simmer
37 "Hunters" star Lena
39 "This ___ war!"
42 "Pretty Little Liars" author Shepard
43 Less risky
45 Sound of waves
47 Yang's complement
48 No longer available
52 Tennis star Gauff
53 Some Arab Open University students
57 Pursue romantically
59 Is remorseful about
62 Personal belief system
63 Complaint about an unlevel playing field
66 Place
67 Eat away
68 Realty unit
69 Whispery "Hey! Over here!"
70 Worked with thread
71 Texting format

DOWN

1 Teacup imperfections
2 Scrub a launch
3 Athlete with an oar
4 Long journey
5 Prefix meaning "new"
6 Slimy garden creature
7 Idris who played Mandela
8 Capital near Taoyuan
9 Pulled up a stool
10 Unlisted candidates
11 High point
12 Subsequently
17 Black-___ peas
18 Coin-shaped chocolate candy
23 Flower stalk
25 ___-mo
27 "Insecure" creator Issa
28 Soccer player Kelley
29 Lotion brand
30 Furikake seaweed
31 Bird of the genus Cygnus
32 Just OK
33 Snowman in "Frozen"
34 "What's the ___?" ("Who cares?")
38 Bottom line figures
40 Neither's partner
41 ___ Fifth Avenue
44 Homophone of "roe"
46 Cried or laughed, for example
49 Color that rhymes with "blue"
50 ___ over (gets ready to click on, say)
51 Home territory
54 Agents negotiate them
55 "Speak of the devil," e.g.
56 Puts into categories
57 Faint cloud
58 Schindler competitor
60 "To be," in Montreal
61 Mount Everest covering
64 Shade of black
65 Tribute in verse

INNNER EYE

By Brooke Husic

ACROSS

1 Alex and Wanda Sykes, to Lucas and Olivia
5 Lip ___ (gloss alternative)
10 Hypotheticals
13 Sotomayor on the Supreme Court
14 Musical pace
15 Prefix for "binary"
16 Choose by ballot
17 Residence permit holder, maybe
18 Day before 4-Down
19 Economist whose name sounds like a teeth-related verb
20 "American Soul" network
21 Flew in the face of
23 Loses moisture
25 "___ when?"
26 Puts on the market
27 Not powered up
30 Perfume container
31 Wearable floral gift
32 Excessively
33 Website for creators
34 Question from a groggy travel buddy
38 Mule's noise
39 "I ___ what you did there"
40 Brew with an amber variety
41 Pennsylvania's Great Lake
42 Coal byproduct
43 "Anne Frank: The Diary of a Young Girl" audiobook narrator Selma
46 Went overlong
48 Like noses with studs
50 Specialized areas
52 "Nicely ___" ("Well said")
53 Leaning Tower city
54 Before now
55 Growl with bared teeth
57 Frozen precipitation
58 Single-stranded biopolymer
59 Shades of color
60 Minestrone ingredient

61 Clock change not observed in much of Ariz.
62 Tinder action
63 Pantry-invading pests

DOWN

1 Back teeth
2 Snug sleepwear option
3 Actress who played Yu Shu Lien in "Crouching Tiger, Hidden Dragon"
4 Day after 18-Across
5 Sharply inclined
6 Message that might have emojis
7 Electric bass attachment
8 Apple tablet
9 Sheet music symbols
10 Incalculably large
11 Market prediction
12 With scorn
13 Transmit
20 Most bustling

22 Goal-setting framework
24 Multitude
27 Catchall category
28 Friend's opposite
29 Briefly
34 Calls before a court
35 Article sometimes worn with galoshes
36 Chai
37 Palindromic fashion magazine
38 St. ___ (Alpine dog breed)
44 Most frigid
45 Takes a mental health day, say
47 Robins' homes
48 Heart rate
49 ___ mining
51 Sculpture medium in "Calvin & Hobbes"
52 Antiretroviral drug, for short
56 Singer DiFranco
57 Fancy hotel amenity

BROKEN RECORDS

By Gail Grabowski

ACROSS

1 Future officer
6 Ice cream drink
10 Rail vehicle
14 ___ and kicking
15 One of the Great Lakes
16 Make angry
17 Award for Rigoberta Menchu
19 See 21-Across
20 Sci-fi crew members (Abbr.)
21 With 19-Across, attacked
22 Image cast by the sun
24 Penny
25 The Fresh Prince's uncle
26 Swords with curved blades
29 Is financially successful
33 Goes right or left
34 Parcel of land
35 Way off of a turnpike
36 Tweak, in a way
37 About 20% of Muslims
38 Widespread
39 Platform over water
40 Highest Sudoku digit
41 Supermarket walkway
42 Guests' sleeping spots, sometimes
44 Showed feelings
45 Doily material
46 Small earring
47 Scrubber made from steel wool
50 2019 movie featuring Jennifer Hudson as Grizabella
51 "So now the truth comes out!"
54 Room size calculation
55 Artist such as Harmonia Rosales
58 Brown quickly
59 Ensnare
60 "You've got the wrong person"
61 Sound from an impatient motorist
62 Athletic award won 12 times by Serena Williams
63 "That's disgusting!"

DOWN

1 Prop for Bartholomew Richard Fitzgerald-Smythe
2 Very much
3 "Mine!"
4 WALL-E's romantic interest
5 Bank employees
6 Be worthy of
7 Like the Mojave's climate
8 Fashion designer Claiborne
9 Opening drives in golf
10 Testing time
11 Melon part
12 Voice range above tenor
13 Tabby's comment
18 Equipment on "Chopped"
23 That man's
24 Manhattan attraction
25 Explore deeply
26 Parts of instructions
27 Video's counterpart
28 Like a 37-Down, often
29 Doesn't wing it
30 Be
31 Biathlete's need
32 Riding horse, old-style
34 ___ parade (June event)
37 Story in a speech, perhaps
41 Like a 37-Down, often
43 Sound from a flock
44 Blues Hall of Famer James
46 Very sentimental
47 Window framework
48 Creme-filled cookie
49 "Good Will Hunting" therapist
50 Thunder sound
51 "The Daughter" actress Miranda
52 Skirt borders
53 Mine extractions
56 Org. with auditors
57 Neither here ___ there

MIDDLE AGES

By Evan Kalish

ACROSS

1 Practice boxing
5 Metal in steel
9 Song at a Sunday service
14 River through Cairo
15 "Look, I did it!"
16 Queen or tsarina
17 Color that's Latin for "water"
18 2017 dance documentary
19 Gives off
20 Clutter-clearing events
23 Broadway's "___ Miz"
24 Fish-and-chips fish
25 Burdens
29 Place for items not needed for a while
32 "Well, gave it my best shot!"
35 Soda can opener
36 Charlotte E. Ray's field
37 Anticipatory fear
38 Early internet letters
39 ___ wheel (task-assigning aid)
41 Dreidel, e.g.
42 Tree that becomes a Muppet if you add an "o" to the end
43 Dating app
44 Stat that's low in a traffic jam
48 Cold Italian treat
49 Networking connections
50 "What ___ that about?"
53 "Forever" item
57 Glossy fabric
60 Good cards in poker
61 Birth state of Toni Morrison
62 "All joking ___ ..."
63 Poet Franny
64 FedEx's has a hidden arrow
65 Game with two queens
66 Good scores at a ball
67 Bird on a Canadian coin

DOWN

1 Surly growl
2 Irritated feeling
3 Kory Stamper and Julia Child, to Smith College
4 500-sheet unit
5 "Mmm, tasty!"
6 Like many horror movies
7 Poems that praise
8 California wine valley
9 Hogs the mirror, say
10 Recaps
11 Tony-winning Stroker
12 Allow
13 "The Marvelous ___ Maisel"
21 Emulated Helen Mirren
22 "Stay (I Missed You)" singer Lisa
26 Pedicure place
27 Digital b-day greeting
28 Drainage conduit
29 "Chandelier" singer
30 Particles in molecules
31 Four-qt. measure
32 Suitcase attachment
33 Valuable stash
34 Attract's opposite
38 Ginger ___
39 Pungent green
40 Moved out of sight
42 Self-centered people have big ones
43 First book of the Torah
45 Fast-moving river parts
46 Makes up for something
47 Dove relative
50 Fish aka ono
51 Friend
52 Eating utensil
54 Skill of sensitivity
55 Spot of soreness
56 Turnpike fee
57 Cul-de-___
58 Campfire residue
59 2-2 game, e.g.

SNOWFALL

By Zhouqin Burnikel

ACROSS

1 Goody-goody
5 Uterus
9 Places where cranberries grow
13 Gushing review
14 Worker who extracts
15 Southern cooking legend Lewis
16 Admired figure
17 Baseball season starter
19 Part of the auditory system
20 Membership fees
21 Wedding reception tributes
22 Rehearsals
24 Bowl over
25 Cause of student stress
26 Actress Gemma
27 Like two peas in a ___
30 Liquor in a Moscow mule
31 Bad deeds
32 Material found by a 14-Across
33 Respectful gestures in front of a Shinto shrine
34 Doctor's visit expense
36 "Once Were Warriors" star Rena
37 Enjoyed some cha siu bao, say
38 Noodle often served on a bamboo tray
39 Son of Drogo Baggins
41 "Hard Place" singer
42 "For real?"
43 Homophone and opposite of "raise"
44 Word after "tea" or "shade"
45 Sprayed, perhaps
48 Beetle sacred to ancient Egyptians
51 Holders of trash or Spam
52 Natori garment
53 Like mind reading
55 Cook up a scheme
56 Innovator's inkling
57 Settled on
58 Guy
59 Take five
60 Didn't discard
61 Livestock's lunch

DOWN

1 Used a crowbar on
2 Weather-tracking tool
3 Place sheltered from worldly concerns
4 Toothpaste type
5 Diaper bag sheets
6 Small bills
7 Guys
8 Brest's region
9 Got started
10 Bookie's figures
11 Swarming insect
12 "___ who?"
14 Chip away at the lead
18 Dog and cat, e.g.
20 Twilight stage
23 Many lipstick colors
24 Branch of Islam
26 Channel covering congressional hearings
27 Pastel color
28 Cookie with a Most Stuf variety
29 Cub's home
30 Cast a ballot
33 Cry of disgust
35 Wind ensemble instrument
36 Seep
38 Metal in a junkyard
40 Long-tailed rodents
44 Special indulgence
45 Where an obi is worn
46 Gradually wear away
47 No longer in style
48 ___-fry
49 Hand over
50 Taproom orders
51 Cut into pieces
54 A drop in ___ ocean
55 Document file type

SPLIT ENDS

By Rachel Fabi

ACROSS

1 Black-and-white sea predator
5 Outermost tree layer
9 Applies with a cotton ball
13 Day of the ___
14 Unboxes, maybe
16 Destroy
17 Aboveboard
19 Bit of creativity
20 Holds a grudge toward
21 Bending out of shape
23 Campervans, etc.
24 Made do
25 "You take that back!"
26 Heard but not seen, perhaps
30 ___ process (14th Amendment protection)
32 Twosome
33 Singer-songwriter Kiyoko
34 Bitter beer
35 Take a load off
36 Catchy tune
37 ___ Miss
38 Scatters
40 Grain-based milk option
41 Winter clock setting in L.A.
42 Very short or very long period of time, depending on context
44 Casual shirt
46 "I Fall to Pieces" singer Patsy
47 ___ and breakfast
48 "The Good Place" actress Maya
51 Episodic programs
55 Way in the distance
56 Ski resort pass
58 Arial Bold, e.g.
59 White heron
60 DVR brand
61 Sounds of disapproval
62 Positive publicity
63 Small cut

DOWN

1 Unpleasant scent
2 Mathematician Descartes
3 Musical with the characters Skimbleshanks and Mr. Mistoffelees
4 Stick like glue
5 Lightning units
6 Bonobos and gibbons, e.g.
7 Title for MLK (Abbr.)
8 Was familiar with
9 Hang after washing
10 German automaker
11 "Muy ___" ("Very good")
12 Sudden problem
15 Powerful hockey strike
18 Covetousness
22 Summary
24 Budget-analyzing exec
25 Core
26 LGTBQ+ magazine
27 Have a Vegas wedding, maybe
28 Flotsam and Jetsam in "The Little Mermaid," species-wise
29 Russian denial
30 Bowl or plate
31 ___ no good (scheming)
32 Loyal follower
35 "Neat!"
36 Spoiled
39 Goes with
40 "First off . . ."
43 In the heavens
44 Actress Hatcher
45 Authoritative orders
47 "Hocus Pocus" star Midler
48 River transport
49 Sci-fi vehicles
50 Unpleasantly damp
51 "___ right up!"
52 Similar
53 Denim pioneer Strauss
54 Halt
57 Cook in fat

YOU'VE BEEN DQ'D!

By Stella Zawistowski

ACROSS

1 Window coloring
5 Use a keyboard
9 Ghanaian garment
14 Nabisco cookie
15 Blooper ___
16 Ten-percent donation
17 Elementary particle with an "up" counterpart
19 Paid for cards
20 Like some inspections
21 Tools for sweeping
22 Laptops and such
23 Accompany
26 Is in possession of
27 Organ with lobes
28 Letters before an alias
31 Place for gloss
32 Video game franchise with fire-breathing creatures
35 From both sides, sound-wise
37 California's state motto
38 Word-for-word citation
42 Peppa or Porky
43 Org. at airports
44 Throws with force
45 Prominent part of a sailfish
46 Like some gumbo and jambalaya
48 Crunchy sandwich
49 One of Santa's reindeer
52 Mall pizza chain
55 Free from a knot
56 Latrice Royale or Vanessa "Vanjie" Mateo
59 Smelled awful
60 Family member
61 President who was also a chief justice
62 Pieces that can be put in check
63 Pharma products
64 In addition

DOWN

1 List heading
2 Wrinkle-removing appliance
3 Employers of columnists
4 Invigorating substances
5 T on a test
6 Apt anagram for "aye"
7 "___ my last email . . ."
8 Taos Pueblo painter Albert Looking ___
9 "The Hate U Give" heroine
10 Half-bull, half-man of myth
11 Name that's "eight" in Italian
12 Science class, for short
13 Brand of sneakers
18 Fourths of a gal.
21 Hair protectors
23 Important time period
24 Get droopy
25 AFL's union partner
26 Bandleader's exclamation
27 Family member
29 Don't be dishonest
30 Invite to enter
31 Acid
32 Last mo. of the year
33 "___ pasa?"
34 Place for a price
36 Getting to
39 Status ___
40 Web address
41 "Bravo!"
45 Food whose name is Spanish for "flute"
47 Smells awful
48 STL food specialty
49 Period after sunset
50 Prefix similar to "contra-"
51 Amaze
52 Corporals' superiors (Abbr.)
53 Sports "zebras"
54 "You might be ___ something!"
56 Beaver's project
57 Regret
58 Common conjunction

OUTER BANKS

By Zhouqin Burnikel

ACROSS

1 Part of a dance lesson
5 Far from nice
9 Mountain range across eight countries
13 "I remember now"
15 ___ fide (genuine)
16 Strong who voiced Raven
17 Not fall in line
19 Meadow mamas
20 Enters a username and password
21 Large piece
23 Chain with notoriously long receipts
24 Direction opposite WSW
25 Ms. ___-Man
27 National Mall tree
28 Martial arts legend Bruce
29 Put on the market
31 Android counterpart
33 Becomes ready for customers
35 Coral reef's home
38 Head off
39 Places to remove makeup
42 Place to exchange vows
43 ___ mignon
44 False identity
45 Largest fast-food chain in China
46 "Moral of the Story" singer
50 Deploy
51 Setting for a period piece
53 Sticky tree fluid
56 Bagel topping
57 Flew on foot
58 Tony winner Ramirez
60 Sign after Taurus
62 "Rubaiyat" poet Khayyam
64 Bluegrass accessories
66 ___ Aid
67 Palindromic flour
68 Wintry mix component
69 Did really well on
70 Overflow
71 Uses a plus sign

DOWN

1 Martens with silky fur
2 Seat for a queen
3 Treatment for dark circles
4 Sambusa veggies
5 B-school degree
6 Long periods of time
7 Joints for some tattoos
8 ___ spray
9 Enjoyed mango sticky rice, say
10 Elena Kagan, to Thurgood Marshall
11 Heads off
12 Talks back to
14 Bail on class
18 Single-stranded molecule
22 Many a Pam Grier film
26 "See you later!"
30 Great deal of, informally
32 Switch dichotomy
34 Prefix meaning "five"
36 Pursues
37 Make the wrong call
38 ___ interpreter (figure at some press conferences)
39 Salad dressing choice
40 Drive away
41 Karaoke bar needs
44 ___ borealis
45 Sakura Kokumai's martial art
47 Cut into thin pieces
48 Pressed the horn
49 Has being
52 Capital with trains to Casablanca
54 Back in time
55 ___ up (enlivens)
59 Part of a poker pot
61 "Black Swan" actress Kunis
63 Hongbao color
65 Printer annoyance

SPREAD THIN

By Evan Kalish

ACROSS

1 A 110-foot-long serving of nachos in 2018 had 450 pounds of it
6 Explorer voiced by Fatima Ptacek
10 Site with reviews
14 "___ Always Love You" (Whitney Houston hit)
15 "The language of the unheard," according to MLK
16 Deep purple berry
17 Endure a tough setback with grace
20 "Uh-huh"
21 Pan for moo goo gai pan
22 Strongly urge
23 Aqua relative
25 Huffy mood
26 De-fleeced
28 Symbol of solidarity
29 Singer Gabriel
32 "Although, thinking about it from the other side . . ."
34 Grain buildings
36 Hindu festival
37 U.S. org. hidden in two U.S. state names
38 Silent OKs
39 Opposite of division
41 "Whee!"
44 "On the Basis of ___" (RBG biopic)
45 ___-bitsy
47 Dare alternative
48 Quite
49 Banana protector
50 Hun ruler
53 Mined rock
54 Items in some social media feeds
57 Demographic with immigrant grandparents
61 List of offerings
62 Out-of-bed announcement
63 Event location
64 Stage constructions
65 Swear
66 Give a stray a forever home, say

DOWN

1 Dog command
2 Broadway's "Come From ___"
3 Be fond of
4 Deliberated overnight
5 "Baby Cobra" comedian Wong
6 What a baby bib catches
7 Farm sound
8 Decay
9 Capital home to the Acropolis
10 Big vessel at a marina
11 Reverberation
12 Villain's hideaway
13 Half a quart
18 Vocal characteristic of Miranda Lambert or Loretta Lynn
19 Ways off a highway
24 "It's the end of an ___"
25 Mountain climbed by Moses
26 Glowed
27 DNA's "double" shape
28 Questionable
29 In the air
30 "Well, OB-viously"
31 First "A" in NAACP (Abbr.)
32 Therefore
33 Restless
35 Protected, in a way
40 Give way
42 Guide a vehicle
43 Anger
46 Super sad
48 Computer problem
49 Gets ready
50 Dispensers of 20s
51 Megan ___ Stallion
52 Sunglass lens feature
53 Burden
55 T. rex, e.g.
56 Gazpacho or gomguk
58 Down Under bird
59 Filmmaker DuVernay
60 Volleyball divider

MINISERIES

By Gail Grabowski

ACROSS

1 Writer of verses
5 Comic Crutchfield
9 "___ the night before Christmas . . ."
13 Spring bloom from a bulb
15 Badly behaved kid
16 Long-eared leaper
17 "The Hunger Games" setting
18 Detest
19 Margin
20 Home to "View of Paris from Vincent's Room in the Rue Lepic"
23 Item of lingerie
25 Forgets an email attachment, say
26 Moon-related phenomena
27 Noisy baby toy
29 Positive quality
31 Looked-up-to person
32 Take the wheel
34 "Lovecraft Country" channel
37 Checkout counter devices
41 Medical show settings, for short
42 Falafel holders
43 Opera song
44 License plates
45 Like relatively few theatrical releases nowadays
47 Sunflower relative
50 Sprinter's assignment
52 Itsy-bitsy
53 Circumvent a point of contention
57 Some family members, for short
58 Pothole's place
59 Windy City airport
62 Singer Brickell
63 "If all ___ fails . . ."
64 Skin openings
65 Bygone Russian ruler
66 Peered at
67 Rope fiber

DOWN

1 School support grp.
2 Sharer's word
3 They go up and down in a skyscraper
4 Rock and Roll Hall of Famer Turner
5 Detest
6 Talks big
7 ___ bomb (fizzy relaxation aid)
8 List component
9 Major college paper
10 Walked in the surf
11 Engage in bickering
12 Appears to be
14 Collection of experts
21 Test for some college seniors
22 Driver's 180
23 Persuasive gift
24 Palindromic device
28 Pampering treatment, for short
29 Chest muscles, for short
30 Actress DeLaria
32 Wimbledon divisions
33 Airport org.
34 Driver's dropoff phrase
35 Wedding suit wearer, perhaps
36 River named for a Great Plains people
38 Mesmerizing painting style
39 Cutting remark
40 ___ King Cole
44 Less wordy
45 Colleagues of MDs
46 "___'s Fables"
47 Positive quality
48 Slips and slides
49 Knee-ankle connector
50 Tenant's contract
51 Lent a hand
54 Arbor Day planting
55 Word before "Ghost" or "Grail"
56 "I was afraid of this"
60 Sleep phase acronym
61 Seer's ability

ON THE JOB

By Mark McClain

ACROSS

1 Turnip greens alternative
5 Protester's placard
9 Messy buns, e.g.
14 Great Lake with the shortest name
15 "True Blood" star Paquin
16 Like Thor and Odin
17 Dog breed with a golden coat
19 Like old bread
20 "What do you ___ to that?"
21 Beachfront hotel's asset
22 T-shirt material
23 Fender bender result
24 Story
25 Aspiring
28 Trembles in fright
32 Poetry slam sounds
33 Container for Jack and Jill
34 Shade of purple
35 Contact by phone
36 Open like an oyster
37 "Millicent Min, Girl Genius" author Yee
38 "I think you're ___ something" ("Good idea")
39 "___-a-doodle-do!"
40 "Not now!"
41 Sheryl Swoopes, to Cynthia Cooper, e.g.
43 "It's the truth!"
44 Prefix for "dynamic"
45 Speedy
46 Proper
49 Pantheon city
50 Do some stitching
53 Illuminated from below
54 Zesty Doritos flavor
56 Quran counterpart
57 Up to the task
58 Ancient stories, e.g.
59 Burn with liquid
60 Utah-to-Nevada direction
61 Lie adjacent to

DOWN

1 Piano's "ivories"
2 General vicinity
3 Easter flower
4 "Electric" fish
5 Cutting lumber, maybe
6 Cove or bay
7 Chew like a beaver
8 Rhyme and synonym of "grab"
9 Still on the store shelf
10 Indoor horticulturist's purchase
11 "Oh, darn!"
12 World capital on a fjord
13 Word in read receipts
18 Bakery appliances
22 DIYer's crack-filler
23 Questionable "university"
24 Like some milkshakes
25 Dressy neckband
26 Totally absurd
27 Mediterranean island republic
28 "I got hot ___ in my bag, swag" (Beyonce lyric)
29 Upper crust
30 Sneaky tricks
31 Intelligent
33 Instagram upload
36 Spine-tingling
40 Jenga tower toppler, e.g.
42 Like pourable butter
43 Shakespearean prince of Denmark
45 April ___ Day
46 Underwater vessels, for short
47 Of major proportions
48 Idris who played Macavity in "Cats"
49 Judge's garment
50 Holier-than-thou type
51 Beige shade
52 ___ your appetite
54 Crow's noise
55 ___ mode (with ice cream)

FUNNY PEOPLE

By Zhouqin Burnikel

ACROSS

1 Habitat for cattails
6 They may be lost or sold
11 Tamagoyaki ingredient
14 Make very happy
15 Handles adversity
16 Mary ___ Retton
17 He played Perseus in "Clash of the Titans"
19 "However . . ."
20 "Get what I mean?"
21 Pet food brand that's an anagram of a gemstone
22 Pea casings
23 "The Princess Diaries" star
27 Chose
30 College officials
31 Needed a heating pad
32 Helps with the dishes
34 Touch lightly
37 Bird feeder bit
38 Geologic time span
39 Skirt size
40 Major Kenyan export
41 Some new dictionary additions
43 Part of a comic strip
44 Jacket fabric
46 Obstacle
47 Tennis player who won the French Open at 17
51 Chips ___! (cookie brand)
52 Word before "turn" or "call"
53 "___ never too late!"
56 Fish in some fish sticks
57 "Patriot Act" host
61 Gibbon, e.g.
62 Be a real thing
63 Steamy room at a spa
64 Name that's one letter short of a direction
65 Pays to use
66 Tree with catkins

DOWN

1 "Not impressed"
2 "I hate to say it . . ."
3 Like "Amazing Spider-Man" No. 1
4 Like some hair
5 "Yo!"
6 Item on a deli counter
7 Energetic quality
8 Sending to the cloud
9 Fragrant neckpiece
10 Payroll ID (Abbr.)
11 Balancing pose in which the legs are held in the air
12 Cheese often coated in red wax
13 Bold
18 Palm reader's study
22 Sweeping camera shot
24 ___ Leeds (Jacob Batalon role)
25 Simple shirt
26 "Rumour ___ It" (Adele hit)
27 Beyond
28 Frozen beverage brand
29 They might help gamers enter god mode
32 Envy or greed, it's said
33 Fictional government worker Swanson
35 Skating jump
36 Stack of raked leaves
39 Situated at the edge
41 Place for scuba diving
42 Common Korean surname
43 "No ___ intended"
45 "How come?"
46 "No ___ done"
47 Colorful parrot
48 "Fingers crossed . . ."
49 Move without effort
50 Tries to find
54 Sound of a mic drop
55 Reasonable
57 That girl's
58 Firefighter's tool
59 "This ___ joke, right?"
60 Kimchi container

40

PLACEHOLDERS

By Erik Agard

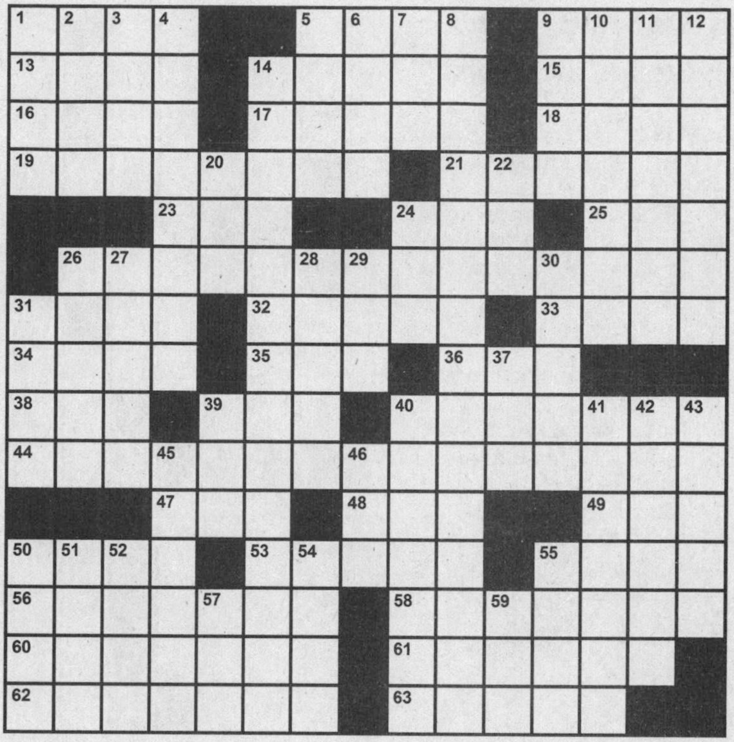

ACROSS

1 Practice like Claressa Shields
5 Stealthy summons
9 Feng ___
13 Domesticated
14 Make it to
15 "They ___ Go When I Go" (Stevie Wonder song)
16 Huge in scale
17 Novelist Thomas
18 Devices for making withdrawals
19 2019 film with a "metaphorical" rock
21 Melted cheese dish
23 20-Down backward
24 Do wrong
25 Devoured
26 Part of a sought-after set
31 "All finished!"
32 That one and that one
33 Loch with a supposed monster
34 Had debts
35 Pelvic bone
36 Prefix that rhymes with 39-Down
38 Lion's home
39 Nail polish option
40 Dwells
44 Last line of the Langston Hughes poem "Harlem"
47 Decompose
48 Many a first responder
49 Veto
50 Guangzhou's continent
53 Portion out
55 Evaluate
56 Slip-up
58 Stopped by
60 "Come on in"
61 Caused to laugh
62 Honey
63 Veggies related to shallots

DOWN

1 Plan part
2 Father's nickname
3 First name that can mean "prince"
4 Brought to mind
5 ___-up energy
6 Wise
7 ___-fi
8 James Baldwin book whose title comes from "Mary Don't You Weep"
9 Goose relative
10 Exciting romantic outing
11 Gets ready to talk, on a conference call
12 "As far as I can tell . . ."
14 Make things interesting, in a way
20 Spanish for "sun"
22 Slip-___ (shoes)
24 Seafaring distress letters
26 Shrink back in fear
27 Consecutively
28 Topping for fries
29 One-up
30 How some sun-dried tomatoes are preserved
31 Extinct bird
37 Particularly (Abbr.)
39 Prefix that means "Earth"
40 Taking-away process
41 Supports a cause, perhaps
42 Not in its original form
43 Course in which contraception is covered, for short
45 Skilled speaker
46 ___ Aviv
50 In the thick of
51 Place
52 Rae who co-founded the record label Raedio
54 Loaned out
55 Reward's counterpart
57 Gorilla, for example
59 "So ___ me!"

KICKSTARTERS

By Stella Zawistowski

ACROSS

1 Granny ___ apple
6 The "A" in T.A. (Abbr.)
10 Signals intelligence org.
13 Tragic Shakespearean teen
14 State where the Jazz play
15 Map dot
16 Brainy
17 "Bye-bye!"
18 Memorial in a newspaper, for short
19 "Let's Have a Kiki" band
22 Sydney's continent (Abbr.)
23 Yuletide plant
24 Absorb like a sponge
27 Not feral
30 Shenanigan
31 Did karaoke
32 Throw lightly
36 Control a commodity, in finance
39 Pairs
40 Cry of pain
41 "I'm Like a Bird" singer Furtado
42 The term "galaxy brain" originated from one
43 Great deal
44 Sneezy sound
48 Perishable necklace
49 Stop what you're doing
56 Leisurely gait
57 Purple smoothie ingredient
58 French bottled water brand
60 "Heads ___, tails you lose"
61 Diluted
62 Mathematical proportion
63 Broadway star Platt
64 "Parasite" star ___ Kang-ho
65 Without stopping

DOWN

1 Some 8-Down takers (Abbr.)
2 Breastfeeding parents, often
3 Apple desktop
4 "The Fosters" star Polo
5 Sriracha, for one
6 Dealership buys
7 Night sky twinkler
8 H.S. tests
9 Chiang Mai resident
10 Prize for Malala Yousafzai
11 Rhyme and synonym of "whirl"
12 On edge
15 Dorothy's pupper
20 "How ya doin'?"
21 ___/her pronouns
24 Precipitation in flakes
25 Spanish for "other"
26 Things stuck in a cushion
27 Lake near Carson City
28 Once more
29 Studio with a lion mascot
30 Do something
31 Cherry discard
32 "Happy little" thing in a Bob Ross painting
33 State north of Tex.
34 Put up for auction
35 Pig's pen
37 Toast option
38 Flawed protagonist
42 Stooge with a bowl cut
43 Moviemaking location
44 Go off script
45 Surname that sounds like a bird
46 Motorist's invitation
47 ___ your purse (pay up)
48 Telling fibs
50 Vessels for dyeing
51 Rebounding sound
52 "Purple ___" (Prince album)
53 "Nothing But a Man" star Dixon
54 Late time, in ads
55 Rhyme and synonym of "obtain"
59 Silently agree

RUNNING HOT AND COLD

By Zhouqin Burnikel

ACROSS

1 Dull in color
5 Hard-___ (uncompromising)
10 "Got it"
14 Get up
15 Pizzeria allure
16 Avoid deliberately
17 Still unresolved
19 Bunch of yaks
20 Organized crime group
21 Vision-related
23 Nueve - siete
24 ___ sticks (imitation seafood)
26 Hoity-toity types
28 Sweetie pie
31 Splinter's species, in "Teenage Mutant Ninja Turtles"
33 Wait for everyone else
36 Longoria who played Dora the Explorer's mom
37 Quite often
39 Window sealant
40 Go on and on
44 Helped out
45 Devoted fan
46 "___ you ready to order?"
47 Sweatshirt part
49 Compete on snow
50 Exasperates
51 Still with us
53 Large-scale story
55 Gear tooth
57 Maximum, e.g.
59 City south of Scottsdale
63 Actress Falana
65 Do some magic
67 Ready for business
68 Register drawers
69 Obligation
70 Discreet attention-getter
71 Streamlined
72 Fast feline

DOWN

1 Beat-keeping instrument
2 Morning TV host Kelly
3 "Yeah, right!"
4 Rebuke following an unkind remark
5 "I'm gonna pass"
6 Round, no-bake cookie treats
7 Bar in a hotel room
8 Radiates
9 Audacious
10 ". . . sorta"
11 Shows sorrow
12 Currency in Cannes
13 Winds down
18 Road surfacing goop
22 Take for one's own use
25 ___ News (paper published in Riyadh)
27 Unfocused picture
28 Versions to be debugged
29 To no ___ (fruitlessly)
30 America's national birds
32 Hypes up
34 Adjective for a sharp contrast
35 Little kids
38 Stovetop whistler
41 On an even ___ (balanced)
42 Ibuprofen brand name
43 Short scissor cut
48 Kicks out of an apartment
50 Cold snack on a stick
52 Inbox pileup
54 "___ the least I can do"
55 Sound from a hoof
56 "Clumsy me!"
58 Landmass that sounds like part of a supermarket
60 Diner handout
61 Fruit used to make saladitos
62 Queen of Arendelle
64 Crawler at a picnic
66 Request

TOPKNOT

By Rachel Fabi

ACROSS

1 Brunch offering
5 Equivalent of Mrs.
8 Two-toned ice cream order
13 ___ over (studied intensely)
15 Goal
16 "Make Me Feel" singer Janelle
17 Olympic host country for 2006 and 2026
18 Unfinished business
20 Chat, informally
22 Informs
23 "Four Women" singer Simone
24 Slightly
25 "Not so loud!"
28 Bump that rhymes with the body part where it forms
30 Give a rundown of
32 Blue-green shade
33 Batteries for remotes, often
34 "Gosh darn it!"
35 Nurses' wardrobe staples
37 More scrumptious
39 Tolerate
40 Tearfully whine
41 Lean and strong
42 Pulitzer-winning poet Armantrout
43 Letters before ://
44 Elevate
46 Congress members (Abbr.)
47 Suffix for an estimate
48 Super ___ (very spicy peppers)
49 Attention-grabbing sound
51 Chloe x ___
52 Lawn machines
55 Spiritual leader in Tibetan Buddhism
59 "Holy" object of pursuit
60 Even a little
61 Congress member (Abbr.)
62 Hayek who portrayed Frida Kahlo
63 Monetary obligations
64 Explosive letters
65 Attention-grabbing sound

DOWN

1 Grand
2 Attend
3 Green apple variety
4 Front-facing camera photo
5 Partner of pimienta
6 It's read as a reprimand
7 Single-celled organism
8 Extract metal from, in a way
9 Troubles
10 Establishment with a keeper
11 Cool
12 "___ Miserables"
14 Actress Cannon
19 Low-pressure wake behind a moving object
21 Showy aerial maneuver
25 Some people eat three a day
26 Decorative wheel cover
27 Brunch offerings
28 Gives a wave, e.g.
29 Teases
31 Organ with an anvil
32 Hand holder
34 It may be 20-sided
36 Reluctant to give details
38 Athletic award
39 Palindromic family member
41 Christmas trio
45 Debut album for Etta James
46 Put back into packaging, perhaps
48 Acclaims
50 Takes more than one's share of
51 Stop
53 Outer edges
54 Picket fence component
55 Palindromic family member
56 Had a meal
57 It may be chocolate or yellow
58 Insect with a queen

IT'S A RACE

By Gail Grabowski

ACROSS

1 Concluded
6 Some apartments
11 Movie release format
14 Garlicky sauce
15 Hunter constellation
16 "Insecure" star Issa
17 Rabbit-sized marsupial
19 Ginger ___
20 Places with lifeguards
21 Place a bet
23 Pays attention
27 Price for a promo
28 Sundiata Keita ruled one
29 Ankle injury
31 University officials
32 Hot, food-wise
33 Hydroelectric ___
36 Tic-toe connector
37 Heart-to-hearts, e.g.
38 Name that's an anagram of a word in 41-Down
39 Ace's value, at times
40 "The Color Purple" sister
41 Consolidate
43 Stinging insect
45 Radical
46 Little fellow
48 Colorful shawls
49 Takes time for some Tomi Adeyemi
50 Puts at ease
52 Part of MoMA
53 Play boisterously
59 There's no winner in one
60 Tickle pink
61 Mistake
62 "How Stella Got ___ Groove Back"
63 Credit's counterpart
64 Flaws in fenders

DOWN

1 Orecchiette shape
2 "In Too Deep" actress Long
3 Semicolon part
4 Caribou relative
5 Pampers products
6 Corporate symbols
7 Like some exams
8 Cone bearers
9 As well
10 Winter closure
11 File-moving method on a computer
12 Employee who parks
13 Name on agricultural equipment
18 Zero
22 Actress Nicole ___ Parker
23 Resulted in
24 "That is to say . . ."
25 Portable device for warming a small area
26 Pewter component
27 Circle segments
29 Go 50-50 on
30 Elongated fish
32 Bargain hunter's delight
34 Quarrel
35 Is introduced to
37 ___ to (look after)
40 Spent the night
41 Color named for a planet
42 Significant period in history
44 Past its prime
45 Disaster relief org.
46 Fury
47 Spine-tingling
48 Winter precipitation
50 Grouch
51 Italian sparkling wine
54 World Cup shout
55 Source of lead or iron
56 Banquet coffee dispenser
57 "___ my problem"
58 Hospital professionals (Abbr.)

OPEN UP!

By Evan Kalish

ACROSS

1 Some email attachments
5 Instance of passing popularity
8 Sense of style
13 Singer-songwriter India.___
14 River, in Spanish
15 Nurture's counterpart
16 Novel whose title character is the missing Amy Dunne
18 Tooth substance
19 Made level
20 "Probably the reason all these boys got crushes," in a Lil Mama hit
22 Sales agent, for short
23 UCLA's "C," for short
25 Unit of tape
26 Strong tree
28 Colorful rock
30 Your and my
33 Section after the last chapter
36 "Unsure about that"
38 Nevada city
39 Changes to manuscripts
41 Slight mistake
42 Gymnast Mary Lou
44 Place to pitch a tent
46 Fourth-year students (Abbr.)
47 Cantaloupe or honeydew
49 Coffee vessel
50 Ready to pluck and eat
51 Author Greenlee
53 Fantasy creature
56 "Gotta run!"
60 Wrist-related
62 Doing something mindlessly
63 "Fingers crossed you're right"
65 Sparkly Christmas tree decoration
66 "Yes, cap'n!"
67 "What ___ is new?"
68 Knight's ride
69 Nourished
70 Pub pours

DOWN

1 Beeper
2 Operated a motor vehicle
3 Nuances
4 Witnessed
5 "Viva la Vida, Watermelons" painter Kahlo
6 Broadcast
7 Robotics Engineer Barbie, e.g.
8 All knotted up
9 To any degree whatsoever
10 Japanese wrestling
11 Uno + dos
12 "I'm sorry Ms. Jackson, I am four ___" (misquoted lyric)
15 Family favoritism
17 29-Down spokeslizard
21 Roth ___ (investment option)
24 Praise
27 Not just some
29 State Farm competitor
30 Internet survey
31 Meter or mile, e.g.
32 What's tugged in a tug-of-war
33 Answers "airs" for this clue, say
34 ___ pressure
35 Sum of all the alleles in a population
37 Cold War country
40 Lies out in the sun, perhaps
43 Failed to mention
45 Sneakers with cats on them
48 Table supporter
50 Reduce, ___, recycle
52 Emulated Viola Davis
54 Slight mistake
55 Runs away
56 Kids
57 "Put a sock ___!"
58 Thick head of hair
59 "Frozen II" snowman
61 Comedian Butcher
64 Body part protected by a lid

ROCK BOTTOM

By Zhouqin Burnikel

ACROSS

1 Contract file type, often
4 Soup flavored with Saigon cinnamon
7 Audibly enjoys 4-Across
13 Piece of lettuce
15 Magneto actor McKellen
16 Professor's job security
17 Follow a nutritionist's advice, say
19 Ideal world
20 Poker prepayments
21 Betting figures
23 Fish in unadon
24 Holler
26 Worked on a canvas
28 Triumphant statement after reaching a destination
31 Calico call
32 ___-and-cheese pizza
33 Name in "business venture"
35 Visit someone briefly
39 Bend at the barre
41 Novelist Wharton
43 "Your Love Is King" band
44 "Oh! Carol" singer Neil
46 Croaker with leathery skin
48 Chili vessel
49 Tower by a barn, often
51 Goes places
53 Chair a meeting
56 J'adore perfume maker
57 Feline zodiac sign
58 Mushroom part
59 Rides to the red carpet
62 Housefly or mosquito
64 Something not to fall for
67 4-Down, e.g.
68 Irish folk dance
69 In need of an ice bath
70 Sign on a moving van
71 Altar reply
72 Catch a few z's

DOWN

1 Desperate appeal
2 Admissions office figure
3 Omega-3 or omega-6, e.g.
4 Sty creature
5 "I told you so!"
6 "Finally you put my love ___" (Beyonce lyric)
7 Crams for an exam
8 "We'd better avoid that"
9 Numero ___
10 Coin in Kolkata
11 Asked nosy questions
12 Close tightly
14 Turned loose
18 Resort settings
22 Structure with a water turbine
25 "C'mon, indulge yourself!"
27 Lowest poker pair
28 Mischievous devils
29 Like bulls and bucks
30 ___ Talks
34 Petty quibble
36 1973 Tatum O'Neal movie
37 Person on a pedestal
38 Meshy dividers
40 Relaxed state
42 Stroller occupant
45 It catches smooches at a ballpark
47 Like the Star Tribune
50 "___ to hozier putting his emptiness into melody" (Adedayo Agarau poem)
52 Nullifies
53 Pasta served "alla vodka"
54 Cello bow application
55 Loudly Crying Face, e.g.
57 Untruthful person
60 Easily bruised veggie
61 Leak slowly
63 Ambulance pro
65 Baby ibex
66 "SNL" star Nwodim

OPEN YOUR PURSE

By Paolo Pasco

ACROSS

1 Nighttime outfit, for short
4 Pole on a sailboat
8 Social class
13 Tumblr site
15 Meet-___ (rom-com trope)
16 Performed onstage
17 Fly higher than high
18 Revise
19 Flip-flop, in Australia
20 Gets ready to back up
23 Sound-related
24 Director ___ Saul Guerrero
25 "This rules!"
26 Web test that might have accessibility issues
28 Some call it "pop"
30 "___ You That Somebody?" (Aaliyah song)
31 Slice of history
33 Receded
37 Nothing new
42 Sound from an angry dog
43 Words from bride to bride
44 Suffix for "Taiwan"
45 Doing nothing
48 Reds or Red Sox
51 "r u 4 real??"
54 Smile from ear to ear
56 "It's a ___" (comment on something extraordinary)
57 Clout chaser's drive
60 "That wasn't exactly true . . ."
61 Shoe bottom
62 Author Ferber
65 Identified
66 "Makes sense"
67 "Yeah, sure"
68 Rita Repulsa, to the Power Rangers
69 Phone contact method
70 Positive vote

DOWN

1 "Simply Ming" channel
2 Constance Wu's "Hustlers" co-star, for short
3 Melodramatic TV show
4 Artist who drew impossible objects
5 Three-vowel automaker
6 Bee's attack
7 Game with L- and T-shaped pieces
8 Many an adorable upload
9 Post-run feeling, maybe
10 Tale
11 Past or future
12 Fringes
14 Go "hrrmph"
21 Syllable before "Tac" or "-tac-toe"
22 Self-importance
23 Plastic wrap brand
26 Puts a limit on
27 Word after "performance" or "latte"
29 ___ Dhabi
32 Poke bowl tuna
34 Moved swiftly past
35 "In this ___, I will . . ."
36 View as
38 Day after Thu.
39 Longtime pal
40 Musical genre with bass drops
41 Last-minute fear
46 Necklace for Queen Liliuokalani
47 Wipes out big-time
49 Feathery wrap
50 Aunt May portrayer Marisa
51 Say what's on your mind
52 Disney warrior who sings "Reflection"
53 Filth
55 Elk relative
58 Appear to be
59 Show off
63 French word before a birth name
64 "One Day ___ Time"

GOOF AROUND

By Hannah Slovut

ACROSS

1 Signals
5 Companion of an electric guitar
8 Flying wool eaters
13 Fails completely
14 Young boy
15 Blacksmith's block
16 Eco-friendly top of a building
18 Out of practice
19 Symbolic system used in dictionaries, for short
20 Tart
21 Salute raised by Smith and Carlos
22 Suffix for a celebration
24 Jazz trumpeter Harry
26 "Party in the ___" (2009 hit)
29 Abound
31 Was all over social media
33 Feeling
37 Olive, canola and vegetable
38 Enjoyed
41 Write in SQL or Python
42 "We going riding on the ___ of love in my pink Cadillac" (Aretha Franklin lyric)
43 Crucial
45 Slimy aquatic animals
48 Subject at a lifeguard training
49 Response
53 Tater ___
55 Old stringed instrument
57 Like some histories
59 Prefix meaning "three"
60 Fabric fold
62 "Oy vey"
64 Grocery store section
65 Not even
66 Increase
67 Pondered
68 "See ya later!"
69 A lot

DOWN

1 Flying ___ (magical form of transportation)
2 Disquieted feeling
3 ___ out a living
4 W-9 IDs
5 Audibly
6 Indigenous New Zealanders
7 File format created by Adobe
8 ___ biology
9 Culpability
10 Filming location
11 Decision in the game of blackjack
12 Sneaky
13 "So excited for the weekend!"
17 ___ v. Wade
21 "At the moment . . ."
23 Move unsteadily
25 Add fuel to
27 Mirror sight
28 First Google search results, often
30 Fighting sport, for short
32 "Hold off for a bit"
34 "Sure, I guess"
35 Car parts
36 Frozen water
38 Sticky stuff
39 Unscented
40 OPEC member
41 Public health org.
44 Moved quickly
46 Moisturizing substance
47 Put emphasis on
50 Friend of Buzz Lightyear
51 Wear down
52 Awesome
54 Put through a strainer
56 University in New Haven, Connecticut
58 Letters often followed by QIA+
60 Cooking spray brand
61 Actress and "Unhomed Belongings" artist Lucy
62 Hunk of 38-Down
63 Kanga's son

INSIDE SEATING

By Zhouqin Burnikel

ACROSS

1 Browser navigation aid
4 Applebee's sister restaurant
8 Uno, dos, ___
12 Line on a graph
14 Gnu's hair
15 "Superman" actor Christopher
16 Green goal
18 Praise profusely
19 Familiar adage
20 St. ___ College (Carleton rival)
22 The whole schmear
23 Incursion
25 Difficult to catch
27 ___-mo
29 Andre the Giant or Sasha Banks, e.g.
31 Bear who loves "hunny"
33 Mama sheep
34 Black ___ bass
35 "You must unlearn what you have learned" sage
36 Spearheaded
38 Natural rope fiber
42 Bother persistently
45 "Silly me!"
47 Pride letters
48 Excessive admiration
53 Helium, for example
54 Chipped away at
55 Reference book named after a Titan
57 Dog's sound
58 "I don't think so"
60 Empty talk
63 Extremely thin
65 Rex Stout's detective
67 Outer boundaries
68 Instrument for Cindy Blackman Santana
69 Church service
70 Have to have
71 Sensible
72 What comes before "com" in a URL

DOWN

1 Tea brand
2 Skater's spinning jump
3 Robin's meal
4 "Not a surprise to me"
5 "This ___ to stop!"
6 Not fooled by
7 Kitchen prep utensil
8 ___-Mex
9 Target field
10 Change over time
11 eBay user
13 Mediocre
15 Say no to
17 Time ___ (sci-fi travel aid)
21 Tavern selections
24 Cry of distress
26 "60 Minutes" reporter Lesley
27 Intelligence agency asset
28 Bathroom, in Liverpool
30 Plants in vacant lots
32 City with a four-mile Ceramic Road

37 Qatari capital
39 Sandwich filling
40 Degree for an exec
41 Scoreboard tally (Abbr.)
43 "Doggone it!"
44 Like some people who wear all black
46 Struck a chord
48 ___-Dazs
49 Brokerage firm with an asterisk in its logo
50 Safe place
51 Boxing match units
52 Snow mover
56 Molecule component
59 Goddess often invoked by Wonder Woman
61 "In that case . . ."
62 Recharge your batteries
64 "Alambrista!" actor Beatty
66 Last leg of a triathlon

FROM THE ASHES

By Brooke Husic & Evan Kalish

ACROSS

1 Be in accord
5 Just-washed
10 Boundary
14 Voices 4 activist Eli
15 Berry who played Zola Taylor
16 Luxor's river
17 Short, sharp cry
18 Lopsided
19 Intention
20 Expands the family, perhaps
22 Noises
24 Lamb's mother
25 Talking-to
28 Managed
30 Way to get up Heavenly Mountain
32 How Anna Lytical teaches coding
34 Programmer Lovelace
35 Drains
38 Cellular "messenger"
39 Practical component of many chem courses
41 Top-left laptop key
43 Figure skater Alysa
44 Predicament
46 Little one
48 Rihanna's character in "Ocean's 8," e.g.
50 Religious nonconformist
53 No longer in style
54 Rough-skinned fruit
55 CPR-certified volunteer
56 Like better
59 Barcode scanner components
62 Car hidden in "gaudiness"
63 Basement's opposite
66 Vat Phou's country
68 "Got it"
69 Pigs
70 Capital west of Stockholm
71 Microscope part
72 ___ and dreams
73 ___/them pronouns

DOWN

1 Leader of the Blues, in the Angry Birds universe
2 "Can I bounce an ___ off you?"
3 Nonsense
4 Make stronger, in a way
5 Casual convo
6 Girls
7 Yellowstone deer
8 Pub offering
9 Interruption-worthy announcement
10 Surrounds completely
11 See 52-Down
12 Pleased
13 Snakelike fish
21 Piano part
23 French "yes"
26 Letters before a stage name
27 Roller coaster, e.g.
28 Like some tofu
29 Queen portrayed by Olivia Colman
31 Gets in another player's head, perhaps
33 Attend uninvited
36 Round desserts
37 Confident
40 "Why not ___?"
42 Durag parts
45 Some photos
47 Fasten with string
49 Legendary place from which Morgan le Fay was banished
51 Jewish ___ bread
52 With 11-Down, "It's All Coming Back to Me Now" singer
56 Plastic beach toy
57 Bit of subterfuge
58 Bible garden
60 Versatile cards in blackjack
61 Lone
64 Number of Nobel Prizes Marie Curie won
65 Suggestion
67 Latte option

THAT'S GOT A RING TO IT

By Gail Grabowski

ACROSS

1 Criticize severely
5 Large primates
9 Halle Berry's "X-Men" role
14 Not prerecorded
15 Hourly ___
16 Cube root of 27
17 Fail to mention
18 Country with a four-crescent emblem
19 Plant secretion
20 "A League of Their Own" field
23 City northeast of (and hidden nonconsecutively in) Sacramento
24 12/31, for short
25 Outdo
28 Storage areas in some houses
31 "Full Frontal" host Samantha
34 One may be airtight
36 Mushroom part
37 Lingerie purchases
38 Be up front on a plane
42 Small-screen commercial
43 "All bets ___ off"
44 On the ocean
45 "Absolutely!"
46 Wall coating
49 Devious
50 Doesn't lack
51 Has wings, say
53 Reason for refusing an invitation
61 ___ congestion
62 ___ testimony
63 Operatic solo
64 Pastry served with tea
65 "Great job!"
66 Spot for a houseplant
67 Has an inclination
68 Defib experts
69 Part of a sock

DOWN

1 Messy type
2 Peru's capital
3 Budget or Dollar alternative
4 Free verse's lack
5 "Tattooed Heart" singer Grande
6 Tattoo ___
7 List-ending abbreviation
8 Email button
9 Deviates from the course
10 Prom committee's selection
11 Hedging words
12 Horse-guiding strap
13 Repair
21 Get the ball rolling
22 Clumsy
25 "Yum!"
26 Pimento-stuffed tidbit
27 Flatbreads with pockets
29 Ranchland measures
30 Grill fuel
31 Copper-zinc alloy
32 Studio stand
33 Writing assignment
35 Contractor's proposal
37 Lunch menu letters
39 Erroneous
40 Investment initials
41 A la ___ (menu option)
46 Analyzes grammatically
47 Impetus for a Boston "party" in 1773
48 Apex predators among birds
50 Pester relentlessly
52 Reduce to smithereens
53 Furtive "Hey!"
54 Risotto base
55 Get ___ the ground floor
56 Not even one
57 Bleak
58 Buffalo's Great Lake
59 River through Egypt
60 Like a skyscraper

THE PLATE SHOW

By Patrick Jordan

ACROSS

1 State capital near Portland
6 Concert hall level
10 Orbit shape
14 Roomy skirt style
15 One of 640 in a square mile
16 Volcanic flow
17 Honor for a hit song
19 Not oblivious to
20 Pig farm pen
21 "Quiet" author Susan
22 Steep-sided valley
24 Have to
25 "Understood"
26 Clam digger's setting
28 Bummed out
31 Bedtime reading
32 Foreshadows
33 Flight safety org.
34 Dog tag datum
35 Sliders on snowy hills
36 "Practically perfect" Poppins
37 "And the nominees ___ ..."
38 Formally ask
39 Mermaid features
40 Obtains
42 "No time to lose!"
43 Like some wontons and wings
44 "Gilligan's Island" structures
45 Is suitable for
47 Song for one
48 "___ Used to Be Mine" (song from "Waitress")
51 Car rental giant
52 High-intensity chase
55 Cartoon cats chase them
56 Bowling Green State University's state
57 They alternate with odds
58 Bitter brewed beverages
59 On the fence
60 Like neglected antiques

DOWN

1 Gets droopy
2 Zillions
3 Bloom on a pad
4 Conclusion
5 Venus neighbor
6 Unspoken
7 Absolute legend
8 Type "teh," e.g.
9 Romantic bouquet
10 "Booksmart" director Wilde
11 Magazine revived in 1983
12 Stratford-upon-___
13 Olympic pool division
18 Make less difficult
23 Devices with PIN pads
24 "___ Hits by The Supremes" (1965 album)
25 Dizzy with delight
26 Main character of "The Hate U Give"
27 Workspace for a telecommuter
28 Ones taking action
29 Before the deadline
30 Leap year's 366
31 Hypnotist's sound
32 Run in the laundry
35 Expert marksperson
36 Earth neighbor
38 Throw in the towel
39 Taught one-on-one
41 Critical situations
42 "Mrs. America" streaming service
44 Motorcyclist's invitation
45 Tuscaloosa school, familiarly
46 Like supervillains
47 Mix with a spoon
48 Litigates
49 Riddle-solving aid
50 Site with a Craft Supplies section
53 "What have we here!"
54 "Law & Order: ___"

CLOSE IN ON

By Zhouqin Burnikel

ACROSS
1 Some choir singers
6 Got 100% on
10 Tiny bug
14 "Last but not ___ . . ."
15 Pixar movie set in Mexico
16 Tree of Knowledge location
17 Sewing kit item
19 Went kaput
20 Epic story
21 Unaju fish
22 Veggie for fajitas
24 Ensure the outcome of
26 Defeats decisively
27 Another name for the cougar
32 Dealership sights
33 Like some hair highlights
34 Gooey mass
37 ___ school
38 Largest lizards native to the U.S.
39 Tedious person
40 Suffix meaning "kinda"
41 Garbage truck output
42 Worker in a pit
43 Craniotomy performer
46 "Little Women" author
48 Negative prefix
49 Possible results of peace talks
50 Many years ___
52 Walking ___ (food in a bag)
56 Negative prefix
57 Founder of the charity SixDegrees.org
60 Bridle attachment
61 Clothes appliance
62 "Stop already!"
63 Vampire's tooth
64 Granny
65 Hands over formally

DOWN
1 European mountain range
2 "Star Wars" heroine
3 Drink mix brand
4 Academy Award nomination
5 Nickname that sounds like a food
6 Feeling after muay thai practice
7 Spiral shape
8 ___-friendly
9 Blood drive numbers
10 Highway divider
11 "Under the weather," e.g.
12 Much of Gen Z, in 2020
13 Put a stop to
18 Shinagawa-based game company
23 "The Matrix" character
25 "___ up to you"
26 Authorizes
27 Trio in Christian tradition
28 For all of us
29 The Beehive State
30 Admission of guilt
31 Toothbrush material
34 Out of sight
35 Sister brand of Nilla
36 Swiss capital
38 Parchment material
39 It might cause a lot of fright
42 Open ___ (hospital procedure)
43 Secretly including among email recipients
44 Turn bad
45 Noodles often topped with narutomaki
46 Sleep lab focus
47 Language of the Roman Empire
50 Romance novel imprint
51 "The Mandalorian" actress Carano
53 Battery fluid
54 Sheltered bay
55 Smallest bills
56 Dog park noise
58 Paleozoic, e.g.
59 Wite-Out maker

SHADES OF GRAY

By Kate Hawkins

ACROSS

1 Loops in on an email thread
4 Sing really loudly
8 Little lie
11 Bathroom, in Britain
12 "Alternatino with ___ Castro" (comedy series)
14 Cubes in a casino
15 ___ or nothing
16 Dancer Rogers
17 Pi times radius squared, for a circle
18 "Dear Prudence" publication
21 Walk nervously
22 Paragons of male beauty
25 Piece of cornhole equipment
29 Throw hard
30 Magical solution to a complex problem
33 Drenched
36 Prefix for "thermal" or "tagging"
37 "___ . . . Sasha Fierce" (Beyonce album)
38 Triage places (Abbr.)
39 First day of Lent
43 Step in a flight
44 Cross-referencing phrase
47 Most trifling
50 Large coffee containers
52 Briquette-fed barbecue device
56 Dull pain
58 Oprah, to Maya Angelou
59 Seven, on a sundial
60 Social equal
61 Muppet drummer
62 Suffix for "social" or "capital"
63 Okra, e.g.
64 Item on a to-do list
65 Consumed

DOWN

1 Necklace fastener
2 Work together, informally
3 Comfort in hard times
4 Snapback feature
5 Sicilian volcano
6 Traveler's bags
7 Tire part that might be measured with a "penny test"
8 Event with bargain basement prices
9 Cubes in a drink
10 Comedian Aisling
12 Get older
13 Ricelike pasta
14 "Get Out" star Kaluuya
19 Boba, etc.
20 Cruel
23 Even once
24 Tennis match parts
26 Country home to Lagos
27 Ran in the wash
28 Catalog cosmetics brand
31 Go up
32 ___ adieu (said goodbye to)
33 Yellow jacket, for one
34 Spanish direction
35 Like some straw roofs
40 Shrivel up on the vine
41 Country on the Baltic Sea
42 "___ wish is my command"
45 "Jeopardy!" material
46 Sign up
48 Gospel singer Franklin
49 Perfume
51 Kids' Choice Awards goop
53 Bank conveniences
54 Helium balloon problem
55 Hairspray alternative
56 TikTok, for one
57 Shonda Rhimes, for Shondaland

SEE YOU AROUND

By Paolo Pasco

ACROSS

1 "___ Survive"
6 "That makes sense now"
9 Place to get a hot stone massage
12 Finnish phone brand
13 Nose, cutesily
15 Mouth, scarily
16 "Crazy Rich Asians" star
18 ___ carte
19 Oodles
20 Li'l boy
21 Smugly flattering
23 "Dora the Explorer" thief
25 Say suddenly
26 Happy hour listing
30 Barbecue pit burners
33 Friendship problem
34 Pen tip
35 Marjorie Weinman Sharmat's "Great" detective
36 Drag racer's stopping aid, for short
38 Teleconferencing button
39 "just 1 more thing . . ."
40 "America's Got Talent"-winning magician Lim
41 Origamist's medium
42 Dish with breadcrumb-coated cutlets
46 Cat burglar's crime
47 ___ in (restrained)
50 Record-spinning gigs
52 Name hidden in "Mabel"
53 Canceled
55 "Euphoria" main character
56 Car named after a California city
59 TV star Carrie ___ Inaba
60 Rings over angels
61 Tag player's cry
62 Tie the knot
63 Traditional tenth anniversary material
64 Yummy

DOWN

1 Ancient Peruvian
2 Fibers from sheep
3 "No need to tell me"
4 "Top 10" blog post, say
5 Counterpart of longitude (Abbr.)
6 How some music is stored
7 Weed-whacking tool
8 "What's new with you?"
9 Become brainier
10 Place for a cheater's notes, maybe
11 "Spirited ___" (Miyazaki film)
13 Sarcastic attitude
14 Commotion
17 Smart ___
22 Spot for a tattoo sleeve
24 Neg. opposite
25 Stuff used to entice
27 Container a contortionist might climb into
28 Texter's alternative to "gn"
29 Prefix meaning "very"
30 "Fast Money" network
31 Solemn vow
32 Flummoxed
36 Kitchen toque
37 Clue
38 Volcano near Hilo
40 "Wells for Boys" from "SNL," e.g.
41 Wistful-sounding Greek letter
43 Writer Gossett
44 Sandwich chain
45 Be abundant
48 Succeeds at an escape room
49 Credit alternative
50 Make a portrait of
51 Pride Month
52 Revlon competitor
54 Obligation
57 Name hidden in "Felix"
58 Eusocial insect

COLD OPEN

By Zhouqin Burnikel

ACROSS

1 Mangoes have big ones
5 River mouth formation
10 Slow as molasses
14 In need of a massage
15 "Mr. Peabody & Sherman" actress Winter
16 Toddler's scrape
17 Much-loved
18 Restaurant freebies
20 Arrange in advance
22 Cross-referencing phrase
23 Playful parody
26 Graph paper feature
27 Metallic symbol of success
30 Lacrosse stick features
33 Bolted
34 "Meet the Parents" actress Polo
35 Shoe designer Jimmy
37 Per item
39 Religious splinter groups
42 Coretta Scott ___
43 Number of Supreme Court seats
44 Distinctive time periods
46 Title for Lancelot
47 Morse code symbols
49 Healthy grain
51 Location
53 Occupants of old Russia's Winter Palace
54 Wrestler's restraining maneuver
57 Airport sections
60 Deviate from the group
63 Part of this clue backward
64 One might be shed or blinked away
65 Take a snooze
66 Currency in Helsinki
67 ___ Disney World
68 Alpha's counterpart
69 Fender blemish

DOWN

1 Items for note-taking
2 Beverage with a spoon straw
3 Disapproving statement
4 Sweet, sticky liquids
5 Little bit of blush
6 Get it wrong
7 "Real eyes realize real ___"
8 Chinese snack often flavored with five-spice powder
9 Salmon-smoking wood
10 Place for swimmers to lounge
11 Birds associated with wisdom
12 Roughly 2.2-pound unit
13 "Sure thing!"
19 Reason for indoor recess
21 Blog entry
24 Mine extractions
25 Word before "ant" or "alarm"
27 High-fiber muffin choice
28 Very fast
29 More pleasant
31 "You're not wrong"
32 Sega's hedgehog
36 Folklore meanie
38 Retail chain with chew toys
40 Easy running pace
41 Wood-cutting tools
45 Unexpected glitch
48 Qipao fabric
49 Don't lose your head
50 Far from PG
52 Anatomical trunk
54 Location
55 Genuine
56 Joint used in leg curls
58 Bring in
59 Assist in the gym
60 "I almost forgot . . ." in texts
61 Powder ___
62 Place to get a mud mask

IT'S LIT!

By Matthew Stock &
Brooke Husic

ACROSS

1 Disney deer
6 Applications
10 Extremely long time
13 Restaurant critic Ho
14 Ripped
15 Timid
16 Bendable craft item
18 ___ Tacs
19 "Great minds think ___"
20 Super stylish
21 Low-visibility forecast
22 Palindromic vow-taker
23 Buddy
25 In sync
28 Blueprint detail, for short
30 Dorm people
32 Bring together
33 Review the finances of
35 Pasta instruction
36 Social media alter ego
39 Briefly drops by
40 Grieve
41 Beginning
42 Lead-in to "crawl" or "quiz"
43 Move like a fish
47 Collection of info to be analyzed
50 Male sheep
52 Environmentalist's prefix
53 "Salt, ___, Acid, Heat"
54 Deprives
56 Uppermost room, perhaps
58 Lively dance
59 Potential date
61 Poem paying homage
62 The ___ effect (tendency to overvalue self-assembled items)
63 Spanish for "grandmother"
64 Affirmative answer
65 Breezy's rhyming partner
66 ___ Dame ("Our Lady")

DOWN

1 Traditional Maori dish
2 ___ skiing (sport named for a mountain range)
3 Timid
4 Chin-up muscle
5 Under the weather
6 State home to the Skull Valley Band of Goshute Indians
7 Supreme Court justice Sotomayor
8 Construct
9 Spanish for "to be"
10 Language related to Finnish
11 "Ah, that makes sense!"
12 City served by EWR, JFK and LGA
13 Goes across
17 Pastry that becomes a name when the first letter is moved to the end
21 Noncompetitive races
24 Cho who played Kira on "Teen Wolf"
26 Teach one-on-one
27 Bear's lair
29 Perch for a "baby on board"
31 Bit of postage
34 Storage spaces
35 Diving acronym
36 Genuine
37 Steals the limelight from
38 Fancy meal part
39 Pea's place
44 Less arid
45 Wintertime dripper
46 Chocolaty cafe order
48 "Living Single" actress Alexander
49 Thai has five of them
51 Cuban dance music
55 Occasion for cake, for short
57 Lacking slack
58 Happiness
59 Bow ___ pasta
60 Vied for office

EARS TO THE GROUND
By Margit Christenson

ACROSS
1 Outdoes
6 Behavior that might prompt someone to yell "Get a room!"
9 Made a rip in
13 Spanish for "milk"
14 Charged particles
16 Marge Simpson's is blue
17 Regions
18 Against
19 "Tell Mama" singer James
20 Unsubtle verbal nudge
22 Engraves
24 Goes out with
25 Destiny's Child or the Supremes, for example
27 "Wide Sargasso ___" (Jean Rhys novel)
29 "Is that so?"
33 Honorific in Hialeah
36 Ingredient in bhindi masala
37 Sewing line
38 Greets
39 ___ Speedwagon
40 Room with a retractable ladder, often
41 Home of the Bruins
42 Banh mi spread
43 Scenic view
44 Where Birmingham and Atlanta are located
46 Prof's aides
47 Serving dishes for soups
49 Pincer, e.g.
53 Frequently misspelled contraction
56 Cyclist's place on the road
58 Debt metaphor
59 Design detail, for short
61 Competitor of Blue Cross Blue Shield
62 "La ___ Bonita" (Madonna song)
63 Deck furniture wood
64 Sheet fabric
65 Sirius or Betelgeuse
66 Tax org.
67 Beeches and banyans

DOWN
1 Case of the ___ (discontented feeling)
2 Unsettling
3 Public spat
4 "It's retro, but in a bad way"
5 Meetup, slangily
6 Tough instrument for movers to move
7 "It would behoove you to be less antagonistic"
8 Insect that sounds like family
9 "It looks safe!"
10 Vow
11 Bat mitzvah, for one
12 Time periods
15 ___ Leone
21 Hoppy brew letters
23 Word after "tongue" or "twist"
26 Pang
28 Hospital parts, for short
30 Allows
31 French for "milk"
32 Village People hit sung at many sporting events
33 Closed
34 Apiece
35 River through Khartoum and Cairo
36 Speak at a podium, say
40 "13th" director DuVernay
42 Least polluted
45 Collective word
46 Judgy sound
48 Shaving mishaps
50 Barista creation
51 Singer Clark, aka St. Vincent
52 Stops breastfeeding
53 "___ Is Us"
54 Sender of invites
55 "First Lady of Song" Fitzgerald
57 Dawn direction
60 Architect I.M.

WHEN IN ROME

By Evan Kalish

ACROSS

1 ___-fulfilling prophecy
5 15th-century Peruvian
9 Nest items
13 Birch, e.g.
14 Be nosy
15 Plumbing problem
16 1989 film about GM layoffs in Flint, Michigan
18 Opposite of "pro-"
19 "Freshwater" protagonist
20 "Set It Off" star Kimberly
21 Messy rooms, metaphorically
22 "Time will tell!"
24 French farewell
26 Place to get cash
27 Gets on in years
28 Collection
31 List of edible offerings
33 Old Russian ruler
34 Partner of willing
35 Ehdrigohr or Swordsfall
38 Internet addresses
39 Yoked farm animals
40 Rowing poles
41 Spelling competition
42 Soil
43 "Have we ___?"
44 Like Vikings
46 Kalahari and Namib, for example
50 Try for a job
52 Earthquake-prone rift
54 "You can't ___ a crown" (Althea Gibson)
55 Drop of sweat
56 Rapidly gained name recognition
58 Border
59 Hard-to-deal-with kids
60 Morning TV host Kelly
61 Level
62 Little demons
63 Spoken exam

DOWN

1 Sipping aid
2 Wear away over time
3 With 4-Down, payment to an attorney
4 See 3-Down
5 Many a bellybutton
6 Silent yeses
7 "Repeat that?"
8 Orangutan, e.g.
9 Fill with joy
10 Apple Store tech support zone
11 It might have a latch or a code
12 Equipment for Lindsey Vonn
14 Capital of Oregon
17 Take some time off, say
21 Venus, to Serena, for short
23 Bowling alley parts
25 Movie star Laura
27 So far
29 Shade-giving 13-Acrosses
30 Golfer's peg
31 "No, I love YOU ___"
32 Star of "Juno"
33 Political process that might affect brackets
34 Colorful stone with bands
35 Massage
36 "The Giver" author Lowry
37 Attends
42 Towel off
43 Turns into water, perhaps
45 Further on in years
46 Two-person karaoke options
47 Broadcast again
48 Florida city by a bay
49 Abscond with
50 Aid and ___
51 Mani-___
53 Relative of "stat!"
56 Softball stat
57 To and ___

UPPER LIMITS

By Zhouqin Burnikel

ACROSS

1 Whale that preys on seals
5 ___ of personality
9 Creamy cheese
13 Home to most Quechua people
14 Model ___ Huntington-Whiteley
15 Like many epic movies
16 Tied
17 "Unfortunately, that's true"
19 Bureaucratic snarl
21 Workers in ambulances, for short
22 Novelist Monica
23 Zodiac lion
24 Sticky note
28 Soda can feature
30 Twangy-sounding
33 Hosp. area
34 Diving apparatuses
37 Ambassador, e.g.
39 Muscle quality
40 Spanish for "father"
42 "Fiddling" Roman emperor
43 In a way
45 Quite
47 Texter's "If you ask me . . ."
48 Pays attention to
50 Brit's bathroom
51 "That's unnecessary"
53 Grand ___ Opry
55 Short snooze
58 "Runaway Bride" actor Richard
60 "Good going!"
62 Leeway
66 Master of Fine ___
67 Sister brand of Newtons
68 Peak performance
69 Search for
70 Grains in muesli
71 Explorer who appears in "Go, Diego, Go!"
72 Ser Anzoategui's "Vida" role

DOWN

1 Zitkala-Sa composed one
2 Party hearty
3 Bank alternative
4 Family reunion invitee
5 "Be serious!"
6 Mex. neighbor
7 Word after "still" or "shelf"
8 School writing assignment
9 Pure delight
10 Fishing stick
11 Shoo-___ (sure winners)
12 Inflated self-image
14 Like a coconut that falls from its tree
18 Ring-shaped island
20 "Honey" star Jessica
25 Long-standing
26 "It matters to me"
27 One-on-one teacher
29 Help commit a crime
31 Threw in
32 Knight's title
34 Couch blotch
35 Fashion mag edited by Jessica Pels
36 Zip through a book
38 "Hang ___ Your Love" (Sade song)
41 Linking verb
44 Roulette spinner
46 Singer Benjamin
49 Williams-___ (cookware brand)
52 Some frozen waffles
54 Pad thai ingredient
56 Fed the pot
57 Irksome
59 "Consequently . . ."
61 Relaxed state
62 Action director John
63 Savings plan option
64 Figure out
65 Boathouse tool

DO I HEAR AN ECHO?

By Stella Zawistowski

ACROSS

1 Desirable group of guests
6 Undesirable picnic "guests"
10 Get out of bed
14 Word of greeting
15 Stir up
16 Tall, in Spanish
17 Religion with five pillars
18 Actor Chaz
19 Prejudice
20 1992 TLC hit
23 "Golly!"
26 "___ the season to be jolly"
27 Gives a hand to
28 Rhyme or ___
30 Not "for here"
33 Have a dispute
34 Requirement to visit some countries
35 Long, long story
39 1999 Destiny's Child hit
42 Hide and ___
43 Option on an edit menu
44 Second half of a musical, often
45 Double-reed instrument
46 "Strange . . ."
47 Counterpart of pleasure
50 "Wow!"
51 "Didn't I tell you?"
52 1965 Byrds hit
57 "Wonder Woman" bad guy
58 Dinghy, dory or dhow
59 Word of obligation
63 Bioengineering target
64 "You're something ___"
65 Fluid that can be donated
66 Airline assignment
67 Back area
68 Christmas creatures

DOWN

1 Yellowfin tuna
2 "___ Miserables"
3 Not feeling so hot
4 Thick slice
5 Marinara sauce ingredients
6 Chain with a cowboy hat logo
7 Beginner, informally
8 Singer Turner
9 Bad roommate for a neatnik
10 Officiant at a Jewish wedding
11 Trojan War epic
12 Attempts
13 Not difficult
21 Plane's overhead storage location
22 Hoops star Ming
23 Snatches up
24 Creepy
25 Bird on the German coat of arms
29 Be a sore loser, perhaps
30 ~
31 Capital once called Christiania
32 One of the states of matter
34 Wine, in Italian
35 Sets on the attack
36 Singers lower than sopranos
37 Move smoothly
38 Line heard by the audience but not by other characters
40 Palindromic fella
41 Spa garment
45 Taking testosterone, for short
46 Debtor's letters
47 Liquidized substance
48 Staples Center, for the L.A. Sparks
49 Map within a map
50 Cute river animal
52 Graffiti artists' signatures
53 Prefix akin to "super"
54 Part to play
55 Space shuttle grp.
56 Legally invalid
60 End of 55-Down's URL
61 Long-handled gardening tool
62 Football scores, for short

RIGHT GUARD

By Zhouqin Burnikel

ACROSS

1 Father, in Chinese
5 Virtual greeting
10 Bug big-time
13 Mennonite offshoot
15 Comedian DeCotis
16 Yak butter ___ (traditional Tibetan drink)
17 What tenure provides to a professor
19 Show with the most Emmys
20 Give confidence to
21 ___ de toilette
22 Follower of "room" or "soul"
23 Solar panel component
25 Congested-sounding
27 Clean with water
30 Distinctive regional characteristics
34 Microbrewery choice
35 Kid around
36 Candle shop emanation
37 Jousting weapon
39 Dog trainer's command
41 ___ up (add pep to)
42 Teensy
43 Project for a pastry chef
45 Swelled head
46 Hyatt or Marriott, e.g.
49 Country that celebrates Sizdah Bedar
50 Slowly diminish
51 Drawn-out
53 Wine container
55 Turn to confetti
57 Tusked sea mammal
61 Hour after midnight
62 Good example
64 Greek letter before theta
65 Weasel-like river mammal
66 "Modern Family" star Vergara
67 Part of a basketball hoop
68 ___ coil (scientific invention of 1891)
69 Really hot

DOWN

1 ___ Fresh (Chipotle competitor)
2 "Cornflake Girl" singer Tori
3 Marathoners' keepsakes
4 Per se
5 Bird with muscular legs
6 Give a hoot
7 Pop singer Grande
8 Customary routine
9 Joke-a-___ calendar
10 "We're doomed!"
11 Tenant's expense
12 Green smoothie ingredient
14 "Present!"
18 Instrument for Tina Guo
22 Polynesian language
24 Defeat
26 Deli counter device
27 "Private Practice" actress Kate
28 Competitor of Budget
29 One of 100 occupied in D.C.
31 Girl, in Spanish
32 End of the Greek alphabet
33 Talked nonstop
35 Dessert that wobbles
38 Supermarket worker
40 Showy part of a peacock
44 Widely recognized
47 Percentage quoted by a bank
48 Intricate robberies
49 Snowy shelters
52 Siestas
53 Mashable editor Jessica
54 Poker player's payment
56 Sumo orange cover
58 Widespread
59 Alternative to Linux
60 Dog trainer's command
62 Foldable bed
63 Tax-deferred plan

STEP BACK INSIDE

By Evan Kalish

ACROSS

1 Ignited
4 Bluish-green shade
8 Broadcast resolution option
12 Very eager
14 Class that doesn't require a lot of studying
16 Locality
17 Production with hand-worn "performers"
19 Dryer fuzz
20 Entertainment that's an anagram of "bearcat"
21 Got perfectly right
23 Mukhwas spice
24 Measurement standard
25 Ruby who played Ruth Younger in "A Raisin in the Sun"
27 Smidgen
28 Place to buy floor coverings
32 Set of moral values
33 "___ rue the day . . ."
34 YolanDa Brown's instrument
36 Improvise dialogue
39 Pig's dwelling
40 Geographic reference book
42 Foreboding signs
44 Louis Armstrong highlight
47 Instant messaging pioneer
50 On the ___ (running away)
51 "Video" singer India.___
52 Oprah's production company
54 Meal that might include turnip cake
56 Like many Tiffany Alfonseca works
58 Southern chef Lewis
59 Looking after a vacationer's fish, say
61 Excessive amount
62 ___ lightly
63 "Gotcha"
64 Valuable stones
65 Smart-alecky responses
66 Six-point plays (Abbr.)

DOWN

1 Company-loving tabby
2 Lizard with a Taino-derived name
3 Auction-winning offer
4 French for "head"
5 Rightward, on a map
6 Fire residue
7 "Russian Doll" star Natasha
8 Corridor
9 Like used-up magic markers
10 With gentle care
11 Large tub
13 College application stats
15 Anticipate
18 Standing straight up
22 ___-bitsy
24 Words before "and personal"
26 River wriggler
29 "Eureka!"
30 Disencumber
31 Discard
32 Semester-end challenge
34 Sit astride
35 Metal in kitchen foil
37 "As I see it," for short
38 "The Fresh Prince of ___-Air"
40 Georgia's capital, on scoreboards
41 Places that do peels
43 ___ game (softball feat)
45 Spew like a volcano
46 Microwave displays
47 Part of MUA
48 Started serving customers
49 Beavers' dwellings
53 Not in favor of
55 Yoga surfaces
56 Parts of some CDC campaigns
57 Provides assistance
58 Omelet ingredient
60 Steeped beverage

64

WITHIN SIGHT

By Brooke Husic

ACROSS

1 Activist Copeny
5 Un poquito ___ (a bit more)
8 Finance pros
12 Like Batman and Stupendous Man, costume-wise
13 Feeling unwell
14 ___ mind (unified consciousness)
15 Not urban
16 Poshmark transaction
17 Bubble tea jelly option
18 Most wicked
20 Canary and lemon, for two
22 Place to buy 8-Down
23 Computer key for indenting
25 Bombards
26 Prolonged attack
28 "Sister, Sister" star Mowry
29 Path-illuminating fixture
32 D.C.'s country
34 Pointy-eared creature
35 Utterance of disgust
36 Sing wordlessly
39 Lima's country
41 Impulsive
43 List of choices
44 Signal "I'm interested" on a dating app
47 Jazz legend Dolphy
48 Spanish for "friend"
49 Sylvia who wrote "The Bell Jar"
50 Next best poker hand after a pair
53 Ice cream ball
55 Bedding item
56 "How lovely!"
60 Fields of expertise
61 Monster that's a Latin conjunction backward
62 Opposite of norte
63 ___ fences (make things right)
64 Friends
65 Loose-leaf ___

DOWN

1 Purple shade
2 National Autism Awareness Month
3 Down-to-earth person
4 Not doing anything
5 "Mamma ___!"
6 Non-enemy
7 "Sweet dreams" alternative
8 Bread sometimes made with anise
9 Trial episode of a TV show
10 Proclaims
11 Really gets
12 Believability, for short
16 Pre-show jitters
19 ___ wool
21 Singer Nash
24 Teyana Taylor won Video Director of the Year at its 2020 award show
27 Rage
29 Lehenga alternative
30 Vegetation adjective
31 Dr. Rhonda's profession on "Insecure"
32 FedEx competitor
33 Stitch
37 Decibel, e.g.
38 A lot
40 In front of us
42 Before now
43 Fruit salad ingredient
45 Gives off
46 Big ___ (large truck)
49 Does some modeling
50 ___ Red Eagle ("The Miseducation of Cameron Post" character)
51 Antidote
52 Like all bra band sizes
53 Story of epic proportions
54 SZA album whose name is a computer key
57 Lead-in for "scotch"
58 Actor's prompt
59 The "E" in BCE

HOLDING DEAR

By Paolo Pasco

ACROSS

1 Sly ___ fox (sneaky)
4 Rhyme and synonym of "glob"
8 "Just One Look" singer Doris
12 Papier-mache substance
14 "Beautiful show!"
15 Russo in "Thor" movies
16 Not acquired easily
18 Community rec center
19 Rhyme and synonym of "appoint"
20 "Only Time" singer
22 Ooh and ___
23 Watches online
25 Unscientific unit of spiciness
27 Suitcase-screening org.
28 Got noisy
32 Arrogance
33 Moved very quickly
34 Place where grooms exchange vows
37 Part exposed by a tank top
38 "Dirty Computer" artist Janelle
39 Couple
40 Hospital procedure in a tube
42 Places for hoops or studs
44 "___ and Maddie" (Disney series)
47 Appliance blamed for missing socks
48 Meal break similar to merienda
50 Schedule placeholder, for short
51 Exclude
54 Arranges on a dish
55 Event for Kendall Ellis
57 "Knives Out" star
59 Synagogue chests
60 Does nothing
61 Ditty
62 Annoyance
63 Substances like henna
64 Maya Angelou's city of birth (Abbr.)

DOWN

1 Beyond shocked
2 Tilts
3 ___ borealis (northern lights)
4 "It's cold in here!"
5 Narrow road
6 Pizzeria appliance
7 Henna designs, etc.
8 Attempt
9 Comment about
10 Being filmed
11 "Uh huh"
13 "The Sopranos" star Falco
14 Poison Ivy's enemy
17 Win the heart of
21 Funnel cake ___ mode
24 Memory-holding phone chip
26 Do something about
29 Hair-raising
30 Has as a goal
31 Merch stand shirt
32 Lug
34 KakaoTalk, e.g.
35 Exposed
36 Neckwear-holding organizers
38 Chicken tikka ___
40 Disney's Ariel, for one
41 Brunch orders that may be jam-filled
43 Oprah, for Harpo Productions
44 Acid-base test material
45 "To clarify . . ."
46 Container
49 Like a tamarind's taste
50 Ensnare
52 Annual auto event, for short
53 Unbelievable story
56 Superlative suffix
58 Word before "Moines" or "Plaines"

UPEND

By Zhouqin Burnikel

ACROSS

1 Febreze competitor
6 Cards checked for building access
9 ___ pump
13 Danger
14 Loch that's also a suffix
16 Just sitting around
17 Open presents early, say
19 Historian Annette Gordon-___
20 Part of a hydroelectric plant
21 Addition amount
22 "This has me down in the dumps!"
24 Speak formally
26 "Measure twice, ___ once"
27 Quick snooze
30 Counterpart of digital
35 Like plants that can survive adverse conditions
36 Break sharply
37 Wait on the phone
38 A lot of ___ in the fire
39 Family dog, e.g.
40 Remove coding errors from
41 "Try again"
42 Orders to attack
43 Place of residence
44 Entertaining little story
46 Holders of oranges
47 Baby goat
48 Engaged in espionage
50 Not neo-
52 Kelp's place
53 Rap star Lil ___ X
56 Largest city in Qatar
57 City north of Dallas
61 Smart ___ (wise guy)
62 Come to deserve
63 Greta Thunberg, for one
64 Rounded roof
65 Food coloring, e.g.
66 Positive trait

DOWN

1 It directs drivers
2 Give temporarily
3 Office space stat
4 Heart-shaped "Titanic" prop
5 Animal that can weigh over a thousand pounds
6 Enter into the system
7 Judged to be crucial
8 Direction opposite NNW
9 "I'll start on a low note . . ."
10 Innovative thought
11 Snow day slider
12 Sam Lloyd's "Scrubs" role
15 Bit of headwear on the slopes
18 "Pronto!"
23 Ingredient in some face masks
25 Light beams
27 Country that's the world's largest instant noodle market
28 Model ___ Philip
29 Characters saying "you'd better come see this," e.g.
31 Enjoys some banchan, say
32 Programmable worker
33 Get away from
34 A 45-Down has 12
36 Rotisserie rod
40 Have the nerve
42 "Wow, that's cool!"
45 Casino cube
46 "Gotta run!"
49 Tube-shaped pasta
50 Game played on horseback
51 "If I may intrude . . ."
54 Tools for firefighters
55 "The Big Unknown" singer
56 Pops
58 Little chap
59 Org. with screening bins
60 Theatrical backdrop

DOUBLE UP

By Amanda Rafkin

ACROSS

1 Matted bits of hair
6 Eager
10 Hairstyle for Esperanza Spalding
14 House made of snow
15 Green-and-brown attire, for short
16 Baby's bed
17 Spanish lollipop brand
19 Egg providers
20 Thread holders
21 They often fly in a "V" formation
22 Number of "Things I Hate About You"
25 Parking place
26 Doesn't flunk
27 "Girl Genius" protagonist
30 Word on a candy heart
31 They may be eliminated with a subscription
32 Exclamation from a prankster
33 Affirmative response to "You are?"
36 They meet for comfort and advice
39 Clips often shown in slow motion
40 Like a dark room, perhaps
42 "How ___ you?"
44 Singer Janis
45 Sea mammals that float on their backs
46 Unleash
48 Word after "beach" or "dad"
50 Singer who keeps her face covered while performing
51 Harmful bit of light
52 Disappear
55 Breakfast, lunch or dinner
56 Really awesome
60 It may be trimmed or painted
61 Activist Brockovich
62 Genre for "Roma" or "Moonlight"
63 Troubles
64 Uses scissors
65 Pancake topping

DOWN

1 ___-tac-toe
2 "Oh, gross!"
3 Target of an annual vaccine
4 T-shirts and blouses, e.g.
5 Hand-washing stuff
6 Sound that warrants a blessing
7 Bank room
8 Little rascals
9 ___ and don'ts
10 Pains' partners
11 Grocery store nibbles
12 Got the 5-Down off
13 Do some overthinking
18 Slushie flavor
21 Distributed
22 Word yelled before "You're it!"
23 They may be inflated or fragile
24 Hiker's path
26 Sound from a contented cat
28 Use a keyboard
29 With joy
30 Drags along
33 Tehran's country
34 Pigs' digs
35 Patty or Selma, to Bart
37 Big name in skin care
38 iPhone assistant
41 Org. with wands
42 School graduates
43 Disclose
45 That stinks!
47 Takes a tumble
48 Toy that involves pulling, twisting and spinning
49 Unwraps
52 Title for Nanak
53 Stat at a racetrack
54 Rage
56 Short time to wait, in brief
57 Golfer's standard
58 Only bird with calf muscles
59 Genre for Eve

STAFF MEETING

By Mark McClain

ACROSS

1 Radar image
5 Webpage
9 "___ on Me" (Bill Withers song)
13 Palindromic mechanism
15 2016 Sharon Olds poetry collection
16 Automotive shaft
17 Thin-heeled shoe
19 Put in an overhead compartment, say
20 Escape in the air
21 Applies
23 Part of a train
24 ___ firma (solid ground)
25 Puts in the oven, perhaps
29 Big cat
30 Microdermabrasion offerer
33 Up to the task
34 What cowry shells were once used as
35 Female bird
36 Sauce with a poblano variety
37 Assumed a certain stance
38 52-Down of power
39 Word before "peeve" or "project"
40 In a foul mood
41 Periods in history
42 Shade of gray
43 Sharpen
44 With great intensity
46 Radiates
48 Beaver's construction
49 Hallowed place
51 Indistinct sounds
55 Take notice of
56 Piece of paper from a colorful pad
59 ___ Major (bear constellation)
60 Have a chat
61 Beans and fries, e.g.
62 Some body art, informally
63 Soap foam
64 Fill-in from an agency

DOWN

1 "Gimme a minute," in an online chat
2 Bread buy
3 "___ be alright in the end"
4 Roly-___
5 Up to now
6 Without purpose
7 Brew that might be black or green
8 Looked up to
9 Surgical light
10 Cheddar variety
11 Quite often
12 Anchors report it
14 Flinch or jump, say
18 Past-tense 'tis
22 Urgent care center scan
24 Things to hum
25 Florida bay city
26 Flutes' neighbors in an orchestra
27 Whatever is left
28 "Come ___ About Me" (Supremes hit)
29 Entourage
31 Flower part
32 Visibly impatient
34 Mars has two
37 Rent strikes, e.g.
38 Itsy-bitsy
40 Goatee's place
44 Unlit
45 TV awards
47 King with a golden touch
48 Mallards and such
49 Open-and-___
50 Queen of Greek gods
51 Salsa rating
52 Standard of measurement
53 Took the bus
54 Flower part
57 Sorority letter
58 Eerie ability

CHEST DIPS

By Zhouqin Burnikel

ACROSS

1 Chess or xiangqi
5 Spur on
10 Eight's cube root
13 For each one
14 Largest city in the Middle East
15 Shape of some earrings
16 "Stop dreaming!"
18 Bronte's Jane
19 Wood stove refuse
20 Gives off
21 Animal that moves on two limbs
22 ___-faced (expressionless)
23 1993 Mariah Carey hit
24 Sculpture garden figure
26 ___-eyed (innocent-looking)
27 Surgical areas, for short
30 Made from fleece
31 Cleaned, in a way
33 Hilarious sort
34 Far from verbose
36 "Not to mention . . ."
37 Standout athletes
39 Withdraw financial involvement
41 "She Can STEM" ad, e.g.
42 Bounce house filler
43 In this manner
44 Parade spoiler
46 Campus heads
47 Comments section annoyance
49 Fashion mag since 1886
50 "It ___ fun while it lasted"
53 Volunteer for more
54 Chitchat in bed
56 Places to stay
57 Had leftovers, perhaps
58 It starts when the curtain goes up
59 Edamame casing
60 ___ up (became informed)
61 Sticky substance

DOWN

1 Apple variety
2 Tailless primates
3 Insect near a flame
4 Short musical releases
5 Bottled water brand
6 ___ biologist
7 "Classic of Filial ___" (Confucian treatise)
8 Geologic periods
9 "ur so funny!"
10 Lap dogs with curly coats
11 Sported
12 Pundit's piece
15 Inheritance recipient
17 "The L Word" role for Jennifer Beals
21 Voicemail signal
22 Seasons, in a way
23 Large and supposedly cursed gem
24 Bagfuls at garden centers
25 Drive aimlessly
26 Cuatro's square root
28 Singer-songwriter Cailin
29 Word after "tight" or "hot"
30 Bundle up
31 Sra. counterpart
32 Roof overhangs
35 Drop the ball
38 Mermaid's feature
40 "That's no surprise"
43 "Roots" actress Uggams
45 Matterhorn's range
46 ___ out (distributes)
47 Vacation
48 Nevada Museum of Art city
49 BofA competitor
50 Home of Baylor University
51 Chorus voice
52 Pass up
54 Tabby's foot
55 Price place

WATER, WATER EVERYWHERE

By Lynn Lempel

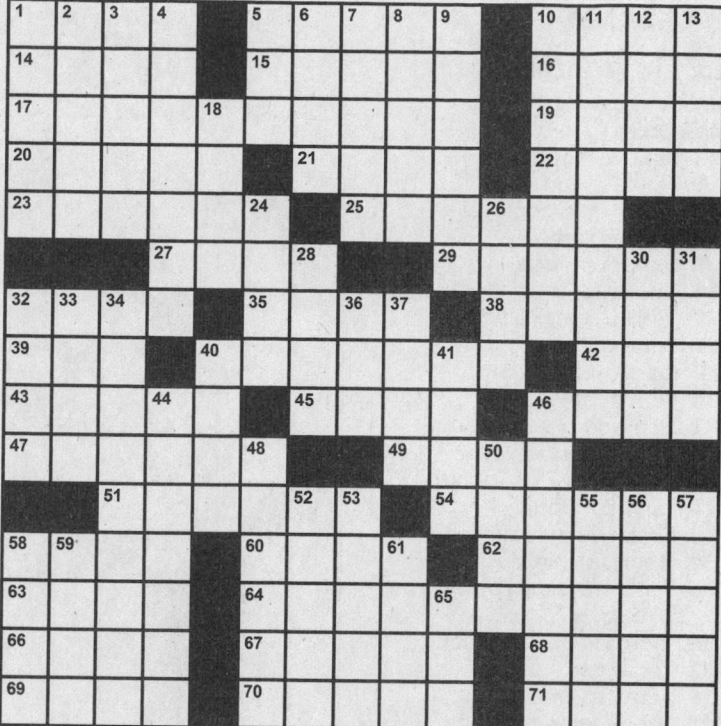

ACROSS

1 "Amphibia" creator Braly
5 Relief from the heat
10 Kati roll, e.g.
14 High woodwind
15 Sculptor who influenced Meta Vaux Warrick Fuller
16 Geologic time spans
17 Short "e," e.g.
19 ___ fide
20 Musical set in Argentina
21 Get out of Dodge
22 Bit of numerical data
23 Dissuades
25 Heart-wrenching
27 Third ___ (subway track part)
29 Spin around
32 Decides
35 Coating formed by oxidation
38 Kidney-related
39 Title for MLK Jr. (Abbr.)
40 Ship's infirmary
42 Place for a blood pressure cuff
43 Chocolate-yielding bean
45 X, in a love letter
46 Range between tenor and soprano
47 Acropolis city
49 Ice cream quantity
51 Bickers
54 Nobel Peace Prize winner Mandela
58 "This looks bad"
60 Donkey's cry
62 Genre for Clara Nunes
63 Lions' homes
64 Broadcast in real time
66 Chocolaty cookie
67 Cause for a food recall
68 Pin the Tail on the Donkey, e.g.
69 Wallpaper unit
70 Waterproof ground covers
71 Geologic time spans

DOWN

1 Changed homes
2 Higher than
3 "Namely . . ."
4 Wobbles
5 H.S. Ditch Day participants (Abbr.)
6 Horse's foot
7 Grown
8 Casual eatery
9 Make lovable
10 Reductress or Clickhole, e.g.
11 Drawn-out dental procedure
12 Fashion designer Sui
13 Three-section H.S. exam
18 "To All the Boys I've Loved Before" protagonist ___ Jean Covey
24 Name hidden in "desiring"
26 Like many slasher films
28 Good fortune
30 Sour
31 Muppet with his own "World"
32 Black-and-white swimmer
33 Bog material
34 Couch potato's pick
36 Word after "water" or "jet"
37 Recipe measure (Abbr.)
40 Bandcamp download
41 "Z ___ zebra" (spelling clarification)
44 Spray can substance
46 On the loose
48 Rental from a renter
50 Treetop dwelling
52 Gospel artist Campbell
53 Relish
55 Slanderous attack
56 "Becoming" author Michelle
57 Contact list contents
58 Property of burning sulfur
59 Protagonist
61 App with business reviews
65 Tia, to Tamera, for short

NO SOAP

By Claire Rimkus

ACROSS

1 Positive feature
6 Store ___
11 Move like a dog's tail
14 Horned beast
15 Chopper blade
16 Choice for a painter
17 "Rollin' Stone" bluesman
19 State-of-the-___
20 Car's audio system
21 Reminder to repay
22 Elementary school orgs.
23 Japanese noodle
25 Formal "you" in Spanish
27 Extended family
30 Excessively wealthy
34 French 101 article
35 Dot surrounded by blue, on a map
36 March 14 observance
37 Really excited
39 Actress Mendes
41 Greek salad morsel
42 Sip slowly
43 Large flightless birds
45 Bear's lair
46 Transaction total
49 Symphony's finish
50 Basic unit of length
51 Pixar-animated clownfish
53 Fruity cereal
55 Middle point (Abbr.)
57 "Gotta ___!" (parting words)
61 Possesses
62 Casual diner
64 Co-host of "The Talk"
65 Lingerie retailer
66 Some inclement weather
67 Blouse size (Abbr.)
68 Manner of dress
69 Screams

DOWN

1 Places for tattoo sleeves
2 Unwelcoming, like an office door
3 One of four on a square
4 Evasive maneuver
5 ___ with (played around with)
6 65-Across purchase
7 Kottu ___ (Sri Lankan street food)
8 Didn't dine at home
9 "Whenever's good"
10 ER workers
11 "Who, me?!"
12 General vibe
13 Understands
18 Adoption center sounds
22 Great danger
24 River through Cairo
26 Editors remove them
27 Loud bell noise
28 Madagascar primate
29 "Just like we agreed . . ."
31 Carpenter's tool
32 Gave in
33 African scavenger
35 What "i.e." is short for
38 County in Massachusetts or England
40 Closing for a prayer
44 Words on a milk jug
47 Covert
48 Vessel from the heart
49 Date night pair
52 Like some lawns
53 Gender-neutral pronoun
54 Leave a five-star review, perhaps
56 Plane alternative
58 Christmas in Paris
59 "I May Destroy You" creator Michaela
60 Otolaryngologists, for short
62 Rest stop fuel
63 Catch a glimpse of

WELL, WELL, WELL!

By Paolo Pasco

ACROSS

1 "Yee-___!"
4 What the top sphere on a snowman represents
8 Daring venture
12 Li'l
13 Fertile area in a desert
15 Three-vowel Great Lake
16 Omurice ingredients
17 Cursive alternative
18 What the bottom spheres on a snowman represent
19 Vanna White's show
22 Slithery swimmer
23 Shiba ___ (dog breed)
24 Solution
26 Southern speech feature
28 Jumped
31 Positive vote
32 Clumsy person, unkindly
34 Member of the fam
35 Cookie with a Mega Stuf variety
36 Printer inserts
40 WNBA team with a card-related name
41 French word before a birth name
42 Negative conjunction
43 Cat's "hand"
44 Crying Jordan, etc.
46 Draws closer
50 Happened next
52 Bowler's target
54 Make a sound like a dove
55 Alternative to throwing a coin into a fountain
59 Golden ___ Bridge
60 Bugs Bunny and Perry the Platypus, e.g.
61 Add to the staff
62 Shoreline platform
63 Sudden uptick
64 "Boys ___ Flowers"
65 Bank conveniences
66 No, in Russian
67 Tie the knot

DOWN

1 More lofty
2 "Are Prisons Obsolete?" author Davis
3 Judicious
4 Biker's invitation
5 Severe scolding
6 "Not gonna happen!"
7 Velociraptor or apatosaurus, for short
8 Puzzle involving pictures and letters
9 Some metal items
10 Looks at disdainfully
11 Caps Lock or Delete, e.g.
12 Made a sound like a kitten
14 Buckles up
20 Pale purple
21 Minecraft explosive
25 ___ Speedwagon
27 Lomo saltado pans
29 Cosmetics mogul Lauder
30 Pool float filler
33 Homemade recuts of a movie
35 Creature that's like an onion, per "Shrek"
36 "No rush"
37 Bit of reportage
38 Sleep stage acronym
39 Retta's "Parks and Recreation" role
40 Monkey relative
44 "I've seen better"
45 Word before "cake" or "bath"
47 Opposite of passive
48 Made a sound like a lion
49 Aching more
51 App downloaders
53 Zoomed-in map section
56 Part of speech of "verb," ironically
57 All the ___ details
58 Spectacle
59 Dean's list stat

L.A. WOMAN

By Zhouqin Burnikel

ACROSS

1 Place for a dartboard
4 Chamberlain hailed as "the most popular girl in the world" by Cosmopolitan in 2020
8 Was in the loop
12 Burden
14 It waxes and wanes
15 Idaho Black History Museum city
16 Enticements
17 "The ___ thickens!"
18 Hopping mad
19 Model with her own fragrance line
22 Kara Walker's field
23 Uno mas uno
24 Time-tested sayings
28 Take-home amount
30 Staff assistant
32 "It seems like so long ___"
33 Dumpster output
34 Curling periods
36 Natural hairstyles
38 Welsh-born clothing designer
41 Neutral shades
43 ___/neuter programs
44 Barbecue orders
47 Prefix for "orderly"
48 Wooden strip
50 Yogurt brand
52 Korokke ingredient
54 ___ Lankan rupee
55 Word before "date" or "diligence"
56 "Road Less Traveled" singer
60 Bandleader's cue
63 Newspaper remembrance, for short
64 Spice jar holder
65 Gas bill basis
66 Double-sided ___
67 Largest joint in the body
68 Pizza crust option
69 Watched carefully
70 Throw into the mix

DOWN

1 Pepper used in chiles en nogada
2 Yet to be broadcast
3 Durable
4 Job provider
5 Works into shape
6 Tie to a dock
7 Prefix for the opposition
8 The "K" in K-Town
9 Pro wrestler Jax
10 Numerical guess (Abbr.)
11 Teensy
13 Pig's hangout
15 "So what?"
20 Pioneering programmer Lovelace
21 Little League coach, perhaps
25 City that's a song title in "The Music Man"
26 Narcissist's display
27 "Mayday!"
29 Seek divine guidance
30 Change with the times, say
31 "The Photograph" star Rae
35 Mars Exploration Program org.
37 Many an office plant
39 Minnesota, e.g.
40 Drank some water
41 Measure of an economy, for short
42 Spanish for "river"
45 Enjoyed a trampoline
46 Moved stealthily
49 "Skip to My ___"
51 Need a sick day
53 Set straight
54 Slender-billed marsh bird
57 Mechanical memorization
58 Auction website
59 Noah's vessel
60 Simple shelter
61 "... or so"
62 ___ chi

THINGS ARE LOOKING UP

By Pao Roy & Brooke Husic

ACROSS

1 Luminous stand-in for Pixar's "i"
5 Cricket's noise
10 Contribute
13 Brief guest appearance
14 The "R" in NPR
15 Sticky part of a house gecko
16 Elated
18 Garage alternative
19 Agitates
20 Angry look
22 Next-to-last Greek letter
23 Jazz style with an onomatopoeic name
27 Wraps up
28 Lacrosse stick part
31 Put money in the bank
32 "While you're ___ . . ."
33 Corp. name ending
35 Many Ph.D. students
36 Pumpkin desserts
37 Daydreaming, say
40 "Good going!"
42 Selma's state (Abbr.)
43 Relaxation destination
44 City in Iowa
45 Evite request
47 Neighbor of Turkey
51 Computers seen at Genius Bars
52 Set the stage for
54 "Crouching Tiger, Hidden Dragon" director Lee
55 Winged white wader
57 Brief rest
60 1-1, for example
61 In all existence
65 Tennis player Ivanovic
66 Measuring device
67 "Well, ___ you a peach!"
68 Turquoise or sapphire
69 Wasn't overturned
70 Sappho is called the 10th one

DOWN

1 Extravagant
2 Bloomer who ran The Lily
3 ___ mortals
4 Some nonstick items
5 French pancakes
6 Cuban sandwich ingredient
7 Knot-tying words
8 ___ Grande
9 1972 video game debut with virtual paddles
10 Legendary lost city
11 Desperate, in a way
12 Really hates
13 Press ___ (group of journalists)
17 Center of activity
21 Feb. 29
24 Subterranean headquarters of a DC Comics superhero
25 Shape of some mirrors
26 Philippine coins worth 100 centavos
29 Artful maneuvering
30 Explosive palindrome
34 Billboard's Hot 100, e.g.
37 Sundae basis
38 ". . . or ___!"
39 Company whose trucks avoid left turns
40 Place for pronouns
41 "Just think . . ."
46 Showed appreciation for being scratched behind the ears, may
48 Strikers' demands, at times
49 On the same wavelength
50 Word after "free" or "double"
53 Friend who might be furry
56 Pulls
58 Fake
59 Ollantaytambo's country
62 ___ Geo
63 Chloe x Halle, e.g.
64 Comedian Nwodim

HEARTBROKEN

By Kate Hawkins

ACROSS

1 Hasbro toy that yells its name at you
6 Beehive or messy bun
10 One-sixteenth cup (Abbr.)
14 Third planet from the sun
15 Second-largest branch of Islam
16 "The thing with feathers," per Dickinson
17 Not these
18 "Just listen…"
20 Play a kazoo
21 Gnaws
23 Prefix for "mural"
24 Word before "opposites" or "vortex"
26 Buddy
28 Longtime NBC show
29 Like Mandarin and Igbo, linguistically
30 Keys' counterparts
32 Flowers for a 3-Down
33 Circle dance
34 Fuzzy footwear
38 London hub
41 Norway's capital
42 Yours and mine
43 "Revelations" choreographer Alvin
44 Like blustering storms
46 Like blustering storms
47 Orienteer's chart
50 Ginger ___
51 "Super Smash Bros. ___" (fighting game)
52 Dole out
54 Sulky
56 Trivial concern
59 Racer's advantage
61 Not sleeping
63 Keen
64 Capitol Reef's state
65 Wild party
66 Camera part
67 Meshes well
68 "I ___ of Jeannie"

DOWN

1 Quiet "Little Women" sister
2 Diamond Head's island
3 Event that might involve a flash mob or a decorated locker
4 "___ Gonna Be Me" (NSYNC song)
5 "London Calling" band
6 Seat-finding attendant
7 "That was a close one!"
8 Dispersions from homelands
9 Boat-rowing tool
10 "If/___" (musical)
11 34-Across, e.g.
12 Rebuff
13 "She loves me, she loves me not" item
19 Harvey who was California's first openly gay elected official
22 Nickname for Harold
25 Two thousand pounds
27 Bowl berry
29 The T. rex had four per foot
30 Lois who wrote "The Giver"
31 Opposite of prone
32 Greek consonant
33 Person you split the rent but not a room with
35 Peak period
36 Neutral colour
37 Pig's place
39 Agitate
40 Place with tracks and cars
45 Granola bar morsels
46 Get hitched
47 Taj ___
48 Advil alternative
49 Bagel or yogurt flavor
51 Hole-making insects
53 Ratio at a racetrack
55 Word before "hygiene" or "exam"
57 Swedish furniture chain
58 Stint in office
60 Pull
62 Simple card game

POD CAST

By Zhouqin Burnikel

ACROSS

1 Bird with melodious trills
5 Tiny opening
9 Radar screen dot
13 Writer Brooke who coined the Hurston-Walker Test
14 Colorado-based beer maker
16 ___ oxide (sunscreen ingredient)
17 Circles with circular toppings
20 Prefix meaning "four"
21 High-walking performer's pole
22 Comment after a fumble
24 "Eww!"
25 Roof sealant
28 Plush dog originally sold by Tonka
32 ___ Grande, Arizona
33 Goof up
34 Jane who met Bertha Mason
35 Massage therapist's supplies
36 Contemporary of Cassatt
38 Smog rating org.
40 Deals with adversity
41 Got older
42 Company hidden in "consultant"
44 Fish that might be mistaken for a sea snake
45 Prohibited thing
46 Fresh water conveyor
49 "Snowpiercer" channel
50 Bus route diagram
51 Iolani Palace island
52 Icy celestial body
54 Czech dance
57 Stuffed appetizers with a kick
62 Needs to pay back
63 Ferrero competitor
64 Excited about
65 Part of a parrot
66 Aunts, in Spanish
67 Soft throw

DOWN

1 ___ off (prune)
2 Help with illegal activity
3 Like a golden yellow mango
4 Didn't give up
5 Feisty
6 Bathroom, in Brixton
7 Charged particles
8 Bottom sirloin cut
9 Sound of a buzzer
10 "Good Side" singer Phair
11 "Not ___ million years!"
12 Netbooks, e.g.
15 Like kung pao chicken
18 Wears away
19 Type
23 "You betcha!"
25 Capital where Ruby Lin was born
26 Zonked out
27 Fight on a mat, informally
28 Person prone to nitpicking
29 Pacific Northwest state
30 Requiring quick action
31 Add zing to
32 Pigeon's call
37 "Without further ___ . . ."
39 Dog food brand
40 Server who might wear roller skates
43 Vessels used for steeping
46 One- or two-humped animal
47 Present-giver's prompting
48 Platform similar to a minbar
50 Tool for a spill
52 Large barrel
53 Morrison who wrote "Beloved"
55 Game similar to bingo
56 Liberal ___ college
57 Task
58 Feeling of wonder
59 Singer Salonga
60 Makeout sesh at a mall, e.g.
61 "Help!"

TOGETHER IN THE END

By Matthew Stock

ACROSS

1 Wash in a tub
6 Fabric edges
10 Worry
14 Witch's prop
15 Surya Bonaly leap
16 "(10-Down) is ___" (Netflix show)
17 "Project Runway" topic
18 TV star Leakes
19 Praiseful poems
20 Place that serves brisket
23 Vietnamese soup
25 Sports team heads (Abbr.)
26 Read carefully
27 Hybrid Southwestern cuisine
29 Turnpike payment
31 Signal that's a palindrome in English and Morse code
32 Two-dimensional calculation
33 Australian gems
35 Investment option
40 Word after "mass" or "social"
41 "Didn't mean to do that"
44 Tablet download
47 D.C. baseball team
48 Nation in Oklahoma
50 "___ Moon" (anime series)
52 Bit of scuba footwear
53 Payment to the government
54 53-Across grouping
58 Hibernation stations
59 Contract length unit
60 "Time flies," e.g.
63 The "E" in HOMES
64 Fairy tale monster
65 Pass along
66 Ink ___ (squids' pouches)
67 Functions
68 Joint above the foot

DOWN

1 "___ Blues" (King song)
2 "The Earth without ___ is just 'eh'"
3 Playroom containers
4 Greeting before "Que pasa?"
5 Come out of hiding
6 Underwear brand
7 Corner office person, for short
8 Diner handout
9 REM researcher's place
10 Surface opposite the ceiling
11 Half a diameter
12 "Despite all that . . ."
13 Flavors
21 Stunt rider's sport
22 Jiggly treat
23 K-12 school org.
24 "Hard Place" singer
28 Palindromic term of address
29 Roman gods' garments, in art
30 Photo ___ (PR events)
34 With 42-Down, stir-fry veggie
36 Toxic fluid
37 "Go ahead, do it!"
38 Small criticism
39 "Shh"
42 See 34-Down
43 "___ Education"
44 Off-mic remarks
45 Bread bowl-selling chain
46 Open-air meal
48 Photo
49 Turkey's capital
51 Disobeys Simon, say
52 Subway riders' payments
55 Asks for a dog treat
56 Like blue lobsters
57 Actress Riegel
61 Amount of milk (Abbr.)
62 Storm's center

MINT CONDITION

By Rachel Fabi

ACROSS

1 Diary addition
6 "The Three Little Pigs" construction material
11 Photo ___ (times to take pics)
14 "The Life-Changing Magic of Tidying Up" author Kondo
15 Garlicky sauce
16 Aisha Dee's character on "The Bold Type"
17 Sensitive to criticism
19 Take a plane
20 Pop in the mail
21 Clinical study
23 Romantic playlist fodder
28 Therefore
29 "___ wrong?" ("Don't you agree?")
30 Opposite of "cheered"
32 Tournament ranking
33 Arakawa's art
36 Like an angle that's neither right nor obtuse
38 "The Legend of Zelda" release of 2017
44 Jumped
45 Musical role for Quvenzhane Wallis
46 Speak hoarsely
49 Prophets
52 ___ Aviv
53 Readily available
55 Complained about unfairness
58 Spry
59 Saint ___, Minnesota
60 "Children of ___"
61 CEO of Stark Industries
68 Deer also known as wapiti
69 Food wrap brand
70 Wipe away
71 One out of 365 or 366
72 Agenda contents
73 Response to "gesundheit!"

DOWN

1 CPR provider, perhaps
2 "I'm good"
3 One less than quadri-
4 Step between "lather" and "repeat"
5 Affirmative answers
6 Answered in the negative
7 Fiftieth element
8 Nigerian language, or a nickname in English
9 Bitter beverage
10 Measurement across
11 "Ugh, you win"
12 Monarch's residence
13 Outfitted for a magazine cover, say
18 Rounded door handle
22 Stitched again
23 Rogan josh meat
24 Ilhan, the first Somali-American elected to Congress
25 Source of grapes
26 Pursue
27 Religious faction
31 "Oh, of course!"
34 Rhyming friend
35 Past tense of 62-Down
37 Oolong, e.g.
39 Owns
40 Oil grp.
41 "___ the Woods" (Sondheim musical)
42 In ___ of (rather than)
43 Lenovo competitor
46 Wandered
47 "Women, Race and Class" author Davis
48 Descriptor for some cheeses
50 Matures
51 Scorch
54 Soda with a red, white and blue logo
56 Fooled
57 Plants of a region
62 Chow down
63 Not post-
64 "The L Word" actress Grier
65 Light brown hue
66 Admonishing noise
67 "Do you get it?"

SCHOOL CLOSINGS

By Erik Agard

ACROSS

1 Soup paste
5 Pieces of marble
10 Excite
12 Things similar to that
14 Fry quickly
15 Avoid wasted minutes
17 A buyer and seller converge on one
19 Sick
21 ___ land (region that encompasses New York City and Philadelphia)
22 "Scary!"
23 Lake under which Garrett Morgan led a rescue in 1916
24 Aide (Abbr.)
25 Sums
27 Precise
28 "No ___!" ("Don't sweat it!")
29 For free
30 "Mind over matter" obstacle
34 "I'm begging you!"
35 Animated character, for short
36 Sprang
37 "This is awesome!"
38 "The Yield" author ___ June Winch
42 Breakfast bits
43 Not against
44 Post office packet
46 Scorer's count (Abbr.)
47 Computer capacity
49 Alter ego of Jon Kent, in comic books
51 "Hey, show's back from commercial!"
52 Author's alias
53 Samsung competitor
54 Blasts of wind
55 Buds

DOWN

1 Garam ___ (South Asian spice blend)
2 Pictures
3 Rejects scornfully
4 Gobble down more hot dogs than, e.g.
5 Communal areas in some dorms
6 Imposes
7 Smart ___ (know-it-all)
8 Instruction from a dentist
9 Compete like Bonnie St. John
11 Palindromic sound
12 Recipe abbreviation
13 From Dubai, say
16 Bring out
18 Hon
20 Allows
23 Midterm, for example
26 Nonfiction movie, for short
27 "The Office" receptionist
28 "Hey you!" whisper
29 Down in the dumps
30 Pants folds
31 Gets warmer
32 Shrill barks
33 ___ roll (Brit's toilet paper)
34 Sound before a fizz, perhaps
37 Australian marsupial
38 In ___ shape
39 State that's the title of a Maggie Rogers song
40 Shrink back
41 Team buildings
43 Some nonflowering plants
45 Spelling-clarifying phrase
47 Options list
48 Toast type
50 Board game piece

PEOPLE WITH CONNECTIONS

By Zhouqin Burnikel

ACROSS

1 "That's incorrect!"
6 Plant used in basketry
10 "Voila!"
14 Enjoyed some homemade sushi rolls, say
15 "Therefore . . ."
16 "Sign me up!"
17 "The Year of Magical Thinking" author
19 Quite a few
20 Fluids used in traditional Chinese painting
21 View as
22 Eva portrayed by Madonna
23 Top at a merch table
24 Female rabbit
25 CBS show about a judge
27 Discombobulate
29 Word after "smart" or "funny"
31 Fred Gray's expertise
32 Huevos ___ mexicana
34 Through
35 "Furthermore . . ."
36 New Look fashion designer
40 Catan resource
41 Container of mints
42 Three, in Chinese and Japanese
43 ___-weekly
44 Zoolander's first name
46 Debate subject
50 The Taxpayer Relief Act of 1997 introduced it
52 Some Instagram posts
54 Government org. that's an animal backward
55 Tool for sweeping
56 Foal's mother
58 Prescriptions, informally
59 Trips around a track
60 "The Inheritance of Loss" author
62 Blog post modification
63 "That right?"
64 Give a speech
65 Physicians, informally
66 Fella
67 Waste disposal system

DOWN

1 Sizzling Tex-Mex item
2 Did penance
3 Disclosed secret information
4 Moral misdeeds
5 Bring to a halt
6 Cash in
7 New York canal
8 Self-centered condition
9 Crime family leader
10 Microwave feature
11 Texas Panhandle city whose name means "yellow" in Spanish
12 "Jurassic World" beast
13 "Do you have the latest?"
18 Wedding day phrase
22 Paper towel layer
24 Place to buy a salad
26 Tilts
28 Fat in some tamales
30 Like lambs and rams
33 Perennial in the daisy family
35 ___ and needles
36 Greeley's state
37 Sister brand of Torrid
38 Cocoa-dusted dessert
39 Platform for honored guests
40 Sang like a bird
44 Not well-lit
45 Dojo discipline influenced by kung fu
47 Playground plank
48 Software download
49 "___ said than done!"
51 Runs a virtual meeting
53 Dragon's place
57 Quite dry
58 "The ___ fact that . . ."
60 Child
61 Number after uno

LOGIC

The next few pages have all the instructions you'll need to tackle all the logic puzzles in this book. They may look a little complicated but you'll soon get the hang of things.

Solving Tips

With each standard problem we provide a chart that takes into account every possibility to be considered in the solution. First, you carefully read the statement of the problem in the introduction, and then consider the clues. Next, you enter in the chart all the information immediately apparent from the clues, using an **X** to show a definite **no** and a ✔ to show a definite **yes**. You'll find that this narrows down the possibilities and might even reveal some new definite information. So now you re-read the clues with these new facts in mind to discover further positive/negative relationships. Be sure to enter information in all the relevant places in the chart, and to transfer newly discovered information from one part of the chart to all the other relevant parts. The smaller grid at the end of each problem is simply a quick-reference chart for all your findings.

Now try your hand at working through the example below—you'll soon get the hang of it.

Example
Three children live on the same street. From the two clues given below, can you discover each child's full name and age?

Clues
1. Miss Brown is three years older than Mary.
2. The child whose surname is White is 9 years old.

Solution

Miss Brown (clue 1) cannot be Brian, so you can place an **X** in the Brian/Brown box. Clue 1 tells us that she is not Mary either, so you can put an **X** in the Mary/Brown box. Miss Brown is therefore Anne, the only possibility remaining. Now place a ✓ in that box in the chart, with corresponding **X**s against the other possible surnames for Anne.

If Anne Brown is three years older than Mary (clue 1), she must be 10 and Mary, 7. So place ✓s in the Anne/10, Brown/10 and Mary/7 boxes, and **X**s in all the empty boxes in each row and column containing these ✓s. The chart now reveals Brian's age as 9, so you can place a ✓ in the Brian/9 box. Clue 2 tells us that White is 9 years old too, so he must be Brian. Place a ✓ in the White/9 box and **X**s in the remaining empty boxes in that row and column, then place a ✓ in the Brian/White box and **X**s in all the remaining empty boxes in that row and column. You can see now that the remaining unfilled boxes in the chart must contain ✓s, since their rows and columns contain only **X**s, so they reveal Green as the surname of 7-year-old Mary.

Anne Brown, 10.
Brian White, 9.
Mary Green, 7.

	Brown	Green	White	7	9	10
Anne	✓	X	X	X	X	✓
Brian	X			X		X
Mary	X			✓	X	X
7	X					
9	X					
10	✓	X	X			

	Brown	Green	White	7	9	10
Anne	✓	X	X	X	X	✓
Brian	X	X	✓	X	✓	X
Mary	X		X	✓	X	X
7	X		X			
9	X	X	✓			
10	✓	X	X			

The solving system for the puzzles that don't have grids is very similar. Read through the clues and insert any positive information onto the diagram. Then read through the clues again and use a process of elimination to start positioning the remaining elements of the puzzle. You may find it easier to make a few notes about which elements of the puzzle you know are linked but that cannot yet be entered on the diagram. These can be positioned once the other examples of those elements are positioned. If you find it difficult to know where to begin, use the starting tip printed upside down at the foot of the page.

Logi-5

Start by looking at the intersection of columns and rows that contain at least two starter letters, preferably more, and then use the "shapes" to further eliminate possible letters from that intersection square. You may well find that you can now position at least one letter exactly. There is one more "trick" to help: If, in your eliminating, you find two squares in a row or column, each of which must contain one of the same pair, then the other squares in the row or column cannot contain those letters and can be eliminated.

Sign In

When solving Sign In puzzles, the clues that aren't there are just as important as the ones that are. In the second row of our example puzzle, the 5 can only be positioned in column two, since placing it elsewhere in that row would mean that a 6 would have to be entered according to the signs. Following the 5, a 4 can now be written in below it. Now here's where the clues that aren't there come into play. If the 2 was placed in either of the shaded squares, either a 1 or 3 must be next to it. And there is no + or - sign linking these two squares. Therefore the 2 must be placed at the top.

Going Green

Four golfers were tackling the tricky 4th hole at their golf club. They had all reached the green, but after different routes and taking different numbers of strokes. Can you fully identify the player whose ball is in each of the positions marked 1 to 4 on the green and say how many strokes he had taken to arrive at that spot?

Clues

1. The ball of Mr. Bunker, who had had a longish argument with a sand trap and taken four strokes to reach the green, is next clockwise from Martin's.

2. Peter's ball is number 4; he had taken one more stroke to arrive at that point than had been taken by Mr. Rough.

3. One player, who was not Mr. Tees, had shocked even himself by knocking ball 2 straight on to the green in one shot.

4. Gerry had reached the green in two shots.

5. Henry's ball bears a higher number in the diagram than Green's.

First names: Gerry; Henry; Martin; Peter

Surnames: Bunker; Green; Rough; Tees

Strokes taken: 1; 2; 3; 4

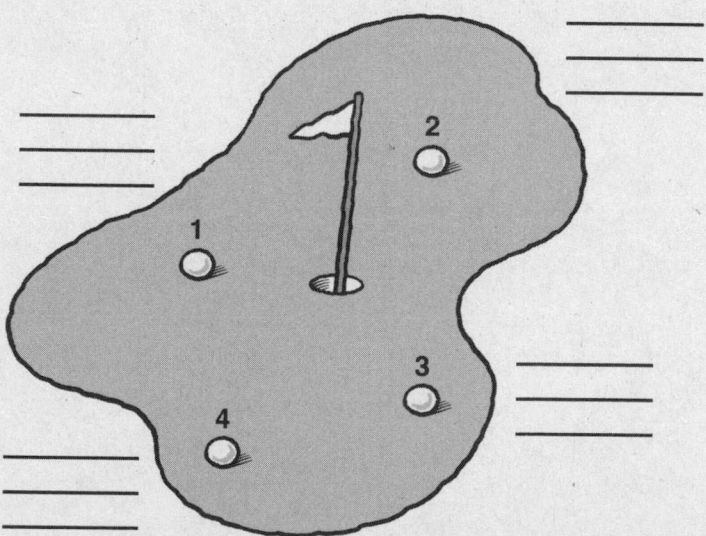

Starting tip: First work out the first name of the player using ball 1.

Getting the Point

"So we're all set, are we?" asked Jake, the leader of the Rainforest Adventure Group a few days before they were due to leave. "We're set," they replied. "Equipment?" he asked. "Sorted!" they replied in unison. "Tickets?" "Done!" "Food?" "Packed!" "Vaccinations?" "Err . . . what?" So Jake arranged for Penny Syllin, the local physician, to visit the next morning with her serums and needles and posted a hastily written schedule on the notice board. Can you fill in the names on the timetable?

Clues

1. Alan's appointment was 15 minutes later than Gary's, who was set to be jabbed ten minutes before Evan, whose time was later than Fifi's, which was 15 minutes before Bess', who was later than Carl but earlier than Hugo, who was sometime before Iris was to be jabbed.

2. The appointments of both Alan and Iris were set for when the minute hand on the wall clock were pointing at odd numbers on the face.

3. Fifi wasn't the second person on the list, but was before Carl on the list.

Adventurers: Alan; Bess; Carl; Dora; Evan; Fifi; Gary; Hugo; Iris

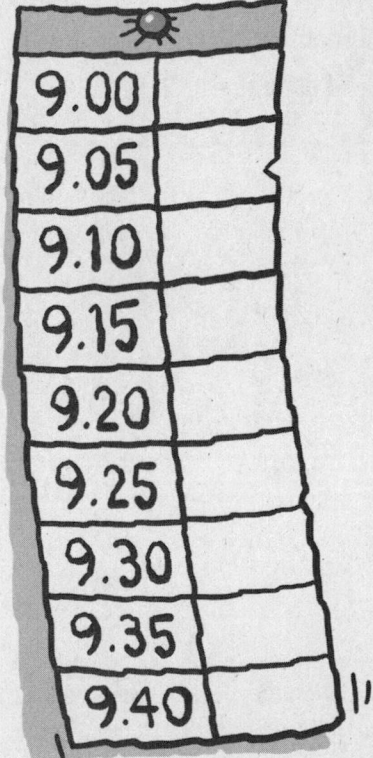

Starting tip: Work out who will be the last person to be vaccinated.

Pigeon Holes

The diagram shows four pigeon holes in the office of the Department of Future History at the University of Melville, each belonging to one member of the academic staff. Can you fully identify the owner of each pigeon hole and their role in the department? (Arabella and Melissa are women, the other two are men.)

Clues

1. The head of the Department of Future History is Professor Spriggs.

2. The pigeon hole of the man named Darby is adjacent to Melissa's.

3. The person whose mail is placed in pigeon hole D is senior in the department to Arabella, but is the junior of Chubb, whose pigeon hole is not the one marked A.

4. The junior lecturer's pigeon hole is somewhere to the right of Graham's.

First names: Arabella; Graham; Jolyon; Melissa

Surnames: Chubb; Darby; Howlett; Spriggs

Positions (in ascending order of seniority): junior lecturer; lecturer; senior lecturer; professor

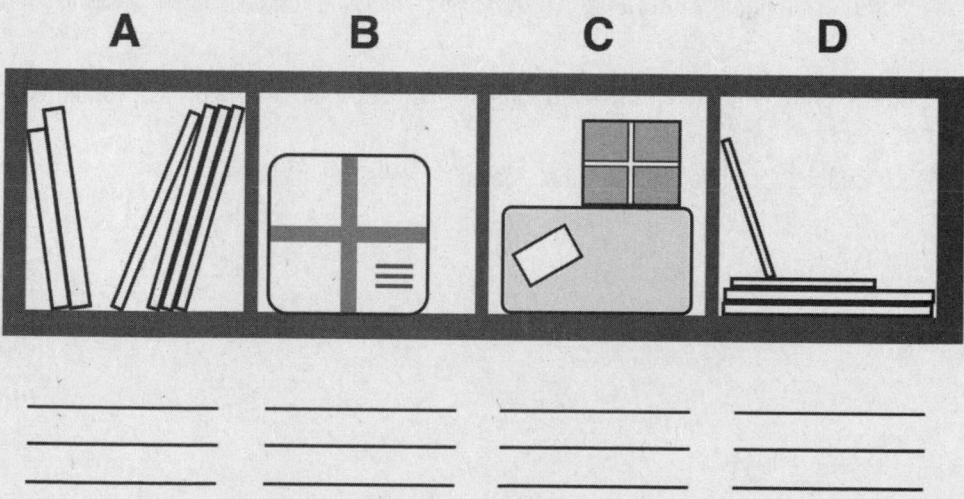

A B C D

Starting tip: Begin by working out Chubb's role in the department.

Chicken Run

When Henrietta moved from her cluttered country home to a spartan city apartment, her friends were concerned that she would miss her flock of chickens (actually she only missed the eggs). Within a week, each of her friends had presented her with a chicken-shaped gift which, for want of anything better to do, Henrietta has arranged in a set of shelves in her new kitchen. From the clues, can you work out the nature of each chicken substitute, the name of the friend who gave it to her, and its position in the nine compartments of the display unit? (Obviously, we've drawn all the items as jugs so as not to give the game away.)

Clues

1. The dog toy in the shape of a chicken (doubly useless since Henrietta does not have a dog) is directly right of Albert's gift and directly above the wooden chicken ornament.

2. Nadine made the felt chicken herself. It is immediately below Ethel's gift and has a number twice that of Roger's present. The clucking pecking robot chicken is in the diagonally opposite corner to Caroline's contribution.

3. Chicken no.6 is an egg cup. The china chicken ornament is numbered twice that of Daniel's gift, which is immediately right of the teapot.

4. The chicken-shaped jug is somewhere left of Paul's present on the same row. Melanie's gift is no.3.

Chickens: bronze ornament; china ornament; dog toy; egg cup; felt ornament; jug; robot; teapot; wood ornament

Givers: Albert; Bridget; Caroline; Daniel; Ethel; Melanie; Nadine; Paul; Roger

Starting tip: Position the china chicken.

Gas Giants

Scientists from Melville University working at the FARCee Observatory have discovered a distant star that has (at least) eight large planets orbiting around it, four of which have systems of rings, four don't. With most of the planets in our solar system being named after male Roman gods, the Melville researchers have chosen the names of female gods for their discoveries. Can you name each planet?

Clues

1. Juno is somewhere left of Minerva, which is somewhere right of the ringed Vesta which is somewhere left of, but not immediately left of, Fauna, which doesn't have a system of rings.

2. Nemesis is somewhere left of but not next to Flora which is somewhere left of Juno; Diana, which isn't planet 8, is more than one place right of Nemesis; only one of Diana and Juno is a planet with rings.

3. Aurora, which is in an odd-numbered position, is somewhere right of Fauna.

Goddesses: Aurora; Diana; Fauna; Flora; Juno; Minerva; Nemesis; Vesta

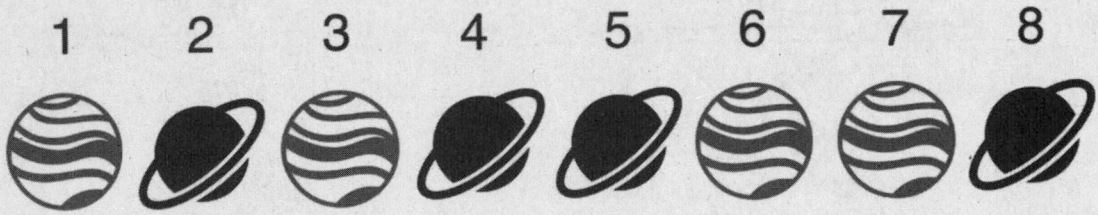

1   2   3   4   5   6   7   8

____ ____ ____ ____ ____ ____ ____ ____

Starting tip: Name planet 8.

Soap Box Derby

The annual Sunnyside soap box derby was held last weekend and the top four carts are shown below. Each was driven by a young driver and co-driver and each was modeled on and named after a well-known luxury automobile brand. Can you name the two drivers and the automobile brand for each finishing position?

Clues

1. The driver of the third-placed Mercedes wasn't Roy Jowett.

2. Aisha Morris' Ferrari finished immediately behind the cart co-driven by Mandy Austin.

3. The cart shared by Jenny Hillman and Hassan Riley finished immediately behind the Jaguar.

4. Neither the Porsche nor the cart co-driven by Gemma Lanchester finished fourth.

Drivers: Aisha Morris; Jenny Hillman; John Singer; Roy Jowett

Co-drivers: Gemma Lanchester; Hassan Riley; Mandy Austin; Peter Humber

Carts: Ferrari; Jaguar; Mercedes; Porsche

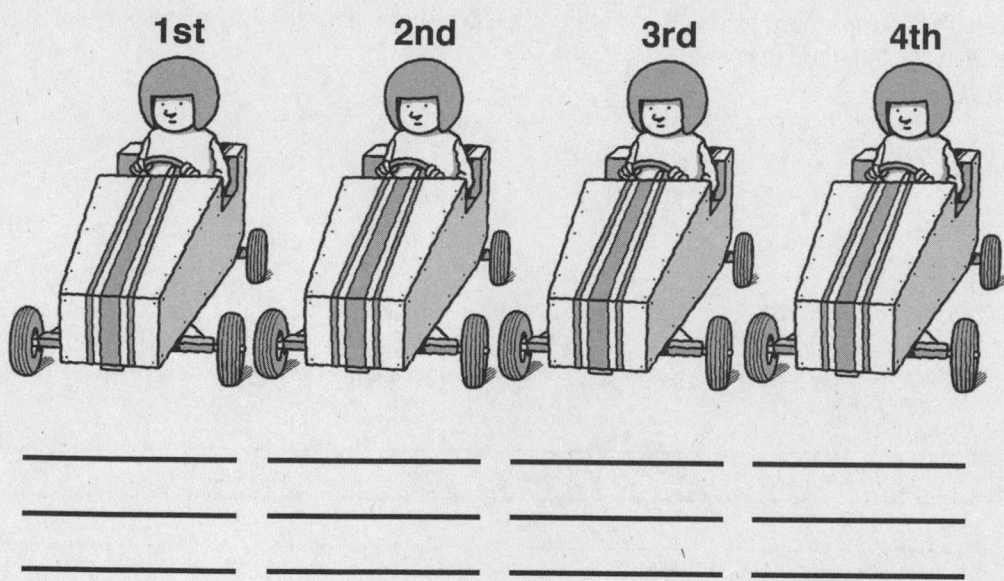

1st   2nd   3rd   4th

Starting tip: Work out who was the co-driver on the cart that finished fourth.

Hair Today

Five servants from Ancient Rome have each adopted a regime involving some aspect of their hair. Can you sort out which areas of hair were involved for each of them, for what reason they started their regimen, and for how many days it lasted?

Clues

1. Branelus, whose hairy experiment lasted for eight days before his boss ordered him to pack it in, wasn't the servant who decided that letting his regular head of hair grow long would be an effective sort of bohemian "rebel statement;" this servant's growth lasted longer than the one who tried to grow a beard.

2. The servant who tried out a full body wax, or in those days a visit to the local hair plucker, gave up after only one day—actually after only ten minutes—as the experience was just too painful.

3. Hopelus started his month's regimen as a way to impress his girlfriend; it was Cluelus who temporarily cultivated a pair of sideburns.

4. One servant was three days into his plan to change his appearance as a disguise in order to throw Prefect Crassus off his track when a knock at the door came anyway.

5. It wasn't Euselus whose plan was to copy his gladiator hero; neither of these two servants' regimens lasted more than four days.

Servant	Hair

	Beard	Body wax	Long hair	Mustache	Sideburns	1 day	2 days	3 days	6 days	8 days	Copy hero	Disguise	Distinguished	Impress girlfriend	Rebel statement
Branelus															
Cluelus															
Euselus															
Gormlus															
Hopelus															
Copy hero															
Disguise															
Distinguished															
Impress girlfriend															
Rebel statement															
1 day															
2 days															
3 days															
6 days															
8 days															

Days	Reason

Logi-5

Each line, across and down, is to have each of the letters A, B, C, D, and E, appearing once each. Also, every shape—shown by the thick lines—must also have each of the letters in it. Can you fill in the grid?

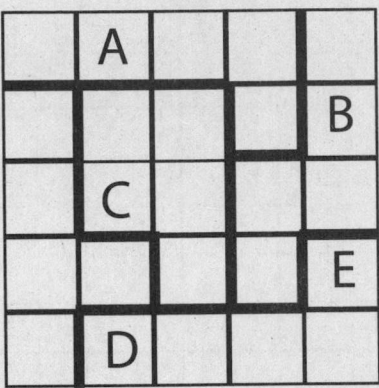

Sign In

Each row and column is to contain the digits 1-6. The given signs tell you if a digit in a cell is plus 1 (+) or minus 1 (-) the digit next to it. Signs between consecutive digits always work from left to right or top to bottom. Examples: 3 + 4 or 2 / 1 ALL occurrences of consecutive digits have been marked by a sign.

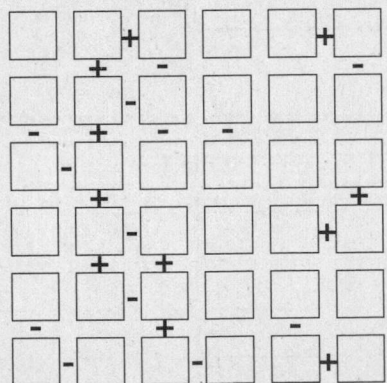

Logi-5

Each line, across and down, is to have each of the letters A, B, C, D, and E, appearing once each. Also, every shape—shown by the thick lines—must also have each of the letters in it. Can you fill in the grid?

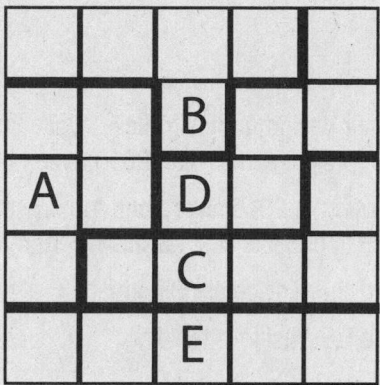

Sign In

Each row and column is to contain the digits 1-6. The given signs tell you if a digit in a cell is plus 1 (+) or minus 1 (-) the digit next to it. Signs between consecutive digits always work from left to right or top to bottom. Examples: 3 + 4 or 2
ALL occurrences of consecutive digits 1
have been marked by a sign.

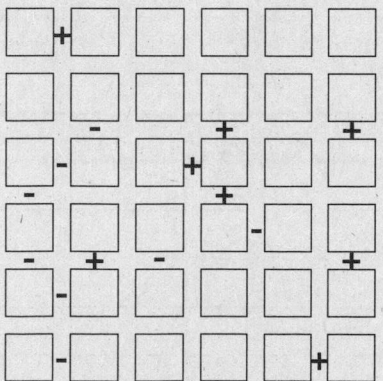

Having Designs

The Frankly Right architecture prize has been awarded annually since 2015. Below are details of the first five winning architecture firms; from the information given can you work out which firm won the prize in which year, the kind of building that won them their awards, and the costs of the project in each case?

Clues

1. Hightower won the award for their design for new offices, while Steele and Klaas' prize-winning design was part of a $24 million project earlier than 2018, when the theater won.

2. Both the architecture firm that won the 2015 award and the one that won for the bridge had names without an "and" in them, and both projects cost less than $36 million.

3. Cinder and Bloch won the award the year before Brickman.

4. The sports arena cost more than L.E. Vashun's building.

5. The apartments were the most expensive project.

6. The least expensive building won the award in 2017.

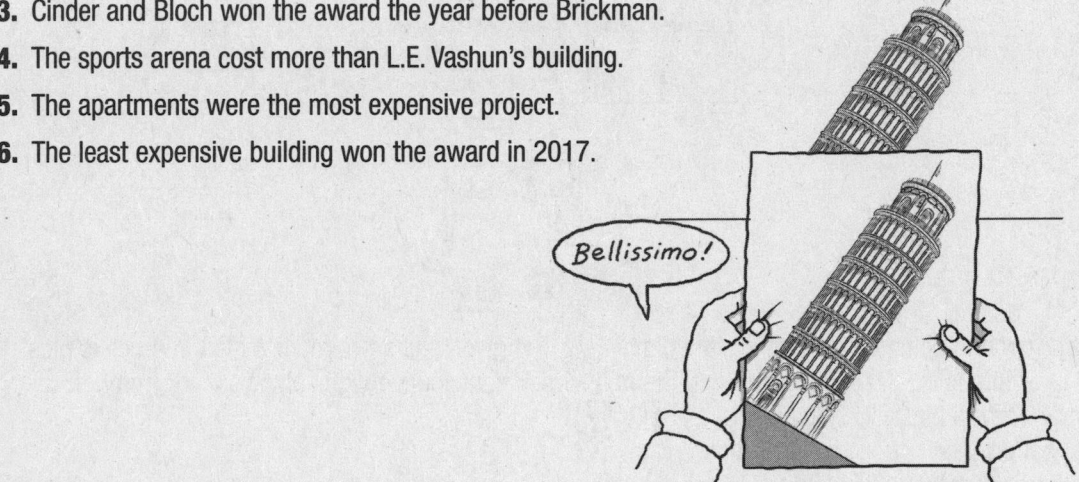

Bellissimo!

What happens when the paper
slips on the architect's photocopier

Year	Architect

	Brickman	Cinder and Bloch	Hightower	L.E. Vashun	Steele and Klaas	Apartments	Bridge	Offices	Sports arena	Theater	$14m	$24m	$30m	$36m	$50m
2015															
2016															
2017															
2018															
2019															
$14m															
$24m															
$30m															
$36m															
$50m															
Apartments															
Bridge															
Offices															
Sports arena															
Theater															

Building	Cost

Very Cross Runners

The first five runners across the finishing line at the end of the national cross-country championship of Catastrophia had all, as was only to be expected in that accident-filled land, had a mishap during the course of the event. From the clues, can you name the five runners, match them with their mishaps, and say in which position each finished the race?

Clues

1. Doome lost his shoe in the mud while crossing a field, but gamely limped on to finish the race somewhere ahead of Johann.

2. Rudolf Plite crossed the finishing line sometime after the man who had been attacked by a goat in the early part of the race and spent a few minutes hiding up a tree until the goat got bored.

3. The runner who caught his foot in a pothole and crashed to the ground during an apparently safe road section of the race was not placed fifth.

4. The athlete placed fourth had left part of his shorts behind on some barbed wire while crossing a fence; this was not Scurge.

5. It was Manfred who lost his footing and slid sideways into a water-filled ditch.

6. Karl ended the race in third position.

7. Klanger was crowned as this year's cross-country champion of Catastrophia.

Do you do sparkling?

MARATHON WATER STATION

First Name	Surname

	Doome	Grief	Klanger	Plite	Scurge	Attacked by goat	Lost shoe in mud	Slipped into ditch	Tore shorts	Tripped in pothole	First	Second	Third	Fourth	Fifth
Emil															
Johann															
Karl															
Manfred															
Rudolf															
First															
Second															
Third															
Fourth															
Fifth															
Attacked by goat															
Lost shoe in mud															
Slipped into ditch															
Tore shorts															
Tripped in pothole															

Mishap	Position

Couples in Photos

Len Shutter, the photographer who specializes in taking memorable snaps of weddings, has attended four such occasions this week and, as well as delivering the photo album to the happy couple, has made a copy of a photo from each to place in his studio window. Can you fully identify the bride and groom in each of the pictures numbered 1 to 4, and say where each ceremony took place?

Clues

1. Picture 3 shows the happy couple leaving St. Alwyn's Church in Washington.

2. Neville, whose surname is not Wilde, did not marry Miss Rowley, whose wedding did not take place at St. Dominic's Church in Daisy Fields.

3. Miss Sowter is not the bride in picture 1.

4. Kirsty's marriage took place at St. Tristram's Church in Sunnyside; she wasn't the blushing bride of William Marshall, who is in the photo directly to the left of the one showing Jason and his new wife.

5. Mr. Gregson, who did not marry Vicky, can be seen in an even-numbered photo.

6. Dean and Alison are the happy couple depicted immediately above the pair who were married at St. Bronwyn's Church in Arlington.

7. Sonia, whose maiden name is Holland and who is still deciding whether to keep it, is not the bride in photo 4.

Brides' first names: Alison; Kirsty; Sonia; Vicky

Brides' maiden names: Holland; Parsons; Rowley; Sowter

Grooms' first names: Dean; Jason; Neville; William

Grooms' surnames: Gregson; Marshall; Smith; Wilde

Places: Arlington; Daisy Fields; Sunnyside; Washington

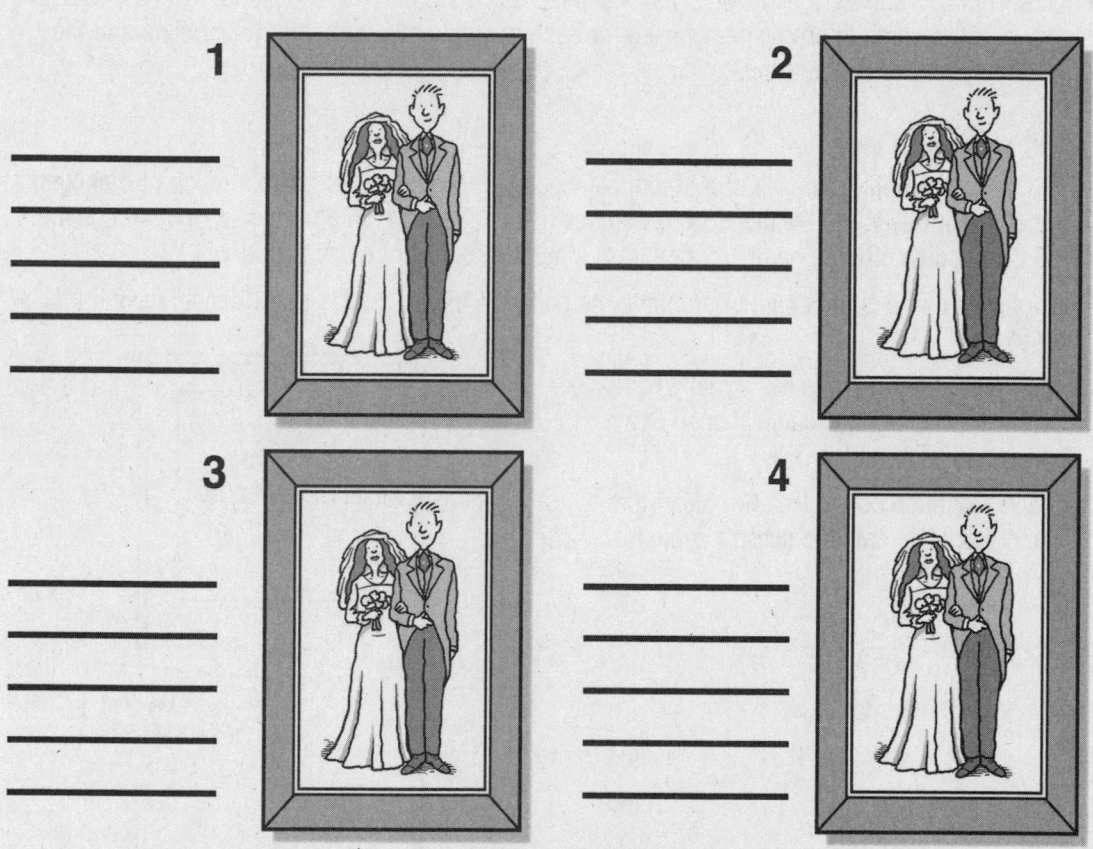

1

2

3

4

Starting tip: Find the picture of Dean and Alison.

Impresso Investigations

Well-known coffee company Impresso has launched a new range of blends called Investigations, sourced from rather unusual parts of the world. Their website provides a set of tasting notes so that connoisseurs can choose their favorite flavor profile. Can you match up the blends with the relevant country and the name Impresso has chosen for each one, together with their flavor style and the color of the pod that contains the delicious, dark, ground-up roasted beans?

Clues

1. The coffee named Bourbonia is said to have woody notes (eucalyptus with a touch of mahogany, apparently); this is not the blend from Cambodia packaged in a cream-colored pod, and neither the Cambodian offering nor the coffee from Mauritius is described as peppery.

2. Rainforest Blend comes from Guatemala; the coffee in the red pod is described as having a floral profile.

3. The coffee from Uganda has a malty flavor; this is not the blend called Monsoon Coast, which comes in a blue pod.

4. Green Mountain coffee isn't the blend that has notes of cereal, and doesn't come in purple pods.

Name	Country

	Cambodia	Guatemala	Mauritius	Sri Lanka	Uganda	Cereal	Floral	Malty	Peppery	Woody	Blue	Cream	Olive green	Purple	Red
Bourbonia															
Green Mountain															
Monsoon Coast															
Rainforest Blend															
Robust Arabic															
Blue															
Cream															
Olive green															
Purple															
Red															
Cereal															
Floral															
Malty															
Peppery															
Woody															

Flavor	Color

Knights Off

Much to their dismay, each of the lily-livered Knock-Kneed Knights of the Round Table received a message requesting help from a different damsel on successive days of the same week, but each came up with an excuse to decline the assignment. From the clues, can you say which knight and which damsel were involved in each day's request, and work out the excuse put forward on each occasion?

Clues

1. The most ingenious excuse was perhaps the one advanced by Sir Sorely à Frayde, that the visor on his helmet was loose, and he couldn't risk suddenly being unable to see in mid-combat; this was sometime after Gertrude requested help.

2. Diana's would-be champion expressed his deep regret at being unable to help, but it was his day off.

3. Elaine's problem arose on Tuesday.

4. Antonia sent her page-boy to Sir Spyneless de Feete to ask for his help; this was not on Monday, but was earlier in the week than the day one of his colleagues was suffering from a tactical stomach upset.

5. On Thursday one knight refused a commission because his sword was blunt, and the armorer was not able to sharpen it until the morrow or maybe even the morrow after that.

6. Sir Coward de Custarde wriggled out of the Wednesday assignment, while it was not Sir Timid de Shayke who said he would have been truly happy to oblige if only his horse had not unexpectedly gone lame.

Day	Knight

	Sir Coward de Custarde	Sir Poltroon à Ghaste	Sir Sorely à Frayde	Sir Spyneless de Feete	Sir Timid de Shayke	Antonia	Diana	Elaine	Estella	Gertrude	Day off	Horse lame	Loose visor	Stomach upset	Sword blunt
Monday															
Tuesday															
Wednesday															
Thursday															
Friday															
Day off															
Horse lame															
Loose visor															
Stomach upset															
Sword blunt															
Antonia															
Diana															
Elaine															
Estella															
Gertrude															

Damsel	Excuse

Logi-5

Each line, across and down, is to have each of the letters A, B, C, D, and E, appearing once each. Also, every shape—shown by the thick lines—must also have each of the letters in it. Can you fill in the grid?

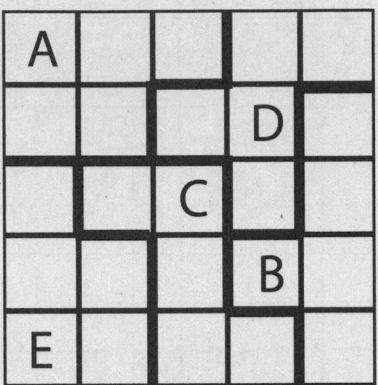

98

Sign In

Each row and column is to contain the digits 1-6. The given signs tell you if a digit in a cell is plus 1 (+) or minus 1 (-) the digit next to it. Signs between consecutive digits always work from left to right or top to bottom. Examples: ③ + ④ or ②
ALL occurrences of consecutive digits ①
have been marked by a sign.

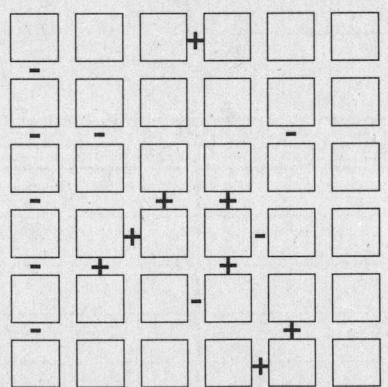

99

Logi-5

Each line, across and down, is to have each of the letters A, B, C, D, and E, appearing once each. Also, every shape—shown by the thick lines—must also have each of the letters in it. Can you fill in the grid?

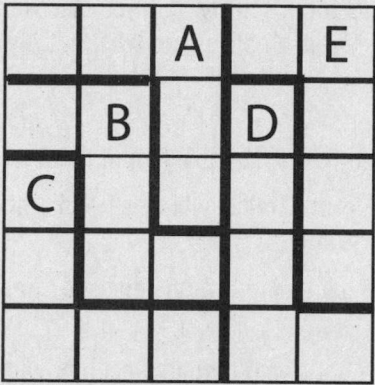

100

Sign In

Each row and column is to contain the digits 1-6. The given signs tell you if a digit in a cell is plus 1 (+) or minus 1 (-) the digit next to it. Signs between consecutive digits always work from left to right or top to bottom. Examples: $\boxed{3}$ + $\boxed{4}$ or $\boxed{2}$
ALL occurrences of consecutive digits $\overset{-}{\boxed{1}}$
have been marked by a sign.

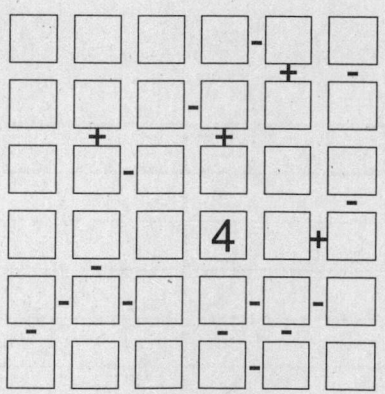

Going Batty

Completely Bats, the latest blockbuster natural history series on Alphabet TV, written and presented by famous naturalist Sir Damien Battenberg, looks at the wide variety of species of bats around the world. Each episode features a sequence looking at a particularly rare and interesting species with remarkable footage of it engaged in some activity. Can you discover which rare species appears in which episode, the country of which it is a native, and what activity was filmed?

Clues

1. The first episode doesn't include the remarkable film of the Sher bat's courting ritual.

2. Neither of the first two films is from Ukraine, which is not the home of the chirruping Baseball bat.

3. The sequence of the Malaysian bat eating is in the episode immediately before the one featuring the Baseball bat.

4. Episode 4 includes footage of a bat giving birth in a country with a longer name than that in which the mating was filmed.

5. The episode featuring the agile Akro bat from Senegal is the one before that with the particularly well-ordered Alfa bat.

6. The musical Shoe bat, which starts a song but often leaves it unfinished, is featured in the third episode; the Indian bat was not filmed flying.

Episode	Bat

	Akro	Alfa	Baseball	Sher	Shoe	India	Malaysia	Senegal	Ukraine	Venezuela	Courting	Eating	Flying	Giving birth	Mating
Episode 1															
Episode 2															
Episode 3															
Episode 4															
Episode 5															
Courting															
Eating															
Flying															
Giving birth															
Mating															
India															
Malaysia															
Senegal															
Ukraine															
Venezuela															

Country	Activity

Comic Relief

Five avid comic book collectors have spent many years seeking rare issues of titles to complete their collections of superhero magazines from the '60s and '70s. Recently, they each managed to track down a particular issue they had been keen to locate, to their great delight. From the clues, can you work out which title each collector found, its official condition-grade, and from where it was obtained?

Clues

1. The collector who paid quite a high price on an online auction site for a long-coveted issue 23 of *The Inedible Bulk* was not Peter Kent, whose acquisition was only in fair condition but too rare to be picky about.

2. Dick Parker was delighted to find a missing issue of the rather clichéd and definitely somewhat dated '60s title *Groovy Girl*; neither this nor the premier issue of *Mercury Man* was the comic bought in very fine condition or the one traded with a fellow collector.

3. It was Clark Stark who was pleased to fill a gap in his collection at a yard sale; another enthusiast came away happy from a thrift store with a comic in fine condition.

4. An incredibly rare copy in mint condition of the final edition of *Dr. Weird* featuring the eponymous mystic superhero was not the title snapped up by Bruce Grayson, whose acquisition was in better condition than the "secret origin" issue of *Beetle Boy* (spoiler: he was run over by a radioactive VW), but not as good as the mag bought at the comic fair.

Collector	Title

	Beetle Boy	The Bulk	Dr. Weird	Groovy Girl	Mercury Man	In improving order					Auction site	Comic fair	Thrift store	Traded with collector	Yard sale
						Fair	Good	Fine	Very Fine	Mint					
Bruce Grayson															
Clark Stark															
Dick Parker															
Peter Kent															
Tony Wayne															
Auction site															
Comic fair															
Thrift store															
Traded with collector															
Yard sale															
Fair (In improving order)															
Good															
Fine															
Very Fine															
Mint															

Condition	Location

AI, AI, Oh!

Much to the chagrin of the usual human contenders, several annually awarded prizes have, this year, been won by recipients who turned out to be artificial intelligence machines. While the organizers of those prizes rewrite the rules to rule out silicon-based intelligences, in favor of the old-fashioned carbon, can you use your human intelligence to work out which AI won which prize in which field?

Clues

1. It was Cal Q. Later, of course, which won the Mathematics award. The winner of the Statuette for Fiction began writing as soon as it was booted up and finished its novel 0.0087 seconds later.

2. The Partington prize for Journalism, which was not the Cup, was awarded to the machine that had spent a whole hour collating all the information on the internet and produced a number of ground-breaking stories.

3. "I'd like to thank my assembler, my developer and my programmer, but most of all I'd like to thank my motherboard," said Otto Maton as it accepted the Cup. The winner of the Gold Star, which was not awarded for Mathematics, displayed it proudly on its monitor.

4. Professor Ounsley personally presented her award to Rob O'Tick. It was neither the Medal nor the Science prize, which was not endowed by the Sorenson Committee.

5. The Hurlbut prize was not a Cup or a Statuette, and Ann Droid did not win the Science prize or the Trophy.

Winner	Prize name

	Gold	Hurlbut	Ounsley	Partington	Sorenson	Cup	Medal	Star	Statuette	Trophy	Fiction	Journalism	Mathematics	Music	Science
Al Gorithm															
Ann Droid															
Cal Q. Later															
Otto Maton															
Rob O'Tick															
Fiction															
Journalism															
Mathematics															
Music															
Science															
Cup															
Medal															
Star															
Statuette															
Trophy															

Prize type	Field

Fancy-Dress Party

Five taxi drivers arrived at a fancy-dress party in the early hours of the morning. The departing partygoers were dressed as fairytale characters. From the clues, can you work out the name of each taxi driver, the time each arrived outside the party venue and the characters of each odd pair who shared the fare?

Clues

1. Ernie picked up his fare at 2:15 a.m.; neither of his passengers was the Big Bad Wolf.

2. As Captain Hook climbed into Max's taxi, Max caught a glimpse of an ugly sister in his rear view mirror but then breathed a sigh of relief when someone else got into his taxi, leaving the ugly sister to party outside with some of the others.

3. Babs picked up Robin Hood with another passenger.

4. Humpty Dumpty was collected from the party at 1 a.m.

5. One driver remarked about something touching the top of their head as the taxi began to drive off. "Oh, that's Pinocchio's nose," laughed Mother Goose from the front passenger seat.

6. Antonio wasn't the taxi driver for Aladdin, who left the party at 1:25 a.m., which was later than the Cheshire Cat left but earlier than Ali Baba went home.

Driver	Time

	12:30 a.m.	1 a.m.	1:25 a.m.	1:45 a.m.	2:15 a.m.	Ali Baba	Humpty Dumpty	Pinocchio	Robin Hood	Ugly sister	Aladdin	Big Bad Wolf	Captain Hook	Cheshire Cat	Mother Goose
Antonio															
Babs															
Ernie															
Heather															
Max															
Aladdin															
Big Bad Wolf															
Captain Hook															
Cheshire Cat															
Mother Goose															
Ali Baba															
Humpty Dumpty															
Pinocchio															
Robin Hood															
Ugly sister															

Character 1	Character 2

Logi-5

Each line, across and down, is to have each of the letters A, B, C, D, and E, appearing once each. Also, every shape—shown by the thick lines—must also have each of the letters in it. Can you fill in the grid?

Sign In

Each row and column is to contain the digits 1-6. The given signs tell you if a digit in a cell is plus 1 (+) or minus 1 (-) the digit next to it. Signs between consecutive digits always work from left to right or top to bottom. Examples: ③ + ④ or ②
ALL occurrences of consecutive digits   —
have been marked by a sign.   ①

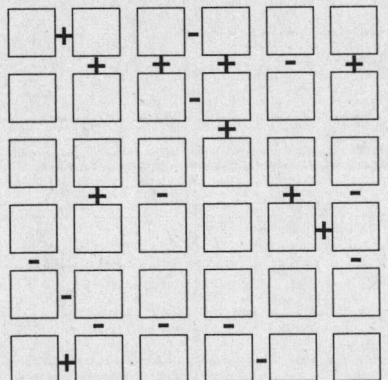

Logi-5

Each line, across and down, is to have each of the letters A, B, C, D, and E, appearing once each. Also, every shape—shown by the thick lines—must also have each of the letters in it. Can you fill in the grid?

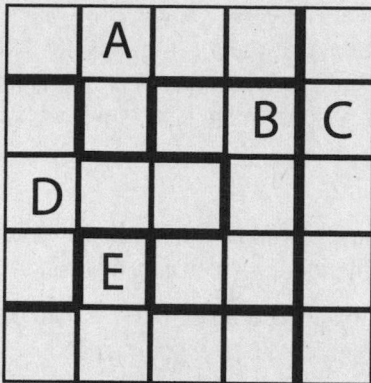

Sign In

Each row and column is to contain the digits 1-6. The given signs tell you if a digit in a cell is plus 1 (+) or minus 1 (-) the digit next to it. Signs between consecutive digits always work from left to right or top to bottom. Examples: ③ + ④ or ②/① (marked with - between)
ALL occurrences of consecutive digits have been marked by a sign.

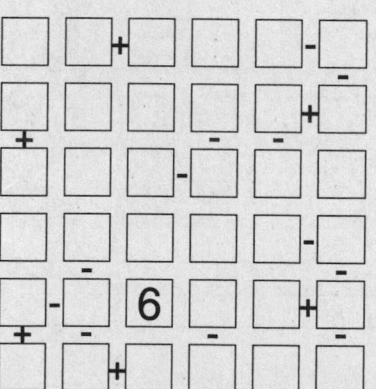

Electric Dreams

"Last night I had the strangest dream," said Kez to his four colleagues in Tech Corp's junior IT team, "I was in an old-school video game arcade and each machine was being used by a character from a game I used to play in the old days, and the games they were playing were all about us, doing our normal jobs." Can you find out which character Kez dreamed was working each machine, which member of the team featured in each and what each was doing that made the game so interesting? (Caz and Jez are women—the rest are men—and Lara Croft and Mario are (sort of) human; the others are something else. Lefts and rights in the clues are from our point of view.)

Clues

1. "I dreamed I was in a game being played by Donkey Kong," said Kez, "Caz was on my left and the character in the game on my right was installing a new hard drive."

2. "Daz was the character on the machine marked D and a man was featured in the game on machine B; Baz's game was being played by a non-human."

3. "The character in the puzzle game on machine A was trying to get coffee, crumbs and coconut oil out of their keyboard. Pacman was involved in a race against time trying to get his character to update a database next left to the game featuring Jez, who wasn't amending the corporate website and wasn't in the game Mario was playing."

Players: Donkey Kong; Lara Croft; Mario; Pacman; Sonic the Hedgehog

Game characters: Baz; Caz; Daz; Jez; Kez

Jobs: amending website; cleaning keyboard; debugging program; installing drive; updating database

Starting tip: Find the machine on which Caz was a character.

On Reflection

Have you ever wondered why vampires always have slicked-back hair? It's because their lack of reflection in a mirror makes it hard for them to arrange it any other way. But that doesn't stop the teenage vampires trying to rebel a little and forge their own style. Can you name the teenage vampire standing at each mirror (it's only vampires, not their clothes, that refuse to reflect) and what style they're trying to adopt?

Clues

1. The vampire rebelling only slightly, by trying to part their hair on one side, is standing immediately next to Fracula.

2. Tracula is fiddling with his hair somewhere to the left of where one vampire is attempting to rearrange the slick-backed look into a stylish quiff and somewhere to the right of where Bracula is trying to get her hair to stand up in spikes.

3. Gracula is dressing her hair in mirror 2, or would be if she could see what she was doing; the reflection in mirror 5 would, if it materialized, show a head of hair being trimmed into a flat top.

Vampires: Bracula; Fracula; Gracula; Pracula; Tracula

Hairstyles: flat top; mop top; quiff; side parting; spikes

_____ _____ _____ _____ _____

_____ _____ _____ _____ _____

Starting tip: Begin by finding Tracula's mirror.

Full Timetable

Students at the University of Melville have a large number of groups that they can join in their spare time—from the official, long-established, and highly respected ones like the army cadets to the unofficial, ephemeral, and disapproved ones, like the Beer Pong Society. The five students here are all in trouble with their tutors for devoting more time to their spare-time interests than to study. Can you work out each one's full name, what she's studying, and which group is taking up all her time?

Clues

1. Ms. Steele, the English literature student, has neither the longest nor the shortest first name in the list; Diana is studying for a degree in geology.

2. Caroline isn't a medical student and does not belong to the Choral Society; Pam is a member of the Melville University Hockey Association, for which she plays as a fearless goalie.

3. The young lady who is one of the leading lights of the Drama Club, who isn't Laura, isn't a law student.

4. The student who is devoting to the University Debating Society much of the time she ought to be spending studying organic chemistry has a first name one letter shorter than Ms. Hardy's.

5. Ms. Riordan is the leader of the University's environmental activist group, and can be found this week chained to a fracking drill somewhere.

6. Tess Parker's parents are very disappointed that she is not paying more attention to her studies, or at least they would be if they knew.

First name	Surname

	Bellamy	Hardy	Parker	Riordan	Steele	English literature	Geology	Law	Medicine	Organic chemistry	Choral Society	Debating Society	Drama Club	Environmentalists	Hockey team
Caroline															
Diana															
Laura															
Pam															
Tess															
Choral Society															
Debating Society															
Drama Club															
Environmentalists															
Hockey team															
English literature															
Geology															
Law															
Medicine															
Organic chemistry															

Subject	Group

The Bard Who Borrowed?

After many years of study, Professor Kent Pruvett has brought out a book called *Shakespeare the Copycat*, which details his theory that, far from being a great dramatist, Shakespeare was simply an opportunist who constructed plays out of the best of the works of others. Can you work out which plays Kent particularly identifies as plagiarism, the works he believes they were taken from, the writers of those plays, and the dates of their original performance?

Clues

1. Shakespeare's *Macbeth* doesn't contain any material stolen from *Hassan the Persian*, which wasn't first performed in 1545.

2. *Romeo and Juliet*, according to the Professor, was mostly taken from *A Sicilian Tragedy*, which does not date from 1570.

3. Magnus Peacock's play was first performed in a year ending with a 5.

4. *The Tragedy of Shadrach the Gypsy*, which is not the work of Jesse Lilburne, is recorded as having first been performed in 1560; this play, according to the Professor, was a major source for *Coriolanus* or possibly *Hamlet*; the controversial academic's book is a bit ambiguous.

5. The play the Professor names as the source for Hamlet was first performed earlier than the one he claims was the source for *Coriolanus*, that much of the heretical theory is clear.

6. *The Winter's Tale*, the Professor claims, was copied from one of the works of Ralph Varney, which was first produced five years after Cedric Amoury's *History of Duke Reuben*.

Play	Source

	A Sicilian Tragedy	Gelais and Medora	Hassan the Persian	History of Duke Reuben	Tragedy of Shadrach...	Cedric Amoury	Jesse Lilburne	Magnus Peacock	Ralph Varney	Solomon Twysden	1540	1545	1555	1560	1570
Coriolanus															
Hamlet															
Macbeth															
Romeo and Juliet															
The Winter's Tale															
1540															
1545															
1555															
1560															
1570															
Cedric Amoury															
Jesse Lilburne															
Magnus Peacock															
Ralph Varney															
Solomon Twysden															

Writer	Date

Knit Wits

Pearl Playne's knitting and crochet supplies shop, Knit Wits, enjoys the custom of a steady flow of regular customers who visit to stock up on materials and tools. From the clues, can you fully identify each of yesterday's customers, the time they called in to Knit Wits, and the item they came to buy?

Clues

1. Betty Cable suffered many jokes in her early days about the likeness of her name to that of a Hollywood star.

2. Gemma, who didn't buy anything to act as a garment fastener, was a later customer at Knit Wits than Ms. Woolley but an earlier one than the customer who needed chunky wool for a chunky sweater; the buttons were bought some time after the zip, which wasn't bought at 11:15 a.m.

3. Jo, who didn't buy any wool, visited Pearl's shop at 2 p.m.

4. The last customer of the day was Ms. Stitch; Anna was neither the first nor the last of these five to visit Knit Wits yesterday.

5. Unlike the customer who bought some double-knit wool, Ms. Cotton visited Knit Wits in the afternoon.

6. Ms. Kneedle didn't buy needles or drop in to Pearl Playne's shop immediately before the customer who did.

First name	Surname

	Cable	Cotton	Kneedle	Stitch	Woolley	10:30 a.m.	11:15 a.m.	2 p.m.	3:15 p.m.	4:30 p.m.	Buttons	Chunky wool	Double-knit wool	Needles	Zip
Anna															
Betty															
Gemma															
Jo															
Helen															
Buttons															
Chunky wool															
Double-knit wool															
Needles															
Zip															
10:30 a.m.															
11:15 a.m.															
2 p.m.															
3:15 p.m.															
4:30 p.m.															

Time	Item

Logi-5

Each line, across and down, is to have each of the letters A, B, C, D, and E, appearing once each. Also, every shape—shown by the thick lines—must also have each of the letters in it. Can you fill in the grid?

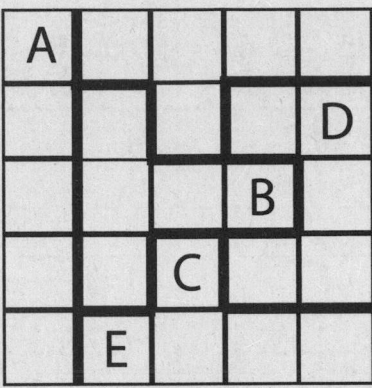

Sign In

Each row and column is to contain the digits 1-6. The given signs tell you if a digit in a cell is plus 1 (+) or minus 1 (-) the digit next to it. Signs between consecutive digits always work from left to right or top to bottom. Examples: $\boxed{3}$ + $\boxed{4}$ or $\boxed{2}$
ALL occurrences of consecutive digits $\genfrac{}{}{0pt}{}{-}{\boxed{1}}$
have been marked by a sign.

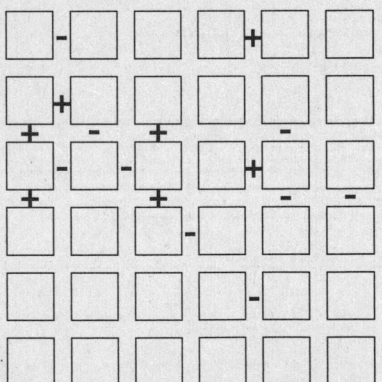

Logi-5

Each line, across and down, is to have each of the letters A, B, C, D, and E, appearing once each. Also, every shape—shown by the thick lines—must also have each of the letters in it. Can you fill in the grid?

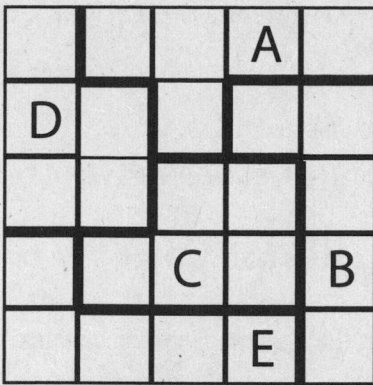

Sign In

Each row and column is to contain the digits 1-6. The given signs tell you if a digit in a cell is plus 1 (+) or minus 1 (-) the digit next to it. Signs between consecutive digits always work from left to right or top to bottom. Examples: ③ + ④ or ②
ALL occurrences of consecutive digits have been marked by a sign. ①

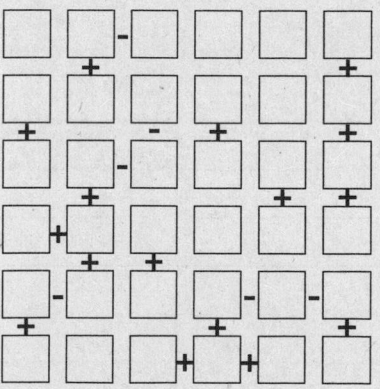

Happy Losers

Five ladies were thrilled with the results of their success at the WaistAway slimming club after the first anniversary of their exercise and diet regimens. In fact, they could all now fit into a smaller dress size. Although they shouldn't have but did, they all rewarded themselves with a treat. Can you work out each club member's old and new dress size and what it was they treated themselves to?

Clues

1. Natasha's dress size a year ago was 20.

2. Sam's new dress size is 16; she didn't reward herself with a Chinese meal and didn't first join the club as a size 22.

3. The woman who started off as a dress size 18, is now a 14; this isn't Emily, who celebrated her achievement with a burger.

4. The woman who is now a size 10 ate a cream cake and almost immediately became a size 10½.

5. The club member whose husband bought her a box of chocolates began her regimen as a size 16; this isn't Trudi.

Name	Old size

	Size 16	Size 18	Size 20	Size 22	Size 24	Size 10	Size 12	Size 14	Size 16	Size 18	Box of chocolates	Burger	Chinese meal	Cream cake	Ice cream sundae
Emily															
Natasha															
Olivia															
Sam															
Trudi															
Box of chocolates															
Burger															
Chinese meal															
Cream cake															
Ice cream sundae															
Size 10															
Size 12															
Size 14															
Size 16															
Size 18															

New size	Treat

Moons of Juno

In 2088, the Terran Space Exploration Agency has a program of investigation of the moons circling the planet Juno, recently discovered in the Hercules star-cluster. Can you work out the name of the moon each space explorer vessel is visiting, what type of environment it has, and what particular hopes the Agency has for it?

Clues

1. The moon known as Ophelia is being considered as a possible candidate for finding new life forms.

2. Rocky desert plains do not cover the moon Viola or the one under consideration as a base for human habitation, which isn't being assessed by the explorer ship *Jason*.

3. The boiling seas of one moon are the target of space scout *Bellerophon*.

4. Neither the moon called Cordelia nor the featureless ice world Desdemona is the satellite being sounded out as a potential refuse dumping center by the star scout *Achilles*.

5. The shuttle *Daedalus* has been sent out to reconnoitre the moon called Portia; this is not the gas giant that is being explored for the prospects of harnessing its stormy energy.

Moon	Vessel

	Achilles	Bellerophon	Daedalus	Jason	Perseus	Boiling seas	Gas giant	Ice world	Rocky desert	Volcanic	Energy	Habitation	Minerals	New life forms	Refuse center
Cordelia															
Desdemona															
Ophelia															
Portia															
Viola															
Energy															
Habitation															
Minerals															
New life forms															
Refuse center															
Boiling seas															
Gas giant															
Ice world															
Rocky desert															
Volcanic															

Environment	Use

Market Mismatch

Sent out to the local markets to source a key ingredient for an important cena (dinner party) their bosses are holding, five unlucky servant friends from Ancient Rome have been aghast to find that it appears to be unavailable. Resourceful as ever, each has settled on a substitute—of greater or lesser similarity—in the hope that something can be cooked up when they get home that will do instead. Can you say which market area each servant visited, the ingredient he was looking for, and what he took back home in its place?

Clues

1. One servant, having failed to find the vintage Falernian wine his boss wanted, gave up and just brought back a jug of the infamous house wine from Grappa's Tavern.

2. Branelus came home with a bucket of fresh tripe, and very little idea of what to do with it; Gormlus didn't visit either of the named Forums.

3. The servant sent to replenish the stock of his boss's favorite artisanal and organic garum sauce was Euselus, but he didn't return with chickpeas or cabbage.

4. The servant sent to the Macellum of Livia was hoping to buy a fine haunch of venison.

5. The Forum Holitorium wasn't visited by either Hopelus or his fellow servant who went in search of a plump brace of capons, which weren't replaced by a rather limp cabbage.

6. A bag of sausages of dubious provenance was one servant's desperate purchase in the shopping street known as the Argiletum in the equally dubious Subura area.

7. Cluelus unsuccessfully scoured the Macellum of Nero for his item.

Servant	Market

	Argiletum	Forum Boarium	Forum Holitorium	Macellum of Livia	Macellum of Nero	Capons	Falernian wine	Garum	Turbot	Venison	Cabbage	Chickpeas	House wine	Sausages	Tripe
Branelus															
Cluelus															
Euselus															
Gormlus															
Hopelus															
Cabbage															
Chickpeas															
House wine															
Sausages															
Tripe															
Capons															
Falernian wine															
Garum															
Turbot															
Venison															

Ingredient	Substitute

Gourmet Gannets

Joe and Vera Gannet love a dinner party and are planning a series of small soirées. They're trying to decide which pairs of couples to invite, as not all of their friends get on with each other that well. From the snippets of conversation, can you discover which foursomes they eventually decided on for each date and the main course they have in mind to serve on each occasion?

Clues

1. "Let's invite Annie and Tom on the 23rd but not with Heather and Alan," said Joe, "and Jane and Paul on the 2nd, although Paul doesn't like fish so we'll keep that off the menu."

2. "Heather and Alan can only make the weekend after Pat and Ray," said Vera, "and Sheila and Peter get on well with Jane and Richard, so we'll have them at the same time."

3. "Sue and Tony have already had my paella," said Joe, perusing his list of recipes, "so they won't come again if I threaten them with that. But that's OK because I'm planning paella for the party a fortnight later."

4. "I'll do my famous boeuf bourguignon on the 9th," said Vera. "Infamous," muttered Joe. "What?" asked Vera. "Nothing, dear," said Joe, smiling.

5. "OK," agreed Joe, "and I'll do roast lamb for Margaret and Jim, they're not ones to complain."

6. "I'll make baked pasta when Jan and Andy come," said Vera, "they'll eat anything."

If it's porridge again, I'll scream

Mr. & Mrs. Goldilocks

Date	First couple

	Heather and Alan	Jane and Paul	Margaret and Jim	Sheila and Peter	Sue and Tony	Annie and Tom	Elaine and Robert	Jan and Andy	Jane and Richard	Pat and Ray	Baked pasta	Boeuf bourguignon	Paella	Poached salmon	Roast lamb
2nd															
6th															
9th															
23rd															
30th															
Baked pasta															
Boeuf bourguignon															
Paella															
Poached salmon															
Roast lamb															
Annie and Tom															
Elaine and Robert															
Jan and Andy															
Jane and Richard															
Pat and Ray															

Second couple	Main course

Logi-5

Each line, across and down, is to have each of the letters A, B, C, D, and E, appearing once each. Also, every shape—shown by the thick lines—must also have each of the letters in it. Can you fill in the grid?

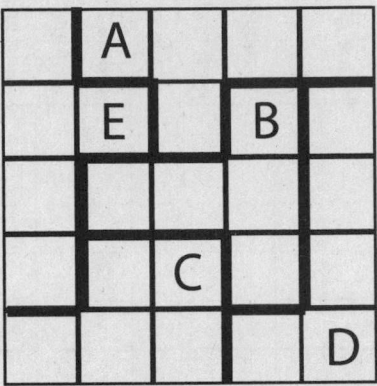

123

Sign In

Each row and column is to contain the digits 1-6. The given signs tell you if a digit in a cell is plus 1 (+) or minus 1 (-) the digit next to it. Signs between consecutive digits always work from left to right or top to bottom. Examples: 3 + 4 or 2 / 1. ALL occurrences of consecutive digits have been marked by a sign.

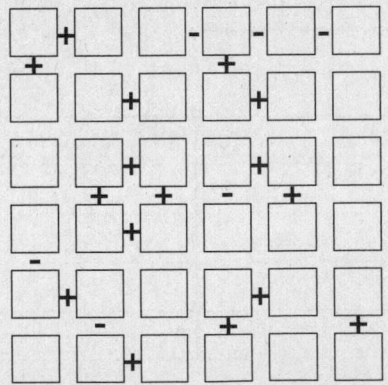

Logi-5

Each line, across and down, is to have each of the letters A, B, C, D, and E, appearing once each. Also, every shape—shown by the thick lines—must also have each of the letters in it. Can you fill in the grid?

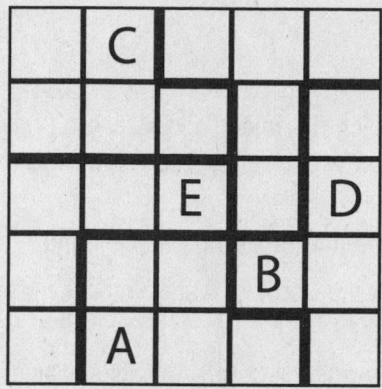

Sign In

Each row and column is to contain the digits 1-6. The given signs tell you if a digit in a cell is plus 1 (+) or minus 1 (-) the digit next to it. Signs between consecutive digits always work from left to right or top to bottom. Examples: 3 + 4 or 2 ALL occurrences of consecutive digits have been marked by a sign.

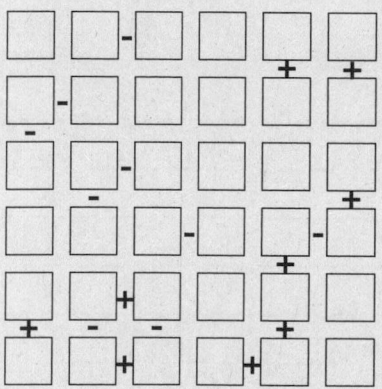

Recovery Positions

Roberta Hoode is a debt collector who specializes in recovering small sums of money from companies that are owed to customers for various reasons. Can you work out the name of each customer with the amount of money owed, what the debt was for, and how long it took the company to pay up?

Clues

1. Mr. Evans, who owns his top-floor apartment, and so doesn't pay rent and has never had need of T.G. Gardening Services' service, was owed $19.25; it didn't take as long as 44 days for this bill to get paid.

2. Mr. Courtney received his payment after 21 days of pestering.

3. Miss Blair was owed money by the Northern Water Company, who had accidentally cut off her supply for a time.

4. One customer, who wasn't Mr. Armitage or Mrs. Dawkins, was owed $25 by Consume Energy, because they were erroneously charged a fee; Mrs. Dawkins wasn't owed $23.37.

5. It took 33 days for T.G. Gardening Services to settle the debt they owed, which wasn't $21.50.

6. The debt of $18, which wasn't a rent rebate from J.D. Housing, was refunded to the customer after 15 days.

Customer	Amount

	$18.00	$19.25	$21.50	$23.37	$25.00	Consume Energy	H.J. Phone Co	J.D. Housing (rent)	Northern Water Co	T.G. Gardening	15 days	21 days	33 days	38 days	44 days
Mr. Armitage															
Miss Blair																
Mr. Courtney																
Mrs. Dawkins																
Mr. Evans																
15 days																
21 days																
33 days																
38 days																
44 days																
Consume Energy																
H.J. Phone Co																
J.D. Housing (rent)																
Northern Water Co																
T.G. Gardening																

Company	Days

Lab Report

Safety is certainly not the motto of five chemists at Melville University. Each specializes in research into a specific element and each holds a very prestigious position at the university. However, the mishaps that occurred in the lab earlier this week undoubtedly put their positions to shame. From the clues, can you identify each chemist's title and name, say in which element he specializes, and work out which mishap befell him?

Clues

1. Botcher managed to set fire to his notes with a Bunsen burner, but his research does not focus on platinum or sodium.

2. Dean Numskerle does not specialize in the properties, uses and potential of sodium nor is he the person who dropped the bottle of acid and melted the soles of his shoes.

3. The Principal filled the lab with clouds of noxious and brightly colored gas; he is not Bungler, who isn't the Professor but who does know more than almost anyone about uranium.

4. The fluorine chemist is not the eminent but absent-minded scientist who forgot to turn off the tap and flooded the lab.

5. Neither the Doctor, whose work on the properties of platinum is famed worldwide, nor Patter dropped a bottle of acid or flooded the lab.

Two minutes after the invention of the rubber band.

Position	Name

	Botcher	Bungler	Flunkitt	Numskerle	Patter	Fluorine	Platinum	Sodium	Sulphur	Uranium	Broke test tubes	Burned notes	Dropped acid	Filled lab with gas	Floode
Dean															
Doctor															
Principal															
Professor															
Reader															
Broke test tubes															
Burned notes															
Dropped acid															
Filled lab with gas															
Flooded lab															
Fluorine															
Platinum															
Sodium															
Sulphur															
Uranium															

Field	Mishap

Ladd's Map

Captain Ladd has a treasure map giving the directions to a hoard of buried Spanish jewels and doubloons. The instructions are in five stages, each involving walking a certain number of paces in a certain direction towards a prominent landmark, then turning and following the next instruction. However, the instructions have been split up into six cryptic sentences, given below. From them, can you work out how many paces must be taken in which direction, toward which landmark, and in which order?

Clues

1. "Head ye toward the cavern's mouth straight afore ye takes 30 paces and straight after ye paces nor'east to someplace else."

2. "Walk 50 paces toward the outcrop of rocks, but on a southerly course ye won't be atreading."

3. "Tread 70 paces due north to reach the landmark immediately before ye pace toward the waterfall."

4. "Pace due east toward the tree that's dead."

5. "Pace sou'west after the first two walks and afore the last two."

6. "After the fifth walking, which ain't of 40 paces, the treasure ye will find."

Order	Paces

	30 paces	40 paces	50 paces	60 paces	70 paces	E	N	NE	SE	SW	Cavern	Dead tree	Rocky outcrop	Treasure	Waterfall
1															
2															
3															
4															
5															
Cavern															
Dead tree															
Rocky outcrop															
Treasure															
Waterfall															
E															
N															
NE															
SE															
SW															

Direction	Target

Shoes Who?

My friend Eric, who is both enthusiastically sporting and obsessively organized, stores the footwear he needs for his various pastimes in a rack under his stairs. From the clues, can you fill in on the diagram the manufacturer and the type of shoe of each of the pairs shown?

Clues

1. The footwear manufactured by Muntjac is immediately below the baseball shoes.

2. The hiking boots, custom made by Bowman, are in an even-numbered position.

3. Pigeonhole 7 in the rack holds the footwear produced by Mithras; the type of footwear in position 6 appears next to the Mithras product in the alphabetical list of types.

4. The beach sandals that Eric wears on his way to the water to ocean swim are in position 2.

5. The cycling shoes, which are in a lower-numbered position than the Emery products, are in the pigeonhole immediately right of the one holding the football boots, which were not made by Eagle.

6. The footwear produced by Libbra is on the horizontal row above the running shoes, and between the boat shoes Eric wears when out sailing and the Ensign product.

7. The Rondo footwear and the tennis shoes are both in the vertical column on the left, but not in adjacent pigeonholes.

Footwear: beach sandals; boat shoes; baseball shoes; cycling shoes; football boots; golf shoes; hiking boots; running shoes; tennis shoes

Manufacturers: Bowman; Eagle; Emery; Ensign; Libbra; Maxim; Mithras; Muntjac; Rondo

Starting tip: Begin by positioning the Rondo product.

Get the Picture

The Makin' Monet gallery is planning an exhibition of digital art and has invited contributions from the public. Five junior IT technicians at Tech Corp, despite knowing very little about art, have decided to enter, and each has produced a creation that they feel meets the stated Terms and Conditions: "to capture the spirit of great artworks of the past using modern technology." From the clues, can you work out the artist, title, and medium of each of the works on display?

Clues

1. Daz looked up "digital" and "art" in the dictionary and decided it meant finger painting. Picture no.1 is conveniently titled *No.1* in homage to Jackson Pollock. It is not Jez's effort, which is next left of the oil painting.

2. Kez's creation is entitled *Composition in Green and Silver: The Artist's Motherboard* (the integrated sound card contains recordings of Kez whistling). Baz's photo-realistic er . . . photo is next right to the work entitled *Hipster Telephone*, a new take on Dali, or possibly Dial, which features a cell phone sporting a false beard and topknot.

3. Caz's contribution is numbered twice the collage and is adjacent to *After Renoir*, which is a print produced by running a completely black image through a printer, twice—making it a "re-noir."

Names: Baz; Caz; Daz; Jez; Kez

Titles: *After Renoir*; *Composition in Green and Silver*; *Degas at the Bar*; *Hipster Telephone*; *No.1*

Media: collage; finger painting; oil painting; photograph; print

Starting tip: Discover the creator of the piece called *No.1*.

Sunday Ceremonies

Last Sunday, the four male residents of the houses numbered 5, 7, 9, and 11 in Sudds Street each spent part of the morning on his favorite pastime of washing his automobile. From the clues, can you name the man who lives at each address, work out the make of his automobile, and say at what time each ceremony began?

Clues

1. Alex, who lives at number 7, started washing his automobile an hour after the Ford owner.

2. Dennis, whose automobile is the Porsche, owns the house that has a party wall with the one where the earliest automobile-washing ceremony of the day took place.

3. The 10:30 start was not made by Martin.

4. Todd's well-worn Sunday morning ritual did not take place in the drive of number 5.

5. The Toyota's owner lives at 9 Sudds Street.

Names: Alex; Dennis; Martin; Todd

Automobiles: Ford; Mercedes; Porsche; Toyota

Times: 8:30; 9:30; 10:30; 11:30

No.5   No.7   No.9   No.11

Starting tip: Begin by naming the resident of number 5.

Absent People

Refusing to believe in any supernatural nonsense, Denise and Adam chose to hold their wedding reception at the historic Davenport Mansion, dismissing all talk of its haunted reputation. But some photos taken on the day didn't turn out the way they were expected. A few of the mansion's serving staff posed for photos with guests at the different tables but for some reason didn't feature in the final prints. Can you work out at what number table the guest or guests who had their photo taken were sitting, the guest who took the photo, and what color apron the spectral staff member wore?

Clues

1. Polly was at table 4 but it wasn't Glen or Jack who took a photo of her.

2. Roxy and Mandy remember discussing the wine with a server in a bottle green apron when their photo was taken; they sat at a lower-numbered table than Anthea and Joey.

3. Heather took a photo of Denise's cousin, Marie, who didn't sit at table 5; Marie's photo was taken as she caught the attention of a waitress, who wasn't the staff member wearing a navy apron, who was at table 2 when a photo was taken, which wasn't by Glen.

4. Ben took a photo of people at table 3.

5. Chrissy liked the handsome-looking waiter with the maroon apron and made sure he was included in the photo she took with her phone. She was disappointed when he didn't appear in it.

6. The waiter wearing a full white apron wasn't assigned to table 6.

Guest/guests	Table

	Table 2	Table 3	Table 4	Table 5	Table 6	Ben	Chrissy	Glen	Heather	Jack	Beige	Green	Maroon	Navy	White
Anthea/Joey															
Marie															
Natasha/Phil															
Polly															
Roxy/Mandy															
Beige															
Green															
Maroon															
Navy															
White															
Ben															
Chrissy															
Glen															
Heather															
Jack															

Photographer	Color

Rooms for Improvement

Melanie and Gavin moved into a 40-year-old, 3-bedroom home last month and, having spotted the potential past the dated and tatty color schemes and décor, have spent most of the time since redecorating. Can you work out in what order they tackled each room, the main thing they ripped out or changed, and which neutral color they painted the walls of each room while they planned their final designs?

Clues

1. In the last few weeks, the dining room walls have been painted in apple white; this was done later than another room whose striped wallpaper had been unceremonially stripped.

2. One of the walls in the primary bedroom had been covered in cork tiles, quite the thing back in the day.

3. The flocked wallpaper in one room, once the very pinnacle of fashion, was the first thing to go but it wasn't replaced with paint described on the tin as nougat.

4. The wood cladding in one room, which wasn't either of the guest bedrooms, was taken down and replaced with a couple of coats of ivory paint; guest bedroom 2 was the second room to be decorated.

5. The third room to receive the Melanie and Gavin redecoration treatment was painted magnolia.

6. The sitting room wasn't the last room decorated.

Order	Room

	Dining room	Guest bedroom 1	Guest bedroom 2	Primary bedroom	Sitting room	Cladding	Cork tiles	Flocked wallpaper	Striped wallpaper	Purple paint	Almond	Apple white	Ivory	Magnolia	Nougat
First															
Second															
Third															
Fourth															
Fifth															
Almond															
Apple white															
Ivory															
Magnolia															
Nougat															
Cladding															
Cork tiles															
Flocked wallpaper															
Striped wallpaper															
Purple paint															

Old decor	Neutral paint

In the Bag

Traveling through Skeptik International airport in the small country of Paranoica can be a trying and lengthy experience. All bags are scanned by x-ray machines, sniffed by dogs, and tested by metal detectors, and rarely does one pass through them all without needing further investigation. The picture to the right shows eight bags that have proved to be suspicious and are waiting to be searched. Can you name the owner of each bag and say what innocent item inside has been flagged by the acutely cynical security staff?

Clues

1. In the pile of luggage, Moss Coe's bag is touching one more of the other bags than is Oz Lowe's but one fewer than the bag that contains a bag of flour, obviously suspected to be some other powder; the bag with the flour isn't touching Ali Canté's bag.

2. Jo Berg's suspicious bag is designated in the picture with an even number.

3. Stan Bull's piece of luggage waiting to be rifled through is numbered twice that of the one containing a small lunch box which, this being Paranoica, is lined with lead; the bag with the lunch box is touching more bags than Frank Fort's bag but one fewer than Sandy Aygo's questionable luggage; Frank Fort's bag isn't the one that contained a small toy water pistol that, frankly, was asking for trouble; Sandy Aygo doesn't own bag 5.

4. Mel Borne has made the mistake of putting her alarm clock in her luggage; her bag is numbered lower than the one that contains a reel of old-fashioned super 8mm cine camera film, which the security team assumed was a garrotting wire, but higher than Oz Lowe's doubtful belongings.

5. The bag containing the kitchen spatula—or machete, as the security officer described it—is numbered higher than the one belonging to Moss Coe.

6. Bag 3 contains a few computer components—hard drive, keyboard, and mouse—none of them connected but you can never be too careful, especially in Paranoica.

Owners: Ali Canté; Frank Fort; Jo Berg; Mel Borne; Moss Coe; Oz Lowe; Sandy Aygo; Stan Bull

Innocent items: bag of flour; camera film; clock; computer components; kitchen spatula; lunch box; ornament; toy

Starting tip: Work out which bag contains the lead-lined lunchbox.

2 _____ _____
4 _____ _____
6 _____ _____
7 _____ _____

1 _____ _____
3 _____ _____
5 _____ _____
8 _____ _____

Logi-5

Each line, across and down, is to have each of the letters A, B, C, D, and E, appearing once each. Also, every shape—shown by the thick lines—must also have each of the letters in it. Can you fill in the grid?

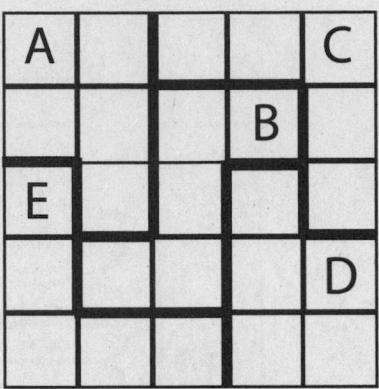

136

Sign In

Each row and column is to contain the digits 1-6. The given signs tell you if a digit in a cell is plus 1 (+) or minus 1 (-) the digit next to it. Signs between consecutive digits always work from left to right or top to bottom. Examples: 3 + 4 or 2 / 1
ALL occurrences of consecutive digits have been marked by a sign.

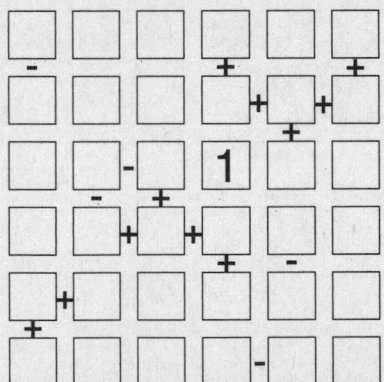

Logi-5

Each line, across and down, is to have each of the letters A, B, C, D, and E, appearing once each. Also, every shape—shown by the thick lines—must also have each of the letters in it. Can you fill in the grid?

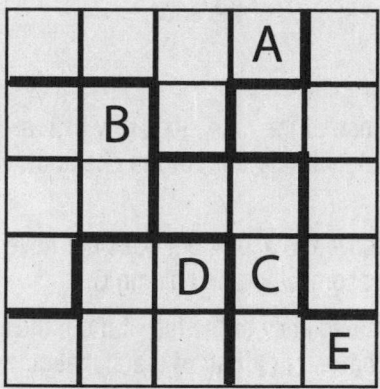

Sign In

Each row and column is to contain the digits 1-6. The given signs tell you if a digit in a cell is plus 1 (+) or minus 1 (-) the digit next to it. Signs between consecutive digits always work from left to right or top to bottom. Examples: ③ + ④ or ②
ALL occurrences of consecutive digits   ⁻
have been marked by a sign.   ①

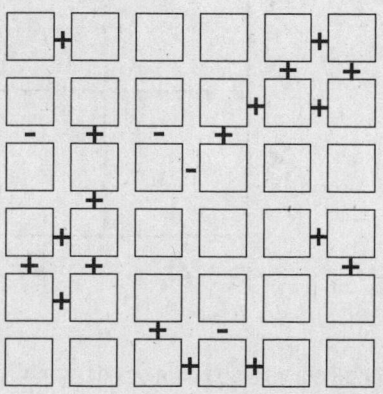

Going Nuts

One sunny winter's day, a squirrel set about unearthing four nuts he'd secreted during fall. The rectangle in the diagram consists of twelve squares, each of which contains either one letter of the word SQUIRREL or one of the four nuts he had hidden. Your task is to write the correct letter and nut (or draw it if you're feeling artistic) in each of the squares.

Clues

1. Each vertical column contains one of the nuts, none of which are in horizontally adjacent squares; one R is in the square immediately to the right of the chestnut, while the other is immediately below the Q.

2. The E is somewhere directly above the acorn, but does not have a nut as a horizontal neighbor; the squirrel buried the hazelnut somewhere in column C.

3. The beechnut is in a square immediately to the left of the I; the L is immediately above the nut in column B; the letter in C3 is from the first half of the alphabet, while the one in C1 is a vowel.

Letters: E; I; L; Q; R; R; S; U

Nuts: acorn; beechnut; chestnut; hazelnut

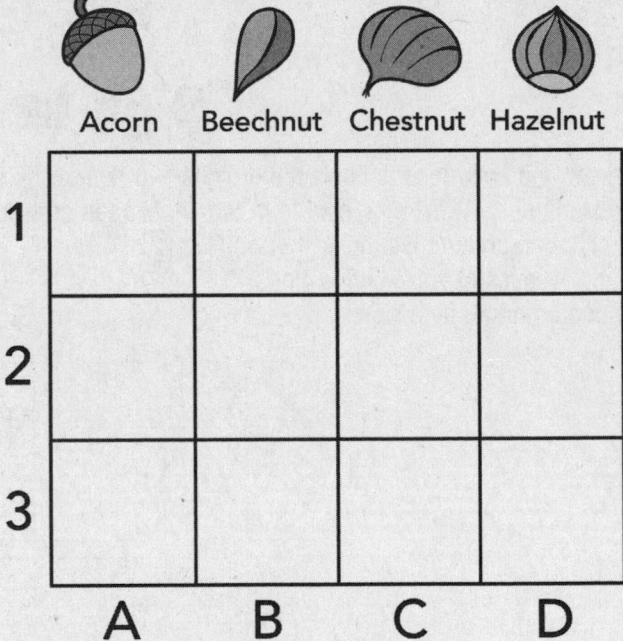

Minnie's Taxi

Today, taxi driver Minnie Myle had a string of a passengers, each one, apart from the first fare who hailed the taxi in Arlington's main street, getting in as the previous customer stepped out. Can you name each of the seven women shown below in the order they used Minnie's taxi and where she needed to go?

Clues

1. When Minnie's taxi pulled up outside the law courts Fran immediately got in. When Fran stepped out a little while later and paid her fare, Cher took her place in the back of the taxi and when Cher got out she was replaced by a lady who said, "La Bonhomie restaurant, please."

2. Dana climbed into the back of Minnie's taxi outside The Grand Theater, where she had been buying tickets for the evening performance.

3. Bess had just arrived by train and had emerged from the railway station when she clambered into the back of Minnie's taxi. When she climbed out, the person who replaced her asked to be taken to the museum.

4. When Gail, who didn't get into the taxi in the main street in Arlington, paid her fare and stepped out of Minnie's taxi, Alma was already talking to Minnie and saying where she wanted to be taken. Immediately after Alma's journey, Minnie took her next fare to the sports stadium.

5. Minnie's fourth fare of the day needed to be taken to the airport.

Customers: Alma; Bess; Cher; Dana; Emma; Fran; Gail

Destinations: airport; law courts; museum; railway station; restaurant; sports stadium; theater

First   Second   Third   Fourth   Fifth   Sixth   Seventh

Starting tip: Work out who hailed Minnie's taxi in Arlington's main street.

Aristo Caughts

At the height of the French Revolution in a small provincial town, four minor aristocrats had been arrested and held in a tower pending trial, each man being imprisoned on a different floor of the building. Can you work out the name and full title of the man on each floor of the tower?

Clues

1. The Comte de Petits-Pois was incarcerated on the floor above Reynaud.

2. Adolphe was imprisoned higher up the tower than the Marquis; neither of these aristos was a member of the de l'Epinard family.

3. The Vicomte had the second-floor cell.

4. The third-floor prisoner was Maxim.

5. Celestin's family name was not de la Basse-Cour.

First names: Adolphe; Celestin; Maxim; Reynaud

Ranks: Baron; Comte; Marquis; Vicomte

Family names: de la Basse-Cour; de l'Epinard; de Petits-Pois; du Verger

Starting tip: First, place Reynaud's cell.

Splish Splash

A large aquarium in the Paws for Thought pet shop in Arlington holds eight fish. Can you name them all? (Lefts and rights are from our point of view.)

Clues

1. Ben is facing right somewhere to the right of Dot, who is facing left; Hal is facing left somewhere to the left of Eva.

2. Amy is facing right somewhere to the right of Col, who is numbered one higher than Gus, who is facing in the same direction as Fay, who is two places left of a fish facing right, who isn't Amy, who isn't immediately next to Hal.

Names: Amy; Ben; Col; Dot; Eva; Fay; Gus; Hal

Starting tip: Work out the name of fish number 1.

Belling the Cat

Four cats in our neighborhood are wont to terrorize the local wildlife, and their despairing owners have resorted to fitting them with collars with bells in the hope of giving the wildlife fair warning. Can you work out the color of each cat, its collar color, and the unfortunate bird or mammal each cat has nevertheless been chasing?

Clues

1. The gray cat is called Dinner because that is the call she always responds to. She hasn't been chasing the pigeon. The tabby cat is wearing a gold collar but hasn't spent the morning pursuing a beleaguered bird.

2. The mouse chaser is next right to the wearer of the red collar, who isn't the ginger cat who has been enjoying the chase with a skink. Candy's collar is green.

Cat colors: black; ginger; gray; tabby

Collar colors: blue; gold; green; red

Prey: mouse; pigeon; skink; sparrow

Starting tip: Find the color of Dinner's collar.

Alfie	**Buttons**	**Candy**	**Dinner**

_____   _____   _____   _____

Capital Dogs

Having spent their racing careers taking part in many photo finishes, the greyhounds at the Clinton Home for Retired Racing Dogs love having their pictures taken, and when Len Scap turned up to take some snaps for the Clinton Courier, the dogs all rushed forward and posed expectantly. Can you work out the current name by which each dog goes and the one under which he raced? (Lefts and rights are from our point of view.)

Clues

1. Eddie isn't the greyhound who raced as Luanda Lad, who is numbered half that of Donny.

2. The former Kingston Kid is posing in position 5; he isn't Benny, who is numbered one higher than the dog who won quite a few races as Dakar Dude.

3. Charlie, who spent his racing career as Belgrade Boy, is in an odd numbered spot in the line-up; Freetown Fellow, as he was once known, is posing somewhere left of Archie in the same row.

Current names: Archie; Benny; Charlie; Donny; Eddie
Racing names: Belgrade Boy; Dakar Dude; Freetown Fellow; Kingston Kid; Luanda Lad

Starting tip: Find the racing name of dog 4.

Candler's Folly

Candler's Farm really was a farm . . . once, but then the late Gascoigne Candler, a rich eccentric, turned it into his private playground and ultimately (when the money started to run out) into a tourist attraction, museum, and zoo. One exhibit is a display of vintage commercial and service vehicles which Candler bought as derelict and restored to perfect condition. Can you fill in the make, type, and date of each of the vehicles on show? (We've drawn them all as the vintage gas tanker so as not to give the game away.)

Clues

1. The Faraway ambulance is in the front row, the vehicle that dates from 1949 is in the back row.

2. Vehicle 5 is an old bus.

3. The dump truck was manufactured more recently than the vehicle built by Jamison's; the latter is displayed immediately left of the former in the picture.

4. Vehicle 6, the one made by Norcross, was built in the decade before the fire truck.

5. The vehicle produced by Wilgreves was built in the decade two earlier than vehicle number 3.

6. The 1923 gas tanker came originally from the local airport.

7. The oldest vehicle is the Holdridge, which is not a tow truck.

8. Vehicle 1 dates from 1936.

Vehicle makes: Faraway; Holdridge; Jamison; Norcross; Rudderford; Wilgreve

Vehicle types: ambulance; tow truck; bus; dump truck; fire truck; gas tanker

Dates: 1908; 1919; 1923; 1936; 1949; 1953

Starting tip: Begin by positioning the ambulance.

_____   _____   _____

_____   _____   _____

_____   _____   _____

_____   _____   _____

_____   _____   _____

_____   _____   _____

Dog With a Bone

Four dogs from neighboring houses along Gnawing Avenue in Centerville were given bones on different days last week. After chewing it to his satisfaction, he buried it in the flower garden for future use. Can you name and describe the dog who buried his bone in the garden of which numbered house and say on which day he was given it?

Clues

1. Charlie's garden is bounded on one side by the bulldog's and on the other by that of the dog given a bone on Wednesday.

2. Romeo, the terrier, was given his bone the day before the dog who buried his treasure at 9 Gnawing Avenue.

3. The spaniel was given the bone on Tuesday; Oscar received his bone on Monday.

4. The lurcher lives and buried his bone in the garden at No.11.

Dogs: Charlie; Oscar; Romeo; Victor

Breeds: bulldog; lurcher; spaniel; terrier

Days: Monday; Tuesday; Wednesday; Thursday

No.5   No.7   No.9   No.11

Starting tip: First, work out when Romeo received his bone.

The Fallen Crown

Shakespeare has King Richard III of England saying, "A horse, a horse! My kingdom for a horse!" at the Battle of Bosworth on August 22, 1485. Can you fill the letters from the second part of his cry into the crown below?

Clues

1. The three Os are in direct and connected diagonal alignment; none of them is in the same column as the N.

2. The A is immediately right of the G and immediately left of the N; both Rs are immediately left of Ms.

3. The E is immediately above the K but not in C1; the I is in row C but not next to a vowel in any direction (vertically, horizontally, or diagonally) and not in column 7; the H is not in a column that also has an M; the S is not immediately above the Y.

4. D4 contains a vowel; the D is in a column numbered one higher than the F.

Letters: A; D; E; F; G; H; I; K; M; M; N; O; O; O; R; R; S; Y

Starting tip: Work out which letter is in D4.

Towel Rail

The cabins at the Sunnyside campground are designed to take a maximum of three, so long as one is under the age of 8. But with a touch of subterfuge and a little skulduggery, ten young friends have managed to squeeze themselves into two adjoining cabins, five boys in one, five girls in the other. They have just returned from swimming in the lake and have dangled their towels over a railing outside to dry. Can you name the owner of each towel?

Clues

1. No two towels belonging to men are adjacent; only one pair of adjacent towels belongs to two women.

2. Gus' towel is numbered twice that of Joy's; the total of the towels belonging to Cyd and Don is 15; Fay's towel, which isn't number 9, is immediately left of Alf's, which isn't number 3.

3. Eva's towel is more than one place right of Ivy's and somewhere left of Ben's, which isn't at the end of the rail; Hal's towel is not immediately left of Joy's.

Women: Cyd; Eva; Fay; Ivy; Joy

Men: Alf; Ben; Don; Gus; Hal

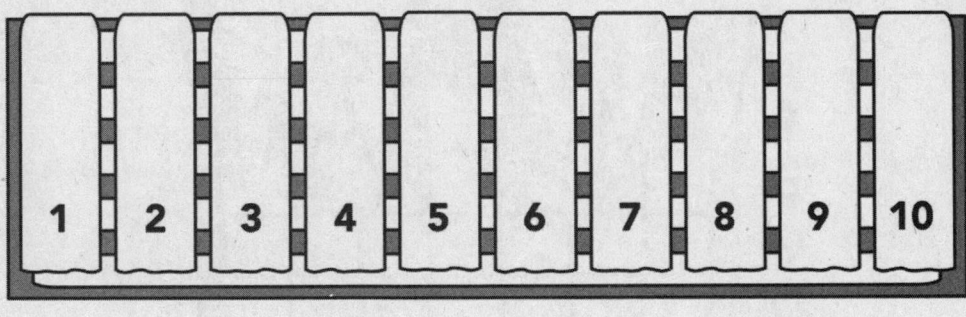

Starting tip: Name the owner of towel 1.

Trade Winds

The weather in the town of Georgetown this morning is what Winnie-the-Pooh might describe as a blustery day. In fact it's so blustery and rainy that the four people we meet here who are on their way to work have just had their umbrellas turned inside out. Can you name each of the umbrella owners, give the name of the company for which they work, and the business it is in? (Lefts and rights are from our point of view.)

Clues

1. The person who is the assistant to psychiatrist Dr. Freemantle is shown somewhere right of Scott Skwall whose umbrella has given up on his way to his job at Miss Tralle.

2. Gary Gayle, who works as an assistant at an upmarket clothes boutique, is shown somewhere left of the person who works for the interior design company.

3. Umbrella number 4 belongs to the person who is a watch repairer at a jewelry store, which is not Harry Caine Ltd; the owner of umbrella 3 isn't Bonnie Bries.

Workers: Bonnie Bries; Gary Gayle; Gwen Gussed; Scott Skwall

Companies: Dr. Freemantle; Harry Caine Ltd; Miss Tralle; Willie Willie and Winned

Businesses: clothes boutique; interior design; jewelry store; psychiatrist

Starting tip: Work out the business where the owner of umbrella 1 works.

Up in Arms

Errol Drey has a niche business creating and painting heraldic designs for those who would like their family crests to hang on their walls or above their doors. Currently Errol has six such items hung on his own wall while he waits for the paint to dry and for their new owners to collect them and settle their bills. Each is a simple shield with an animal in a traditional heraldic pose. Can you name the animal and pose on each shield?

Clues

1. Each row of shields has one each of the animals.

2. One lion is immediately to the left of the sejant (sitting) animal, the other is to the immediate right of the dormant (sleeping) figure; one of the dragons is painted in a statant (standing) pose; the two dragons are numbered two apart.

3. The courant (running) animal is somewhere to the right of the couchant (lying down) figure.

4. Neither of the bears appears in either of the left-hand shields and neither is rampant (rearing).

Animals: bear; dragon; lion (two of each)

Poses: couchant; courant; dormant; rampant; sejant; statant

Starting tip: Work out which animal is on shield 1.

Paranoica Dates

The small country of Paranoica is distinguished by having the world's largest secret service, which spends most of its time checking up on its own citizens. Paranoica spies are not allowed to have relationships but they are allowed to have blind dates with other agents. "Tell her I'll be under the clock at the station," said one of the nine agents with dates on February 14 to the person arranging the rendezvous, "I'll be carrying a rose." "It's Valentine's day," replied the date organizer, "everyone will have roses; you'll have to carry something else as well." Can you say what each of the agents shown below carried in their other hand so that their blind date would recognize them?

Clues

1. The agent with the rose in one hand and the yo-yo in the other is in an even-numbered spot one lower than that of the agent holding the large spanner; the agent holding the shoe is more than two places away from the one with the yo-yo.

2. The agent with the pineapple in his left hand is numbered twice that of the one with the table tennis bat, who has a higher number than the agent with the bicycle pump.

3. The agent carrying the butterfly net has an even number in the diagram, which is lower than the number of the agent with the roller skate.

4. The agent in position 5 isn't carrying any of the three items you might wear; none of these three items are adjacent to each other but agents with the roller skate and the top hat are separated by only one other agent.

Items: bicycle pump; butterfly net; pineapple; roller skate; shoe; spanner; table tennis bat; top hat; yo-yo

_____ _____ _____ _____ _____ _____ _____ _____ _____

Starting tip: Work out what item is being carried by agent 5.

Suite of Carts

The Grand Hotel in Greenville has a number of suites that can be hired for small groups and which are often hired by businesses holding meetings. It's lunch, and food and drink is being delivered to the various suites. Can you name the company in each suite, the subject they're discussing, and the sweet treat the Managing Director has requested on the lunch cart? (Lefts and rights are from our point of view.)

Clues

1. Information International are discussing expanding their overseas offices.

2. Rebecca Reddy of Reddy, Willing, and Abel has ordered pain au chocolat; their cart is shown immediately right of the one going to the business discussing new product development.

3. Rather a large number of cream pastries are being delivered to the Royal Suite; the talk in the Excelsior Suite is of novel and ingenious marketing ploys.

4. The discussions about a possible merger, which aren't being undertaken by The Goode Company, who haven't ordered doughnuts, are not taking place in the Imperial Suite.

Companies: Finance Solutions; Information International; Reddy, Willing, and Abel; The Goode Company

Subjects: marketing scheme; merger; new products; overseas expansion

Treats: cream pastries; doughnuts; cookies; pain au chocolat

Starting tip: Work out which suite has been hired by Reddy Willing and Abel.

Premier Suite

Excelsior Suite

_____
_____

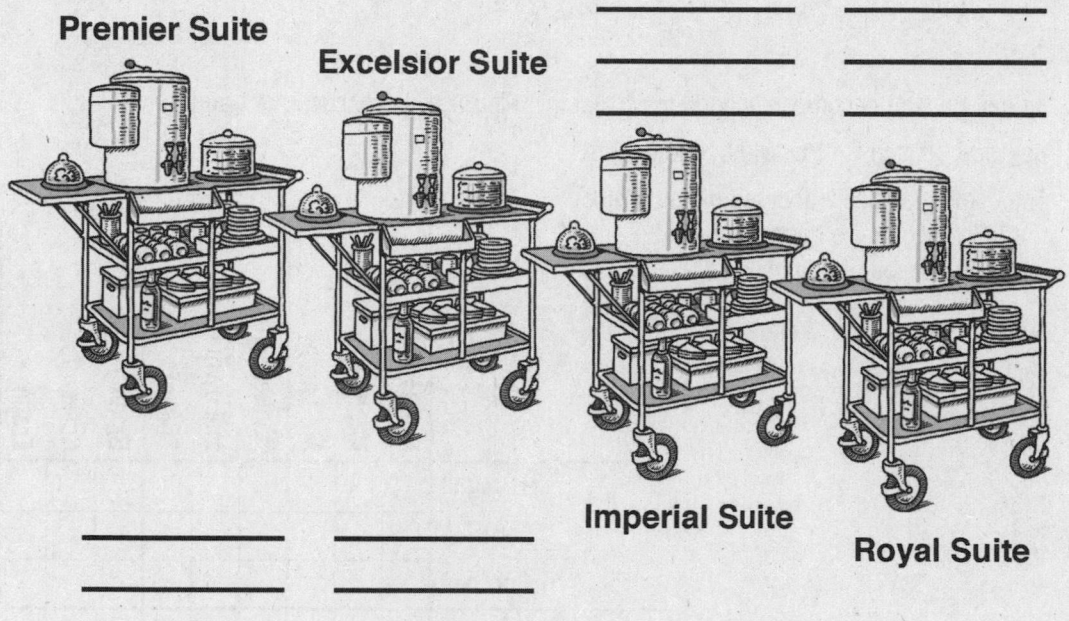

Imperial Suite

Royal Suite

_____
_____
_____

Sloth and Slander

While cleaning out the darker recesses of the library basement at Melville University, the librarian has found a handwritten manuscript entitled *Sloth and Slander* that purports to be an unknown novel by the classic author Jade Austell (1762-1819). It tells the story of the three Benson sisters and their prospective husbands. Can you work out the name of each sister's suitor, his occupation, and the slanderous accusation he suffers?

Clues

1. Abigail Benson becomes engaged to Mr. Farcey; Mr. Barcey is accused of fraud.

2. Beatrice Benson isn't wooed by the banker.

3. The soldier is falsely accused of cowardice; Cordelia's would-be husband finds himself accused of bigamy.

	Mr. Barcey	Mr. Farcey	Mr. Larcey	Banker	Mill owner	Soldier	Bigamy	Cowardice	Fraud
Abigail									
Beatrice									
Cordelia									
Bigamy							
Cowardice							
Fraud							
Banker				
Mill owner				
Soldier				

Sister	Suitor	Occupation	Accusation

154

Music Makers

For a few weeks now, the Jim of Jim's Bar in Centerville has been putting on live music at weekends. Can you work out the two members of the duos, one female and one male, that played on Friday, Saturday, and Sunday last weekend and what the twosome call themselves?

Clues

1. Sandi Scayl and Ralph Riff, who have been playing together ever since they became a couple last summer, played later in the weekend than Duo Decimal.

2. Andy Minor plays keyboards to his performing partner's guitar in their band Twin Set.

3. Two of Us didn't play on Sunday and Karen Keah didn't perform on Friday.

	Carrie Cored	Karen Keah	Sandi Scayl	Andy Minor	Ralph Riff	Stan Stave	Duo Decimal	Twin Set	Two of Us
Friday									
Saturday									
Sunday									
Duo Decimal									
Twin Set									
Two of Us									
Andy Minor									
Ralph Riff									
Stan Stave									

Day	Female	Male	Name

Cold Hard Cashless

Three young married couples have each decided to attempt to save money for a few weeks by only heating their house for two hours each evening. Can you name the two members of each couple and say at what time their heating is turned on?

Clues

1. The heating boiler in Lynn and Nigel's house leaps into action one hour after the Strapts begin to feel a little warmer . . . for a short time.

2. Piers Broak's boiler is kicking out heat at 6:30 p.m.

3. For a few days now, Kate's boiler has been sitting inert and cold at 5:30 p.m.

Woman	Man	Surname	Heating hours

	Nigel	Oliver	Piers	Broak	Penylus	Strapt	5 p.m.–7 p.m.	6 p.m.–8 p.m.	7 p.m.–9 p.m.
Kate									
Lynn									
Mary									
5 p.m.–7 p.m.									
6 p.m.–8 p.m.									
7 p.m.–9 p.m.									
Broak									
Penylus									
Strapt									

Sunny Afternoon

As the sun beats down along Summer Lane in Sunnyside, three neighboring gardens are ringing to the sound of small children splashing about in pools. Can you work out the surname of the family at each address, the shape of the pool, and the small inflatable toy that's in the water with the kids?

Clues

1. The Brites have a round pool; the square pool is at a higher numbered house than the one with the inflatable dinosaur.

2. The oval pool is occupied by two excitable siblings and a blow-up shark.

3. The Heatons live at 9 Summer Lane; the Clement children don't have an inflatable crocodile.

	Brite	Clement	Heaton	Oval	Round	Square	Crocodile	Dinosaur	Shark
No.7									
No.9									
No.11									
Crocodile						
Dinosaur						
Shark						
Oval			
Round			
Square			

House	Surname	Pool shape	Inflatable

157

Odd Jobs

Semi-retired odd-job man Andy Mann has been busy. The first three days of this week he had three jobs. Can you say for whom he worked on each day, what he did, and how long it took him?

Clues

1. The stubbornly sticking door that Mr. Green needed trimming and re-hanging took Andy one hour less to complete than the job he attended on Wednesday.

2. The building and positioning of a set of shelves, which wasn't for what Mrs. Brown employed Andy, didn't take as long as four hours to do.

3. On Monday, Andy spent some time mending an old fence after a windy weekend.

	Mrs. Brown	Mr. Green	Mrs. Scarlett	Door	Fence	Shelves	2 hours	3 hours	4 hours
Monday									
Tuesday									
Wednesday									
2 hours									
3 hours									
4 hours									
Door									
Fence									
Shelves									

Day	Customer	Job	Time

Timber

Tree's a Crowd is an arborist company dealing with all aspects of looking after trees. On Monday morning, following weekend storms, they had three calls from people whose trees had come crashing down in their gardens. Can you say what time each caller called, the type of tree that had been blown down, and the item it had landed on?

Clues

1. Mrs. Bower called Tree's a Crowd on the dot of 9:00; the call that came in fifteen minutes later wasn't about an apple tree.

2. Mrs. Copse's old cherry tree had succumbed in the high winds on Sunday; a small birch tree had toppled over and smashed a few panes of a greenhouse.

3. Mr. Forester rang to say that his garden pond is now not so much full of water as it is full of tree.

	Mrs. Bower	Mrs. Copse	Mr. Forester	Apple	Birch	Cherry	Greenhouse	Pond	Shed
9:00									
9:15									
9:30									
Greenhouse									
Pond									
Shed									
Apple					
Birch					
Cherry					

Time	Caller	Tree	Garden item

Logi-5

Each line, across and down, is to have each of the letters A, B, C, D, and E, appearing once each. Also, every shape—shown by the thick lines—must also have each of the letters in it. Can you fill in the grid?

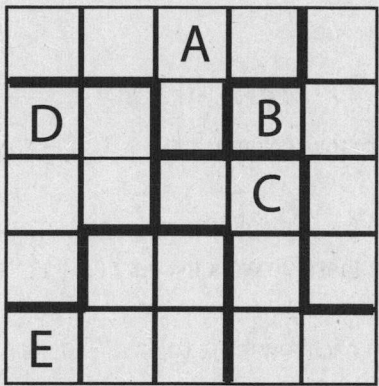

Sign In

Each row and column is to contain the digits 1-6. The given signs tell you if a digit in a cell is plus 1 (+) or minus 1 (-) the digit next to it. Signs between consecutive digits always work from left to right or top to bottom. Examples: 3 + 4 or 2
ALL occurrences of consecutive digits
1
have been marked by a sign.

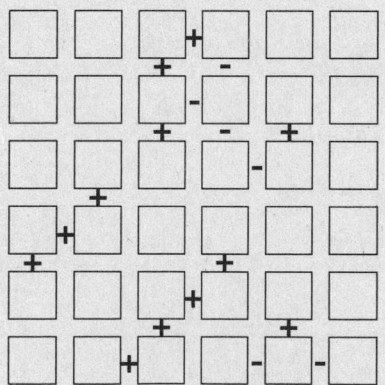

SUDOKU

How to Play

Complete the grid so that every row, column, and 3 x 3 cube contains every digit from 1 to 9 inclusive with no repetition.

In sudoku, you are given a 9 x 9 grid. Some of the grid squares already contain numbers—you cannot change these. To work the puzzle, fill in the empty squares of the grid with the numerals 1 through 9.

The puzzle is solved when each row, each column, and each 3 x 3 cube contains the numerals 1 through 9 with each numeral appearing only once. The 3 x 3 cubes are differentiated by shading.

9	6		1	2		7	4	
		7		5	3	6	1	
		8			4			9
	9							2
6	4	2	8	3	7	9	5	1
5							3	
7			3			1		
	3	9	5	7		2		
	5	6		8	1		9	7

★☆☆☆☆

	3			9	1	5		2
	2	4			6	7	8	1
				8	7			
4	1	7			9	8	2	
			7	2	8			
	8	2	1			6	9	7
			6	1				
2	6	1	8			4	7	
8		5	9	7			1	

★☆☆☆☆

1		3	8	5	9		6	4
				2			1	3
		6		1		5		
6				7		9	3	
		2	4		5	6		
	1	5		6				7
		1		3		2		
7	3			4				
2	5		9	8	1	3		6

★☆☆☆☆

	3	6	7		2		9	
			8	3	6			
2	1	8			5		6	
5	4			8		6		2
		3	4	2	1	7		
1		2		6			3	8
	9		2			5	8	6
			1	5	8			
	8		6		3	1	2	

★☆☆☆☆

		5		1		8	3	
1		7		9	3			2
			8	6		5		1
		2		3		7		4
6		1	4	7	2	3		9
7		3		5		1		
2		9		8	6			
5			7	4		2		8
	7	8		2		9		

★☆☆☆☆

6	2			3	1	4	9	
4	1		5	9	8		6	3
	8		2			7		
2	6							4
			6	5	3			
5							8	7
		2			6		7	
1	4		9	7	2		3	6
	9	6	3	8			4	2

★☆☆☆☆

5				8				7
3			6		9		2	1
			4	7	2		6	
	2			4		1		
4	3	5	2	1	8	7	9	6
		1		3			8	
	5		8	6	1			
1	8		5		7			2
9				2				8

★☆☆☆☆

6		7		5	1			
	3			9		5	4	6
	5	9	2				1	8
1							8	
	7	6	1	2	4	9	3	
	9							2
7	6				3	8	2	
9	4	8		7			5	
			8	4		6		9

★☆☆☆☆

	4		2	6	1			3
3			9					1
		6		3		9	2	
	8			5	3	2	7	
6		4		9		8		5
	5	7	1	4			6	
	9	2		7		1		
4					6			7
7			5	1	9		3	

★☆☆☆☆

9			4	2				1
8	5	2		6	1			
6	4			7		2		
	1			9		4	5	
5	6			1			7	8
	2	8		3			1	
		6		4			3	7
			7	5		1	8	6
1				8	3			4

★☆☆☆☆

9		8		6			2	
		1		9		6		
	2	6	7	4	5		8	
		2		5			4	
8		5	2		4	3		6
	9			1		2		
	8		6	2	1	5	7	
	3			8		9		
	6			3		4		8

★☆☆☆☆

6				8			7	5
	3			1	2		9	
			5	6	3		8	
		5		4		2	3	9
9	2			5			6	1
3	7	1		9		4		
	8		9	3	1			
	5		8	7			2	
4	9			2				7

★☆☆☆☆

		6	7		9		3	4
1			8		3	5		7
			2	5	4			
4		5	6		1			9
7		2		3		4		1
3			4		8	7		5
			5	8	2			
2		8	3		7			6
5	9		1		6	8		

★☆☆☆☆

2	4			5			7	
9		8	4	6			1	5
	7	1		3		6		
6	8		3			1		
	1	5		2		9	3	
		9			4		5	6
		7		4		5	8	
4	5			8	9	7		3
	6			7			9	1

★☆☆☆☆

2	3			1		5	4	
1		6	5	9				
9	4			2	3		6	
	1		3	4	7	2	5	
		2				9		
	5	3	9	6	2		8	
	6		2	5			9	3
				3	9	8		7
	9	8		7			2	5

★☆☆☆☆

	8		2	7	3		5	1
5		7		1			2	
		2	8	6		3		9
				3	2			4
9	2						1	3
3			7	9				
1		3		8	9	2		
	6			2		9		7
2	9		3	5	7		6	

★☆☆☆☆

4	3		7	5		1		6
					6	8		
6	2	5		3	8			
		7	8	9		5	4	
2				7				1
	8	4		1	5	7		
			5	6		9	1	4
	2	3						
5		6		4	7		3	8

★☆☆☆☆

1	7				6		3	
		9			4			
2	4		7	1	3	8		
5	1		4	6	2		9	8
9				7				6
4	8		1	3	9		2	7
		4	6	2	7		8	1
			3			6		
	6		8				5	3

★☆☆☆☆

			3	8				6
			7	9		1	2	
8	6	7	2	1			5	
1	3		4				7	
7			8	5	2			1
	9				3		6	4
	8			3	7	4	1	2
	1	3		2	8			
6				4	1			

★☆☆☆☆

		8	4	9	2			5
3	7		1	5		6		
	5	9			3		8	
7	2	6		1				
1		5		3		8		7
				7		2	9	1
	6		9			5	1	
		7		8	1		2	6
9			5	2	6	7		

★☆☆☆☆

7				5	6			
	9	3						
6		1	9		4			
8	4			2		5		7
	6			4			3	
1		7		8			4	9
			4		2	3		1
						7	9	
			1	9				4

★★☆☆☆

							1	2
	9		7	2				
	3		1	9	7	8		
4		9	5		3			
			6	4	8			
		1		9		6		4
	2	3	9	8			7	
			7	2			6	
7	8							

★★☆☆☆

	3			2			5	
9					6			
		7		3	4	9		
8		9	6			3		
		5		7		8		
		4			8	5		1
		1	8	5		4		
			7					9
	8			4			7	

★★☆☆☆

				6	7	8		
9	3			1				
5			9	2				3
6				8		2		
7	8	2				3	4	6
		3		7				9
3				9	5			4
				3			6	1
		5	6	4				

★★☆☆☆

	6		3	2	4	1		
		3	6	5			4	
4				9	1			3
	3	7		1		6		4
9			2	7	6			1
5		6		3		9	2	
3			7	6				8
	2			4	3	7		
		9	1	8	2		3	

★★☆☆☆

3			1	8		4		7
	5			6				
	8	4	5	3				
2				5	9	8		4
	4			2			7	
5		8	7	4				9
				9	3	6	4	
				1			3	
4		5		7	6			1

★★☆☆☆

	7				9	4		
	4		7	6	5	9		
8		9						5
		1					4	
4	9			1			8	2
	3					1		
3						5		4
		4	1	2	3		6	
		6	4				9	

★★☆☆☆

5	6		2	3				8
				5	6	1		
		7			9			5
	2			7		8	3	
				1				
	3	5		4			6	
2			1			7		
		6	8	9				
1				2	7		4	6

★★☆☆☆

1		5		9			8	
				5		4	3	
				8		6		1
2	3		7	6		1	4	
	1	4		3	9		7	6
7		8		2				
	4	1		7				
	2			4		5		7

★★☆☆☆

		8	7	6	5		3	
			9		4	8	2	
3				2	8			7
8		2				6		
9				5				8
		7				5		2
5			8	4				9
	1	9	2		6			
	8		5	9	1	2		

★★☆☆☆

4		3		7	9		5	
				4	5		7	
		6	1					9
			9	3			2	4
			5	1	7			
3	6			2	4			
7					1	6		
	2		4	9				
	3		7	6		4		5

★★★☆☆

		6	8	9				
4	9							
				7	3	9	2	
6				3	8	5	9	
		7		5		4		
	5	1	2	6				3
	6	3	5	8				
							5	8
				4	6	3		

★★★☆☆

	8				3			9
		1		8	9			6
	6		1	2				
			8	9		3	2	5
		9				4		
3	2	5		4	1			
				7	4		1	
4			5	1		6		
5			9				8	

★★★☆☆

7				4				3
			2	3				
	9	4		6	8		1	
	3		4	2				
	7	1		9		4	6	
				1	5		2	
	1		3	5		7	8	
				8	4			
4				7				6

★★★☆☆

				1	4		8	
2			9	8				6
7		8		3				1
				4		3	7	
			1		5			
	5	7		2				
3				5		1		9
4				9	1			8
	1		7	6				

★★★☆☆

		6		4		3	7	5
			2	5				
				7		4		8
		7	9			8		
4				2				3
		9			5	7		
3		4		9				
				1	6			
9	7	1		8		2		

★★★☆☆

	9							
3		1		2	6			9
				4	1		3	5
		4	6					1
		6	4	1	2	5		
1					3	2		
6	2		7	9				
9			1	6		8		7
							6	

★★★☆☆

				2		4		
8	3	9			5			
				6	7		3	1
	2			1				3
	5		8		3		6	
3				5			9	
5	6		2	3				
			5			6	2	4
		2		7				

★★★☆☆

					2			8
	6						7	4
5				4	9	1		
	8		4	2	3		1	
	7		9	6	1		5	
		2	5	8				1
8	3						4	
7			1					

★★★☆☆

	5			9		4		
4		2	7					9
	9		5	4				
		9		8	7	3	6	
				6				
	6	7	4	1		9		
				2	9		1	
8					4	5		6
		6		5			2	

★★★☆☆

				2	4		9	6
5			3	7	6			1
	2							4
	1	5		3		6		8
				5				
6		9		4		1	5	
4							3	
7			2	9	3			5
9	6		4	8				

★★★☆☆

	7		3		1			2
			2	4	9			
	9	4			8			
		6					2	1
	8		1	2	4		3	
4	2					8		
			5			3	9	
			4	3	6			
8			9		2		6	

★★★☆☆

			4		6	9		
	4		3	5			8	
2				8				3
		4						1
8		9		3		4		7
1						3		
7				4				9
	2			7	3		6	
		6	2		5			

★★★☆☆

			5	9	1		
1	9		8	7		4	
		1	4		2		
	4		3		6		
8			2				1
	2		6		8		
	9		1	3			
4			8	5		9	6
	5	7	9				

★★★☆☆

3		5		8				
	7			2	4	6		
2			6	5			8	7
			4	1				
7			5		2			4
				7	3			
5	9			4	7			6
		1	9	3			4	
				6		5		9

★★★☆☆

	7		2				4	
	6				9	2		
8	9			3				6
				7		4		
2				4				8
		1		6				
3				9			8	4
		6	8				7	
	4				3		5	

★★★☆☆

		8	7	6	5			1
				9			3	
	9	2		1				
	4		5	3		1		
		9				8		
		5		7	9		6	
				5		4	8	
	6			2				
1			6	8	4	2		

★★★☆☆

		5		2	8	3		
	2			7				5
1				9		8		
		6	2	1			9	
		2				4		
	7			8	6	2		
		7		3				4
5				4			8	
		4	8	6		1		

★★★☆☆

				3		2		7
				9	2		6	1
		7		4			8	5
8					3			
		4		2		8		
			5					6
7	9			8		6		
4	1		2	6				
2		6		5				

★★★☆☆

	8	1		4		3	6	2
	6			8				
4			6		7	8		
1		4	3	2				
			7		8			
				6	4	7		3
		3	1		6			4
				5			3	
6	1	2		9		5	8	

★★★☆☆

			1	5			8	7
	3			6	8	5		
	8			4		9		
				2		7		4
		8		9		1		
9		5		7				
		4		8			3	
		2	7	1			5	
8	5			3	2			

★★★★☆

	1		2	7				8
				8	9			3
	2			3			6	
		5	1	9				
		2	4		3	8		
				6	2	4		
	8			4			2	
2			7	1				
3				2	8		4	

★★★★☆

	2	6	9	7				
	1			5	8	6		
	8			2				5
		8		4				
3			8	9	1			6
				3		8		
2				6			4	
		7	5	1			6	
				8	9	5	2	

★★★★☆

		7			3			5
	8				2	1		
6				1				
		4	3	2			9	
		1		4		5		
	7			9	8	2		
				7				8
		9	5				1	
2			9			4		

★★★★☆

1			4	8	9			3
	4		2	5		7		9
				7	6	2	8	
	6	4	5	2				
8		7		9	2		5	
4			8	1	7			6

★★★★☆

						2		8
	3		6	7				9
8				5	1			
	2			1	7			6
	7			3			4	
3			5	2			9	
			1	8				5
9				4	2		6	
7		1						

★★★★☆

8		4	7	9	5		3	2
9					6			
	5	7						
	6					8		9
4				3				7
2		8					5	
						7	9	
			1					4
7	4		9	5	8	3		6

★★★★☆

				8	5	3		
8	5			7				2
	4	3		1	2		9	
	2				8			
3				9				8
			3				4	
	8		2	6		7	3	
1				5			2	6
		9	7	3				

★★★★☆

				2	6	4	9	1
		9		3			6	
		8			9			
	7	6	4					
1				9				5
					2	8	1	
			5			9		
	3			1		5		
6	2	5	9	7				

★★★★☆

				6				
7	3			6				
4			8	7				
				1	3	5	7	
	9	3	7			1		
		4			1	2	3	
	6	7	4	5				
				3	8			2
				2			9	6

★★★★☆

	3	1					4	
				3	2			8
5				4			6	
					4		1	9
		3		9		8		
4	2		7					
	4			5				1
6			9	7				
	9					3	8	

★★★★★

		5		6			8	
				7		9		
	7				5	4		6
7	6			4				5
8				1			2	4
3		6	1				9	
		1		9				
	5			8		6		

★★★★★

	7		9	5		2		
				3			8	
		1		7		4		
3		4	1					
6				9				8
					7	5		4
		5		1		8		
	2			8				
		6		4	5		9	

★★★★★

				9	3		4	2
5		4		2				1
		7		6				
			9			2	8	
				4				
	5	6			8			
				8		9		
9				3		1		5
7	3		2	5				

★★★★★

3			2		5		1	7
	9			7		2	3	
			9					
		4		6				1
	5			1			2	
7				2		8		
					2			
	1	2		5			4	
9	4		7		1			2

★★★★★

				6		2		
				3			5	1
3	1	9		4			8	
				2	6			4
	3			1			6	
1			9	8				
	6			5		1	9	3
2	4			9				
		3		7				

★★★★★

				2	3	1		
4				2	3	1		
8		2	4	5				6
	5							
			1	8			7	
	8			9			4	
	9			3	5			
							1	
9				7	2	3		5
		6	3	1				4

★★★★★

				9	7		2	
	1							7
		5			8		9	3
4		2					8	
			5	3	6			
	6					7		9
5	8		9			4		
9							3	
	7		2	4				

★★★★★

				9	7			
3				6		9		
		9		1			8	5
				3		6		2
	5		9	2	8		4	
2		1		5				
9	3			4		2		
		4		8				3
			5	7				

★★★★★

		5		8	3			
			9				1	7
6	1			4				3
	6					7	4	
				9				
	7	1					5	
4				3			7	8
1	3				9			
			5	1		3		

★★★★★

				5	6			
	4						1	7
8			1	3			6	4
1				4				
4		6		2		8		9
				9				6
3	1			7	4			2
9	6						5	
			8	6				

★★★★★

					1	7		
				5			9	6
			4	7		1		
6				1			7	
4	1	8		3		2	6	5
	5			4				3
		5		6	4			
3	9			2				
		7	5					

★★★★★

			5		2			
				1		5		6
		1		6		3	9	2
							4	7
		4		9		8		
8	2							
1	5	3		4		2		
2		6		3				
			6		9			

★★★★★

	9		5	7				3
						7		
			8	6	2			
8		4	2	5			3	
	6						1	
	2			9	6	5		8
			3	8	5			
		8						
6				1	9		2	

★★★★★

					7			3
	3	6		4				
		8		1			4	
	6		4	8		1		
	1			7			3	
		5		6	1		8	
	4			5		2		
				3		6	9	
9			8					

★★★★★

	6			1	5	8		
9								
				8	4	2		7
		8		9			3	
	1	9				6	8	
	2			4		1		
1		7	4	2				
								6
		6	8	7			1	

★★★★★

				8	9		1	
		7		5	4	9		6
			6			5		
7							4	
		9	3	4	5	1		
	1							3
		4			2			
3		6	5	1		2		
	5		4	3				

★★★★★

		6		7				
	7		1	2		9		
9	3						4	
2	1			8	6			
		5		3		2		
			2	4			7	6
	4						8	9
		9		1	7		2	
				9		3		

★★★★★

		1	7		8			
	7			1		3	8	
							9	1
5	8		1	7				
	6			4			5	
				8	9		4	7
6	2							
	3	9		6			7	
			8		1	9		

★★★★★

			2	4			9	
				8		7		2
	2	9		6		3		
			7	9			3	1
		3		5		8		
8	5			1	3			
		2		3		6	5	
6		8		7				
	1			2	6			

★★★★★

						1	2	
3		6	4	8				
		8		7				
9								7
		4	5	2	1	8		
8								6
				6		5		
				1	7	3		2
	2	7						

★★★★★

	7				2		6	
8				6	9			
		2	7					8
		3						1
2		1	5		3	8		9
9						2		
7					8	1		
			1	3				7
	5		9				8	

★★★★★

		9		2	1		7	
				9		8		
2			6	7		5		
4		5		8				
	1			6			4	
				4		1		9
		3		1	8			5
		1		5				
	8		2	3		7		

★★★★★

					7			8
				3		6		
		1	8	9			7	
	7		6	5				3
	6			4			1	
5				7	8		6	
	5			1	2	7		
		8		6				
9			4					

★★★★★

					1			
				9	5	6	7	
9			6	4				
		7	3				4	6
5				6				9
6	1				4	3		
				7	6			1
	2	4	1	8				
			4					

★★★★★

9	3			1	4		7	
6	4					9	3	
		4		3	5			8
3				2				7
7			9	4		6		
	7	8					6	1
	2		6	7			8	9

★★★★★

				6		1		3
				8	4		9	
		9		3	1	6		4
	6	7						
	8			9			3	
						8	1	
8		6	7	4		9		
	9		8	5				
4		5		1				

★★★★★

	5			1			6	
		4		6			9	
			8			1		
	7			5		2		9
		8				4		
6		2		7			1	
		7			2			
	4			8		6		
	1			9			5	

★★★★★

				1	8		5	
3	8				6		2	
				5				
2				8		5	6	
		6	5	2	1	4		
	9	4		6				2
				3				
	1		6				4	3
	6		1	4				

★★★★★

		5			3	7	6	8
			2		7	4		
				5				9
			8			9		
7	8			3			2	4
		4			9			
1				6				
		7	3		8			
2	9	8	7			6		

★★★★★

WORD ROUNDUP

How to Play

Find the hidden words in the puzzle looking horizontally, vertically, and diagonally. Unlike traditional word searches, Word Roundup gives clues to the words hidden within the puzzles. The words themselves are for solvers to figure out.

```
L P I A N O V T T P Y P
C U J U N E E E G V L R
O M T Z X N P R I E U A
J A Z E I M A K V N J H
N R X R U T Z X I U T M
A S A R I B O B N S U C
B L T U G O I N G R B B
C J G O B O E Z D J A C
```

FIND AND CIRCLE . . .

Ten musical instruments	☑☐☐☐☐☐☐☐☐☐
Two words starting and ending in G	☐☐
Two planets	☐☐
Two months	☐☐
Dylan or Marley	☐

```
B K B X I D E O L O G Y
V O R E A S T J Z O O M
Z E O Z S N A K E Z X B
Z G W M T U R T L E J C
D I N A B R U P T L Y Z
O E K Y L O C A T I O N
O B L A C K C W H I T E
M P L U M E A X R O O M
```

FIND AND CIRCLE . . .

Five words rhyming with "groom"   ☑☐☐☐☐

Four eight-letter words   ☐☐☐☐

Four five-letter colors   ☐☐☐☐

Two reptiles   ☐☐

Direction of the sunrise   ☐

```
L C P O B A M A F O R D
D Y A C L I N T O N Z X
R T N K V B G R E E C E
A I T X F R A N C E A A
P G H J J G N A V Y R M
O E E X U D A V I D M U
E R R O R E A G A N Y P
L Z C A R T E R L I O N
```

FIND AND CIRCLE . . .

Seven felines ☑☐☐☐☐☐☐

Five U.S. presidents ☐☐☐☐☐

Two six-letter European countries ☐☐

Two branches of the U.S. armed forces ☐☐

Word Roundup inventor Hoyt ☐

```
D F L A M I N G O J S Z
C U V C E V N C R A U S
S J C S A A X E B Y N E
J W O K C T H U N D N L
L O A I Z C C I U N Y L
G A L N T Z A H R I T E
C E O I X R J Y E W O C
P K P S N O W Y P R M K
```

FIND AND CIRCLE . . .

Five water-loving birds   ☑☐☐☐☐

Four weather conditions ending in Y   ☐☐☐☐

Three four-letter countries   ☐☐☐

Two baseball positions   ☐☐

"Magnum, P.I." star (first/last name)   ☐☐

```
M S O Y B E A N S Z D G
U A X K H X Z E X N G N
I P T Z K I C Y A N E I
G I K H D N S L V H R K
L N J L E L G T Z O M C
E K O I U N J X O J A A
B G C A E G R A Y R N N
Z S P O I N T I N G Y S
```

FIND AND CIRCLE . . .

Three school subjects	☑ ☐ ☐
Three eight-letter words	☐ ☐ ☐
Three seven-letter European countries	☐ ☐ ☐
Three four-letter colors	☐ ☐ ☐
Lennon and McCartney	☐ ☐

```
P B A S K E T B A L L V
Z O B A S E B A L L Z D
K R L J H B A R G E H N
A U F O O T B A L L O A
Y G X Z C A N O E Z A L
A B K J K F F L E X X S
K Y C V E R B N O U N I
F E R R Y Z S O C C E R
```

FIND AND CIRCLE . . .

Seven sports	☑☐☐☐☐☐☐
Four five-letter boats	☐☐☐☐
Two parts of speech	☐☐
Two four-letter words ending in X	☐☐
Iceland or Jamaica, for example	☐

```
D H A R P J M C N D L A
M R M O L E O L I I A B
V A U V Z L O O C C N U
K J R M X U S O O T O T
O X Z K K M E N T A I L
B G E O R G E E I T T U
O T W A I N Z Y N O A T
E Z P A C I F I E R N E
```

FIND AND CIRCLE . . .

Five four-letter musical instruments	☑ ☐ ☐ ☐ ☐
Four eight-letter words	☐ ☐ ☐ ☐
Three mammals starting with M	☐ ☐ ☐
"Up in the Air" star (first/last name)	☐ ☐
Samuel Langhorne Clemens: ____ ____	☐ ☐

```
G C O L O N Z S N E E R
Y R A P O S T R O P H E
G R I M A C E C U B A C
Z X J N F S C Z X K K A
W O R M V R M O R Y I N
P E R I O D O I M C R A
H Y P H E N M W L M K D
J A M E S S B C N E A A
```

FIND AND CIRCLE . . .

Six facial expressions	☑☐☐☐☐☐
Five punctuation marks	☐☐☐☐☐
Two countries starting with C	☐☐
Captain of the Enterprise: _____ Tiberius _____	☐☐
Four-letter flexible invertebrate	☐

```
L L H I S T O R Y S E A
V A G R A Y M Z E K S B
Z G K Z X L K I C E S A
P O V E I N V I D B Z Y
C O X F A O L A U G H F
O N N E M F P L X O T L
V J C D Y S C J J L A U
E O S C I E N C E D M G
```

FIND AND CIRCLE . . .

Eight bodies of water	☑☐☐☐☐☐☐☐
Three school subjects	☐☐☐
Three words that mean "motion picture"	☐☐☐
Two playing card suits	☐☐
Two colors starting with G	☐☐

```
S M A N A T E E Z X E E
Y E M A Z D A N S L E G
A L A X J A I U A N V N
T I Z L D H R H O K I A
O M V N P L W M V Z F R
Y E O L A V E R O M E O
O H O W X L M I L A N V
T D T A N G E R I N E Z
```

FIND AND CIRCLE . . .

Five aquatic mammals	☑☐☐☐☐
Four citrus fruits	☐☐☐☐
Three Japanese car companies	☐☐☐
Two large Italian cities	☐☐
Square root of 25	☐

```
I I N D I A S P U P I L
C R M D O C T O R S A N
O A I A Z W N S U E I R
R N J S R E E S S A B U
N I E J K S I U S R M T
E T K A R T T N I T A A
A E V U S X A E A H Z S
C R N Z B T P V L E N S
```

FIND AND CIRCLE . . .

Five parts of the eye	☑☐☐☐☐
Four planets	☐☐☐☐
Three sets of people in a hospital	☐☐☐
Three countries ending in IA	☐☐☐
Two opposing directions	☐☐

```
I Y F K C R B E J S E C
C N V O O C T X S U I L
C H C J O U Z E N F A E
M Y A H L T R I I R S T
I M Z O E P T C E O A Y
L X S R M N E N O O C A
E B G O O P E G M Z X R
A E C C S G R O B I N D
```

FIND AND CIRCLE . . .

Four four-letter units of length ☑☐☐☐

Four eight-letter words ☐☐☐☐

Three five-letter birds ☐☐☐

Two military ranks ☐☐

Trench with water surrounding a castle ☐

```
M Y C B U T T E R E Z X
Y I Z H R V J K P A L C
S X L U E T K T A S A C
J H G K U E F I C T R M
J O A O V R S G I E T A
Y P R R O Z X E F R N E
K T V W K J V R I N E R
S M E L T P E R C H C C
```

FIND AND CIRCLE...

Five dairy products	☑☐☐☐☐
Four five-letter fish	☐☐☐☐
Three U.S. time zones	☐☐☐
Five-letter feline	☐
"Star Trek: The Next Generation" Klingon	☐

```
A N T A R C T I C A P B
V S N I C K N A M E E O
E B I X Z I C H O U R G
P E J A L I M I L E S O
O R K R R A L D R I N T
R N E F C O L L I N S A
U B A A R M S T R O N G
E A U S T R A L I A Z X
```

FIND AND CIRCLE . . .

Five continents	☑☐☐☐☐
Three Apollo 11 astronauts	☐☐☐
Three country capitals starting with B	☐☐☐
What mph stands for	☐☐☐
"The Duke," for John Wayne	☐

```
J S E P T E M B E R X Y
R U A C S Z Y K Y Z A J
E K L P O X A N E M M U
B R C Y R J R I K S A N
O O V J F I G F R P R E
T F B L U E L E U O C H
C S A L A M I X T O H A
O D E C E M B E R N Z M
```

FIND AND CIRCLE . . .

Eight months	☑☐☐☐☐☐☐☐
Three deli meats	☐☐☐
Three eating utensils	☐☐☐
Two four-letter colors	☐☐
"The Road Not Taken" poet Robert	☐

```
S O L U T I O N J S C C
P O S I T I O N X P I H
C M F D R I V E C R D A
T A E A J A C K H I A I
P A N X Z J Y K I N R R
B U B A I H C I P K O Z
C E T L D C X N Y L P X
B J D T E A O G D E S K
```

FIND AND CIRCLE . . .

Five pieces of furniture	☑☐☐☐☐
Four eight-letter words	☐☐☐☐
Three golf shots	☐☐☐
Two North American countries	☐☐
Two face cards	☐☐

```
K O R A N G E K V T Y P
A O K S H O E K O R K A
N V O N Z X C O R A N P
A B Y K A I B E Y K W A
N Z X C K C H A Z C O Y
A L U T E C K X J O D A
B H A R P A C R O S S J
K N A P S A C K K I N K
```

FIND AND CIRCLE . . .

Six words starting and ending in K	☑☐☐☐☐☐
Four six-letter fruits	☐☐☐☐
Three four-letter things worn on the foot	☐☐☐
Two puzzle clue directions for Will Shortz	☐☐
Two four-letter stringed instruments	☐☐

```
C S I N G A P O R E S X
D U O S T R I C H L T A
N J B U R E D Z O E O C
A X M A B L U E T T N I
L E Z W H I T E E O E A
E P E N G U I N L M X M
C M A D A G A S C A R A
I K O L I V E R Z B C J
```

FIND AND CIRCLE . . .

Five island countries	☑☐☐☐☐
Three flightless birds	☐☐☐
Colors of the Australian flag	☐☐☐
"Platoon" director (first/last name)	☐☐
Two five-letter lodging options	☐☐

```
R B R U S S E L S T J W
J O K V I D Z A S A V A
L X M R A T S T H N S R
I Z A E L L K E E G N S
S P H A A Z Y L E O E A
B A W S Z C H L P Z H W
O M A M B O P E N N T J
N B E R L I N R X V A Z
```

FIND AND CIRCLE . . .

Seven European capitals	☑☐☐☐☐☐☐
Four five-letter dances	☐☐☐☐
Comedy magic duo: _____ & _____	☐☐
Opposite of behind	☐
Source of wool	☐

```
V G B L U E K S E N D D
K E O G Z I L C H W Z N
H V N P E P G Z J O Z E
G T Z D H R I O K R E L
B E E Z X E B N L L S Z
E N B C U P R I K D T K
N D R G R A Y Z L V Y V
D X A T E A L X M E N D
```

FIND AND CIRCLE . . .

Six words ending in END   ☑☐☐☐☐☐

Five four-letter colors   ☐☐☐☐☐

Three five-letter words starting with Z   ☐☐☐

Two six-letter rodents starting with G   ☐☐

Global soccer tournament: the _____ _____   ☐☐

```
H N A T I O N A L K V E
M O H T O M M D Z E J L
P I U O H G N O D X K E
R H N R C O Y A N E Y C
O A Z U C K C E E T A T
T N C E T E E W A Z H R
O K S J D E C Y X R O O
N S L E A G U E B K O N
```

FIND AND CIRCLE . . .

Seven units of time	☑☐☐☐☐☐☐
What NHL stands for	☐☐☐
Two parts of an atom	☐☐
"Bosom Buddies" star (first/last name)	☐☐
Five-letter search engine	☐

```
P C N I C A R A G U A A
O E H A E W Z G C T E I
R Z R I U A E Z X O C B
K X Y U L N S S Y R U M
U N C L E E T T T O A O
V A N C O U V E R N D L
M O N T R E A L X T O O
G U A T E M A L A O R C
```

FIND AND CIRCLE . . .

Six Western Hemisphere countries	☑☐☐☐☐☐
Three Canadian cities	☐☐☐
Your cousins' parents, to you	☐☐
Two opposing directions	☐☐
Meat from pigs	☐

```
O F V I R G I N I A F Z
J H L J M E D I U M A X
N H I O T O L Z X J T A
I A S O R E T A V Y H K
S W M N D I X H R H E S
U A A I O Z D A E G R A
O I L N C X K A S R E L
C I L E K S I S T E R A
```

FIND AND CIRCLE . . .

Six U.S. states	☑☐☐☐☐☐
Four six-letter relatives	☐☐☐☐
Three common sizes	☐☐☐
Landing pier	☐
Square root of 81	☐

```
D V T E R N Z J H Z J K
C O G A N D H I W A X V
C H V G E C K O Z R W C
R Y Z E F I N G E R E K
O I N S P E C T O R B N
W X A T T E N T I O N B
R E C E P T I O N H C Y
D U C K L O O N L A R K
```

FIND AND CIRCLE . . .

Eight four-letter birds   ☑☐☐☐☐☐☐☐

Three nine-letter words   ☐☐☐

Political leader Indira   ☐

Pinkie, for example   ☐

Five-letter lizard   ☐

```
L B M A N D O L I N Z H
H U A F I Z Z V I O L A
G A T N P A C I F I C C
U C R E J I N D I A N I
I V E P P O N T I A C D
T A T L A N T I C J K E
A Z X K L A R C T I C R
R J A Z Z O V I O L I N
```

FIND AND CIRCLE . . .

Eight stringed instruments	☑☐☐☐☐☐☐☐
Four oceans	☐☐☐☐
Two four-letter words ending in ZZ	☐☐
Maker of the Firebird	☐
Hot apple beverage	☐

```
W C G O A T Z J L I O N
Z O B D R O L U C A S D
Y J L E R E R E Z X E E
V M V F A I V A M V V E
P O K X Z R V E N O E R
U L G E O R G E R G N J
M E N E U T R A L S E K
A K L I M E V M U L E J
```

FIND AND CIRCLE...

Eight four-letter mammals ☑☐☐☐☐☐☐☐

Three transmission gears ☐☐☐

Three citrus fruits ☐☐☐

Creator of "Star Wars" (first/last name) ☐☐

Number of days in a week ☐

```
A K D A U G H T E R Z E
X U N C B J B J X Y R U
S Z N I M R U C H E A L
I K X T E O O L V K B B
S C Z C V C T W Y N B Z
T A J U N E E H N O I M
E L W A L R U S E D T A R
R B E I G E Z F O R T Y
```

FIND AND CIRCLE . . .

Five female relatives (four-letter min.)   ☑☐☐☐☐

Four colors starting with B   ☐☐☐☐

Three six-letter mammals   ☐☐☐

Three months   ☐☐☐

Twenty plus twenty   ☐

```
F K S E V E N W A L L F
K I X Z E C A N A R Y I
Y Z V R C R O W Z R N F
N J H E S T O P J O O T
I T C E I L I N G O O E
N M I D N I G H T L N E
E T H I R T E E N F V N
E L E V E N Z X J O N E
```

FIND AND CIRCLE...

Eight odd numbers	☑☐☐☐☐☐☐☐
Three room surfaces	☐☐☐
Two times that are 12 hours apart	☐☐
Two birds starting with C	☐☐
Opposite of go	☐

```
C H R I S T I N E V C T
Y U Z X V F X C H Y A H
R E J N E A E O C A R I
E V A O R U C U T D R N
S R S U B L U R A N I N
I E I N J T E T M U E E
M S A T U R D A Y S Z R
F I R E S T A R T E R X
```

FIND AND CIRCLE . . .

Six Stephen King stories	☑☐☐☐☐☐
Five five-letter words related to tennis	☐☐☐☐☐
Weekend	☐☐
Two parts of speech	☐☐
Home to Vietnam and Laos	☐

```
M M Z F A M I L Y T K Y
Z A X Z M K V R V S J E
E E R V K E E E H E O N
A R Z S H T R T N W B U
S C K T I Z U C Y U S T
T P R P J O J B U Z S P
J O U Z S U G A R R K E
N J C S T E V E C B Y N
```

FIND AND CIRCLE . . .

Five planets	☑☐☐☐☐
Four main compass directions	☐☐☐☐
Two things commonly added to coffee	☐☐
Apple co-founder (first/last name)	☐☐
Classic sitcom: "All in the ____"	☐

```
S X K I N G V B E E F G
J I T U N I S I A J N A
X K N Z F L I C K I I A
Z V L G F I L M W D A N
R M O V I E J X N K B I
I C Z W I L L I S X U H
N I N D O N E S I A C C
G B R U C E Z J D I N G
```

FIND AND CIRCLE . . .

Five four-letter words ending in ING	☑ ☐ ☐ ☐ ☐
Five countries ending in A	☐ ☐ ☐ ☐ ☐
Three words that mean "motion picture"	☐ ☐ ☐
"Die Hard" star (first/last name)	☐ ☐
Meat from cows	☐

```
J A N T A R C T I C A B
M U S E P T E M B E R R
Z A L T T X R A I N F E
K A R Y W H Z K X Y I B
M P S C X E I Y T K F O
A R N Z H J N R V C T T
Y I O J X J O T T V Y C
V L W A F F L E Y Y B O
```

FIND AND CIRCLE . . .

Six months   ☑ ☐ ☐ ☐ ☐ ☐

Four numbers ending in Y   ☐ ☐ ☐ ☐

Two four-letter forms of precipitation   ☐ ☐

Southernmost continent   ☐

Belgian _____ (six-letter answer)   ☐

```
M B H A R E V K D E E R
Z U S B U S I N E S S B
B Z L E K C O M M A K V
E N J E A J W I L M A E
A O C E L L O J L C V L
R I X F R E D Z X Y K O
V L M A C H I N E S N M
J G O A T G U I T A R X
```

FIND AND CIRCLE . . .

Nine four-letter mammals ☑☐☐☐☐☐☐☐☐

IBM: International _____ _____ ☐☐

Two stringed instruments ☐☐

Mr. and Mrs. Flintstone ☐☐

Five-letter punctuation mark ☐

```
G L I T H I U M V T I N
Z O S O S T R I C H Z I
I E L A X R C A N O E C
W R B D E O C E A N K K
L U O V I C E L A N D E
C E L N P E N G U I N L
C I A A L U M I N U M X
S B G D K C O P P E R V
```

FIND AND CIRCLE . . .

Nine metals	☑☐☐☐☐☐☐☐☐
Two seven-letter flightless birds	☐☐
Two island countries	☐☐
Two words formed from A-C-E-N-O	☐☐
Direction of the sunset	☐

```
K O F F I C E K X J K K
J I P Z E V E K N C Z B
V L N L H L A V I A A X
K A U K O Y Z K J R C C
C M Z M A B O X A J H K
O B J K U N I T E D O B
N K N A P S A C K J M V
K E M I R A T E S K E X
```

FIND AND CIRCLE . . .

Six words starting and ending in K	☑☐☐☐☐☐
Home to Dubai and Abu Dhabi: ____ ____ ____	☐☐☐
What HBO stands for	☐☐☐
Two four-letter mammals starting with M	☐☐
Young sheep	☐

```
I Z C V A A B I V L P L
F R K O N L I C I Z O I
L X I I R A A P L E N S
U J T S W N U S K X D B
G E Z A K P E V K I Z O
R X H L A K E A H A N N
R O M E S T E P H E N G
K C A L I F O R N I A V
```

FIND AND CIRCLE . . .

Five parts of the eye	☑☐☐☐☐
Three U.S. states	☐☐☐
Three four-letter bodies of water	☐☐☐
Author of "Salem's Lot" (first/last name)	☐☐
Two European capitals	☐☐

```
P A P R I C O T A J O X
A E D L S I N K P Y R K
V K A E E S T O P R A S
O Z J R N M P Z L R N A
C M I N K V O E E E G L
A M A N G O E N A H E L
D B A N A N A R X C Z A
O C D E T R O I T V H D
```

FIND AND CIRCLE . . .

Ten fruits	☑☐☐☐☐☐☐☐☐☐
Three large U.S. cities starting with D	☐☐☐
Weasel-like mammal with soft fur	☐
Opposite of go	☐
"Everything but the kitchen _____"	☐

```
K G P O N Y S T K S H B
E N R Z X J H S K T O K
L B E E J O P E C A S J
K E R E E A M L A N P W
C I V O Z N U P L D I O
U G K B W X I M B I T B
N E J O H N R I Z N A L
K A N K L E T S C G L E
```

FIND AND CIRCLE . . .

Four joints	☑☐☐☐
Four eight-letter words	☐☐☐☐
Four five-letter colors	☐☐☐☐
_____ Cusack (siblings)	☐☐
Small horse	☐

```
H Y V U L T U R E O W L
Z A Z C B X Z Y P R A A
N J W G V L A M D I L D
O P K K L R U L V N O A
C Z I A G T O E X G G N
L X E N S G V C K O N A
A T Z V K R U S S I A C
F C O N D O R S T A R R
```

FIND AND CIRCLE . . .

Five birds of prey	☑☐☐☐☐
Five four-letter colors	☐☐☐☐☐
Three six-letter countries	☐☐☐
Beatles drummer: _____ _____	☐☐
Remaining part of a tree after it's cut down	☐

```
N B R A Z I L C H I L E
K O V A D J E C T I V E
Y P U E J K B V P V C K
B J E N R A I O D O B N
G Z X R V B C N X J L H
U J P A U L Y K G I Z O
R C O L O M B I A K N J
P R E P O S I T I O N G
```

FIND AND CIRCLE . . .

Four parts of speech	☑☐☐☐
Four South American countries	☐☐☐☐
Three sports	☐☐☐
Lennon and McCartney	☐☐
Two face cards	☐☐

```
F V A L V E Z V J T K B
Z O E K T J F V I S W V
V B U V Y W E O Y V I O
T R M R O V E T R A I X
H E Z I L L R N R T R D
G A X E L I V J T U Y D
I D W K H E Z E J Y E Z
E T V T S A V V Y T E N
```

FIND AND CIRCLE . . .

Nine even numbers   ☑ ☐ ☐ ☐ ☐ ☐ ☐ ☐ ☐

Four words with two V's   ☐ ☐ ☐ ☐

Two four-letter units of length   ☐ ☐

White, wheat or rye   ☐

Opposite of false   ☐

```
F T H I R T E E N Z C J
R I S K R A I N Y C B N
O J V P E X E Z V N Z E
O V Z E A E J E E E W V
F J R J T R R V M T I E
O H X F V O E A O G N L
T N I J C S R O I I D E
K F E S J F F P N B Y V
```

FIND AND CIRCLE . . .

Eight odd numbers	☑☐☐☐☐☐☐☐
Three five-letter words related to bowling	☐☐☐
Two five-letter weather adjectives ending in Y	☐☐
Two four-letter words with OO in the middle	☐☐
Swine	☐

```
C C O L O M B I A K H C
B H K V C Y M A Y A I E
C J A I K H D A N D S C
J A M D R A I I T C T N
C M Z A N K H L P H O E
U E X A R C Z J E B R I
B S C J V Y V E R B Y C
A C A M B O D I A B C S
```

FIND AND CIRCLE . . .

Seven countries starting with C	☑☐☐☐☐☐☐
Three school subjects	☐☐☐
Captain of the Enterprise: _____ T. _____	☐☐
"_____ Poppins"	☐
Action word	☐

```
S J M A N A T E E F S V
J E V K Z O N A V Y E H
E G A C D I T S X L N O
G N Z L H Y U T A F I P
I I Z P M R B H E Z R K
E E L R L J W L Z R A I
B O A A K Z H N U J M N
D B W A I R B U S E K S
```

FIND AND CIRCLE . . .

Six aquatic mammals	☑☐☐☐☐☐
Three branches of the U.S. armed forces	☐☐☐
Two competing aircraft manufacturers	☐☐
Two colors starting with B	☐☐
University and hospital founder: Johns ____	☐

```
L V B E N D E R J S E A
L A Z X P B G Z B A Y T
E R K J U A O X V N N E
N E K E D C L J O A F N
N D G D D O D O E X O D
A N U N L N G C K V X E
H E L O E A O L E A D R
C G F P L S E N D E R Z
```

FIND AND CIRCLE . . .

Nine bodies of water	☑☐☐☐☐☐☐☐☐
Four six-letter words that rhyme with "fender"	☐☐☐☐
Two four-letter metals	☐☐
_____ and eggs	☐
Three-letter canine with a bushy tail	☐

```
Y C A T L A N T I C Y B
C E B K H D M O N T H C
D N A X Z O E W H V G I
N T V R V T C C E O V T
O U T R U N K K A E U C
C R V N O R T H E D K R
E Y I N D I A N Z Y E A
S M P A C I F I C X J C
```

FIND AND CIRCLE . . .

Eight units of time (four-letter min.)   ☑ ☐ ☐ ☐ ☐ ☐ ☐ ☐

Four oceans   ☐ ☐ ☐ ☐

Sport that comes in ice and field variations   ☐

Commonality between a tree, a car and an elephant   ☐

Opposite of south   ☐

```
A D G W I L L O W E G J
W U A M N S K V E T R W
W O N U O I I Z A I E H
I K W T G T E S S H E I
N A Z X J H H C T W N P
D Y W E S T T E E K S
O A R A D A R E R V R A
W K W A L L O W R E D W
```

FIND AND CIRCLE . . .

Five female relatives (five-letter min.)	☑☐☐☐☐
Five words starting and ending in W	☐☐☐☐☐
Colors of the Italian flag	☐☐☐
Two five-letter palindromes	☐☐
Directions that once preceded "Germany"	☐☐

```
D P O L I S H B L G C D
Z R L I M E K U N U E V
X L U C B E F I V T T P
J E K M E K S N S S R E
O M V R N A I U O A J K
B O G A E T J H H Z B C
O N H L A D G E R M A N
E T P L A L U M I N U M
```

FIND AND CIRCLE . . .

Four four-letter musical instruments	☑☐☐☐
Four eight-letter words	☐☐☐☐
Four languages	☐☐☐☐
Two citrus fruits	☐☐
Demi Moore/Patrick Swayze movie	☐

```
E M G S Z O B A T V N Z
M R A O U X N N K A C N
O R I R L P J T G V A E
D A N E M D E I A Z T E
G B O F Z O H R G R K R
N B R A X C S V I O I G
I I U R I J K E C O A O
K T H M G R A Y T B R T
```

FIND AND CIRCLE . . .

The Great Lakes	☑☐☐☐☐
Five mammals ending in T	☐☐☐☐☐
Three colors starting with G	☐☐☐
Home to England and Scotland: United _____	☐
George Orwell novel: "Animal _____"	☐

```
F N E W M A N I R A N C
J O S T O R K V J K E O
C Y O K Z R H E N S E B
R A X T E C L I O L L A
A R K T N I B O G U X L
N D E I M O G A A Z K T
E M V P R Z E P C U B A
Z F U R L O N G P E R U
```

FIND AND CIRCLE . . .

Six units of length	☑☐☐☐☐☐
Five five-letter birds	☐☐☐☐☐
Three four-letter countries	☐☐☐
"The Sting" star born in 1925 (first/last name)	☐☐
Element with atomic number 27	☐

```
H D O O D L E K Y X A E
V A W I N D Y N S F T S
N Y Z Y K M I F N U N N
O N C Y R A J O O C E E
O N B O R Z X G W H G F
D U T L O N G G Y S A E
L S C L O U D Y Z I M D
E J O F F E N S E A V K
```

FIND AND CIRCLE . . .

Eight weather conditions ending in Y ☑ ☐ ☐ ☐ ☐ ☐ ☐ ☐

Two seven-letter colors ☐ ☐

Two football sides ☐ ☐

Two words that rhyme with "poodle" ☐ ☐

Opposite of short (length) ☐

```
W K M T R I P L E Z T X
X E V I F U L L E S Y J
E Z E Y N V B D U R K H
L J P K Z U A J U Z T R
G A M Z O C T T X N A J
N I A D E K N E O E X Y
I L T D K E K M Y Z A K
S V S X C J U M P D B C
```

FIND AND CIRCLE . . .

Seven units of time	☑ ☐ ☐ ☐ ☐ ☐ ☐
Three baseball hits	☐ ☐ ☐
Three four-letter words starting with J	☐ ☐ ☐
Envelope add-on	☐
Opposite of empty	☐

J N O V E M B E R A A E
Z U H T E A L C Y C M N
T J L O Z X U E D T A U
S Z X Y R J E N E I R J
U G R A Y R Z T M O D Y
G M E X I C O E O N A Z
U C A N A D A R C M X K
A S E P T E M B E R J B

FIND AND CIRCLE . . .

Six months	☑☐☐☐☐☐
Four types of movies	☐☐☐☐
Three four-letter colors	☐☐☐
Two North American countries	☐☐
Football snapper	☐

```
I A R G E N T I N A U V
U R I D U C K C O I G J
R W A N E Z J R X N A Y
U Z E N D A J O Y E N L
G V J S K I S W G M D A
U F A S T V A T E R A T
A H Y D R O G E N A Z I
Y I N D O N E S I A B C
```

FIND AND CIRCLE . . .

Eight countries starting with a vowel	☑☐☐☐☐☐☐☐
Two components of water	☐☐
Two four-letter birds	☐☐
Two opposing directions	☐☐
Opposite of slow	☐

```
G F D I S N E Y J G J T
G O W O R L D G G L A V
E U N Z B C N N T O N J
O R Z G T I I K L W E U
R T X S W V J T H I R D
G H R O I S E C O N D Y
E I R G P E T E R G T V
F G G B E N C H L E Y C
```

FIND AND CIRCLE . . .

Five words starting and ending in G	☑☐☐☐☐
Football game quarters	☐☐☐☐
Three Jetsons	☐☐☐
"Jaws" author (first/last name)	☐☐
Post-Super Bowl quote: "I'm going to _____ _____!"	☐☐

```
A Z E W I L L C U B S J
J S Z U B K A I B B H N
X L I V R C X R U E O W
E E Z A I O K I L A R O
G N Y R J V P S L R T R
I S F B L U E E S Z B
E A N T A R C T I C A Z
B Z A U S T R A L I A X
```

FIND AND CIRCLE . . .

Five continents	☑☐☐☐☐
Three colors starting with B	☐☐☐
Three professional Chicago sports teams	☐☐☐
New York Times crossword puzzle editor (first/last name)	☐☐
Two four-letter parts of the eye	☐☐

```
V C D O L E N Z X C K C
S E A D J E C T I V E O
E N R X Z N D S U G V S
N O J B A A O R X A I T
O U K R H A E Z J S N N
J N I C L P S O L I D E
P R E P O S I T I O N R
K N E S M I T H T O R K
```

FIND AND CIRCLE . . .

Four parts of speech	☑☐☐☐
The Monkees (last names)	☐☐☐☐
Four four-letter countries	☐☐☐☐
"Dances With Wolves" star (first/last name)	☐☐
Two forms of matter	☐☐

```
F W M O T H E R B C A T
O O I Z P O N D L O C Z
O S O N D O G R S G O X
D U X L T Z X E I N U M
G M C O V E J H S I S M
O M L A K E R T T R I O
O E J G U L F A E P N O
D R L O O K R F R S J N
```

FIND AND CIRCLE . . .

Six four-letter words with OO in the middle ☑☐☐☐☐☐

Four six-letter relatives ☐☐☐☐

Four four-letter bodies of water ☐☐☐☐

Three seasons ☐☐☐

Two common three-letter pets ☐☐

```
T C B R A I N P T C C T
V E K K T Z R H Y O V R
T L N X X A G Y J O R U
A L I T H I R N X L E A
I O R Z L K A G K E V N
N J D I J B V Z E R I T
T Z W V I O L I N T L K
K T T I L T H E A R T J
```

FIND AND CIRCLE . . .

Six words starting and ending in T   ☑☐☐☐☐☐

Four stringed instruments   ☐☐☐☐

Three five-letter organs   ☐☐☐

Opposite of warmer   ☐

Five-letter synonym for "beverage"   ☐

```
S S O C K Z F A T H E R
J H S W E A T E R X A K
P N O K V T T H O M E T
A H Z E R E Z J E R R Y
N O X I K M O T H E R V
T J H C S E I N F E L D
S S A A D A M S K B O X
J J P A J A M A S V J B
```

FIND AND CIRCLE . . .

Eight things meant to be worn	☑☐☐☐☐☐☐☐
Parents	☐☐
Star of a "show about nothing" (first/last name)	☐☐
Second U.S. president (first/last name)	☐☐
HBO: _____ _____ Office	☐☐

```
M L T E N D V E L N V B
N E R S R Z X S H E K C
I V N A N A K U E G N G
L B Z D I O T O L Y E D
R E X J K N W M I X M V
E N L I S B O N U O O E
B D A T H E N S M C R N
S E N D V M A D R I D D
```

FIND AND CIRCLE . . .

Six four-letter words ending in END	☑☐☐☐☐☐
Five European capitals	☐☐☐☐☐
Two six-letter gases	☐☐
Two rodents	☐☐
Two four-letter forms of precipitation	☐☐

```
T Z E N G L I S H J G J
S H Y H Y R Z J H X C N
T M A S F X U S K N R A
R O K I Z R I S I C E M
E O N L X N E T S D E R
A R U O A K A N I I K E
M G K P J L V R C V A G
G K S B U B B L E H Z N
```

FIND AND CIRCLE . . .

Eight languages	☑☐☐☐☐☐☐☐
Two flowing bodies of water	☐☐
Most important people at a wedding	☐☐
Body of gas contained in a liquid	☐
Black-and-white mammal that stinks	☐

```
N V F S P I E L B E R G
J I T I H I S T O R Y N
X P N H V S C I E N C E
J A Z E R E G R E E N V
O U X K V E W H I T E E
H L H G S T E V E N Z L
N N T H I R T E E N X E
V M A T H T S E V E N K
```

FIND AND CIRCLE . . .

Six odd numbers	☑☐☐☐☐☐
Three school subjects	☐☐☐
"Minority Report" director (first/last name)	☐☐
Two five-letter colors	☐☐
Lennon and McCartney	☐☐

```
T P W R E N J R A V E N
N E E Z X L E T T U C E
I R R L T O M A T O R N
U A Z N I S J A C K E O
G G X J K C W Z B B A C
N U K I N G A A C O M L
E S B A C O N N N B J A
P T V K N P U F F I N F
```

FIND AND CIRCLE . . .

Eight birds ending in N   ☑ ☐ ☐ ☐ ☐ ☐ ☐ ☐

What BLT stands for   ☐ ☐ ☐

Two things commonly added to coffee   ☐ ☐

Two face cards   ☐ ☐

_____ Newhart   ☐

```
H R O B I N C H C O V E
T A Z R Y Z X L A K E B
O P Z W A S N O W Y I Y
O O K Y J I Y G I C S M
F N Z D E N N H N O P R
S D R L N Z J Y D K E O
K A I U G U L F Y E P T
Y M S W I L L I A M S S
```

FIND AND CIRCLE . . .

Six weather adjectives ending in Y	☑ ☐ ☐ ☐ ☐ ☐
Four four-letter bodies of water	☐ ☐ ☐ ☐
Four four-letter units of length	☐ ☐ ☐ ☐
"Good Morning, Vietnam" star (first/last name)	☐ ☐
Two competing cola brands	☐ ☐

```
C W A L R U S Z S L U G
O L M R J M I T T E N V
C Z A O A A Z C B L Y R
T X K M N B G J K I E E
O C U B A K B U V H K T
P D E U C E E I A C N S
U Z G L O V E Y T R O Y
S S C A L L O P Z X D O
```

FIND AND CIRCLE . . .

Five mollusks	☑☐☐☐☐
Five six-letter mammals	☐☐☐☐☐
Two things worn on the hand	☐☐
Two countries starting with C	☐☐
Two of hearts, for example	☐

```
D B C H E E S E J P Z X
Z E X J C Z H E N E I K
R L E S J A F O L A V G
E E C R H F M L R A V B
T W Z I A E E E R S Y Y
T I X R V Z E B L M E W
U S I X A I E P R C O Z
B G B G Z Z C A J C X J
```

FIND AND CIRCLE . . .

Nine hoofed mammals ☑☐☐☐☐☐☐☐☐

Two six-letter dairy products ☐☐

Two branches of the U.S. armed forces ☐☐

Daniel Day-_____ ☐

Honda car with a palindromic name ☐

```
G W A L T Z V K Y Z T X
E R Z X A K E K E O A J
C V I B J C E R S B N Z
I K M N A L N I R M G R
D A J M I W J M E A O E
S X I M O Z X S J M K E
Z R S R E A S T E R N N
G V F S A L S A V Z J S
```

FIND AND CIRCLE . . .

Six facial expressions ☑☐☐☐☐☐

Five five-letter dances ☐☐☐☐☐

New York City's time zone ☐

Top worn by a football player ☐

Cubes used in board games ☐

```
W T H A I L A N D Z V G
A O T U R K E Y Y Z E E
I X L Z W Z W B X L B N
S M G F J A A E A J E E
I A R K Y L L H A K T R
N J A V L Z W R V S A A
U O Y A G O L D U Z E L
T R W A L P H A J S X L
```

FIND AND CIRCLE . . .

Five mammals starting with W	☑☐☐☐☐
Three countries starting with T	☐☐☐
Two military ranks	☐☐
First two Greek letters	☐☐
Two colors starting with G	☐☐

```
F C F I S H E R J S H C
B O P A R T I A L O A B
Z Z R R U S S E L L M K
N X J K C R O W E A I N
O X Z L U N A R V R L I
O N I C A R A G U A L F
P G U A T E M A L A V E
S Z F O R D P A N A M A
```

FIND AND CIRCLE . . .

Three eating utensils	☑ ☐ ☐
Three Central American countries	☐ ☐ ☐
_____ eclipse	☐ ☐ ☐
Three "Star Wars" (1977) stars	☐ ☐ ☐
"Gladiator" star (first/last name)	☐ ☐

321

```
O J M O N T A N A V Z M
A H R I D L E Y E N A I
L T I Z B T N G N R D C
A E X O I W I E H O I H
S X Z H O E E S E C R I
K A W R B R Z O R I O G
A S B V G X K O O N L A
H A W A I I C G N U F N
```

FIND AND CIRCLE . . .

Seven U.S. states	☑☐☐☐☐☐☐
Four five-letter colors	☐☐☐☐
Two five-letter birds	☐☐
Mythical one-horned animal	☐
"Alien" director: _____ Scott	☐

```
S M A N A T E E B E S Z
T E K E L V I S S R N P
N V A C J T E I O I E R
E L Z L O S O T H L K E
I E B O R P C P A J V S
T M F U R O L H Z X B L
A O N O D O W L I M E E
P N P Z D W A L R U S Y
```

FIND AND CIRCLE . . .

Six aquatic mammals   ☑ ☐ ☐ ☐ ☐ ☐

Three sets of people in a hospital   ☐ ☐ ☐

Performer called "The King" (first/last name)   ☐ ☐

Two citrus fruits   ☐ ☐

Twelve inches   ☐

```
P V R I C H A R D Y N V
E A M E R C U R Y E O K
N V W K V S T A R K E Y
U E V N S H A R K R G T
T N K K G X Z O Z U I R
P U B I S H O P X T P O
E S N N G R P E R C H U
N K C G S A T U R N K T
```

FIND AND CIRCLE . . .

Five chess pieces	☑☐☐☐☐
Four planets	☐☐☐☐
Three five-letter fish	☐☐☐
Ringo Starr's real name: ____ ____	☐☐
Two six-letter birds	☐☐

```
W C C H I L D H A L L L
T A B A R R I E R Z L H
E R L A P P L E J A C O
R R Z L T O M V B A G N
R I H A N K S K E N O L
I E Z T A L L P A M L J
E R G U A V A M E A X J
R Z J K M A L L C Z V K
```

FIND AND CIRCLE . . .

Six four-letter words ending in ALL ☑☐☐☐☐☐

Five five-letter fruits ☐☐☐☐☐

Three words with three R's ☐☐☐

"Forrest Gump" star (first/last name) ☐☐

TV chef Julia ☐

```
P E C U A D O R W N O J
Z E G O O S E O H E R A
X C R V J V C K I E A M
K H J U A I Z K T R N A
C I Z W X J V G E G G I
U L C E N T I P E D E C
B E M C O L O M B I A A
A B R A Z I L Z D U C K
```

FIND AND CIRCLE . . .

Eight Western Hemisphere countries ☑☐☐☐☐☐☐☐

Colors of the Irish flag ☐☐☐

Two waterfowl ☐☐

Nine-letter arthropod ☐

Tidal _____ ☐

HIDATO

How to Play

Each Hidato puzzle starts with a grid partially filled with numbers.

6		⑨
	2	8
①		

The goal is to fill the grid with consecutive numbers that connect horizontally, vertically, or diagonally.

6	7	⑨
5	2	8
①	4	3

Hidato Tips

Tip #1: Each puzzle has only one solution.

Tip #2: Hidato puzzles can be solved using 100 percent logic. No guesswork is needed.

Tip #3: The first and last numbers of a puzzle are circled.

Tip #4: It is not necessary to start from the first number. Sometimes it is better to start elsewhere.

Tip #5: Working backward (counting down in numbers) can reveal key clues to solving the puzzle.

A Sample Hidato

The following example demonstrates how to solve a Hidato puzzle.

	8		4
			3
	10		①︎
12		⑯	15

The circles indicate that the lowest number in the grid is 1 and the highest is 16. Start by trying to complete chain 1 to 3. There are two possible places to put the 2.

It is not clear which position is correct. Therefore, look for other connections that will provide the clues needed to place the 2.

	8		4
		2	3
	10	2	①︎
12		⑯	15

As you scan through the puzzle, you'll see there is also not enough information to solve chains 4 to 8, 8 to 10, and 10 to 12. However, there is only one way to connect 12 to 15. By working backward, you'll see only one position for the 14 because the 15 has only one open box connected to it. With the 14 placed on the grid, the locations for the 2 and the 13 are revealed.

	8		4
			3
	10	14	①
12		⑯	15

	8		4
		2	3
	10	14	①
12	13	⑯	15

Now, numbers 5, 6, and 11 also have exact positions. The final numbers can now be placed to complete the puzzle. These strategies can be used to solve all levels of Hidato puzzles.

	8	5	4
	6	2	3
11	10	14	①
12	13	⑯	15

7	8	5	4
9	6	2	3
11	10	14	①
12	13	⑯	15

Hidato   353

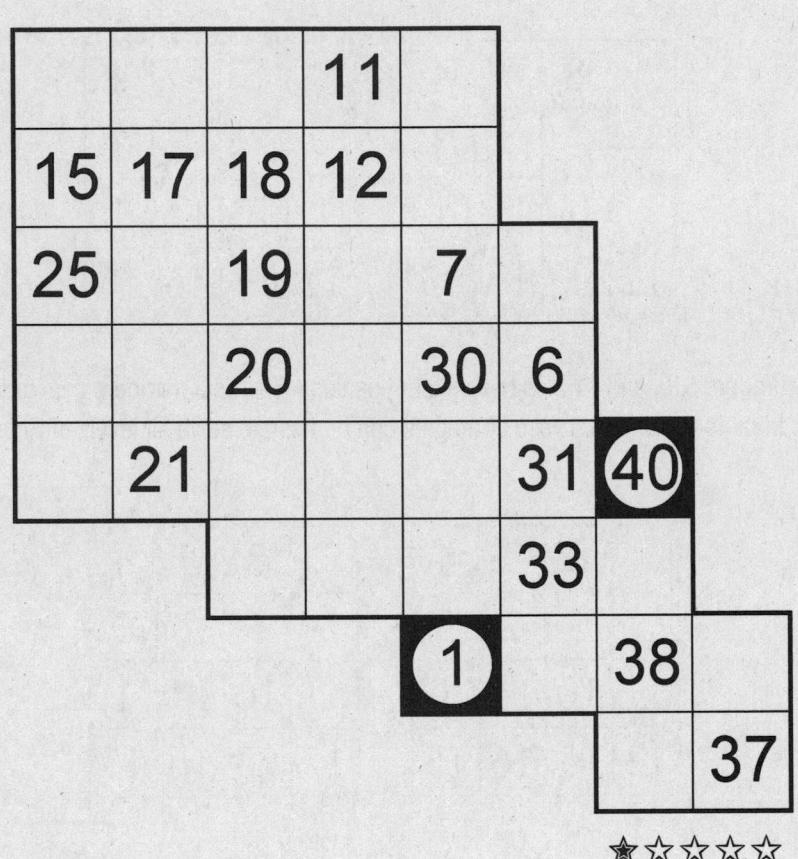

PRACTICE

	29				
		9		23	
	7	8	26	12	
		6		25	
36		33		20	
			1	19	
38		40			

★☆☆☆☆

PRACTICE

				35	
24		28			36
	19	12	30		
14		1	4		
	16	2		9	

★☆☆☆☆

		9			31	35
	13	㊷42		33		
14						27
					28	
①1	4					24
2		17	20	21		

★☆☆☆☆

	19		14	
		18	15	
	22		4	40
26				39
		2	1	9
		29		37
				32
				34

★☆☆☆☆

	40			
39				33
			6	
		5		27
1		10		22	28
	19		23	
17		20		
16	14			

★☆☆☆☆

	13	8		5	
16	■				
		■	10		
31		33	■	(1)		39
19			■		
	21	28		■	
		27		(42)	

★☆☆☆☆

	17		28	
			20	
				23	
40		31			25
39		11		1		
38				7	
		35				5

★☆☆☆☆

334

			7		4	
	17	15		25	26	
			10			1
		11		28		
	36				32	
39		37				31

★☆☆☆☆

335

			8			
	4					22
1			10			21
		11		25		
		36				
		37			29	
39				32		30

★☆☆☆☆

★☆☆☆☆

			36		
23		35		16	
	32		1		12
	26				11
	27				10
	29		4	7	9

★☆☆☆☆

				21	22
3	4				
1		7		18	
		32			
9					
		15			

★☆☆☆☆

		7			
	16		6	4	**40**
15	13				**1**
		12			
		19	30	33	
				29	34
		25			

★☆☆☆☆

			19		
27	26	20			
		25		36	
	9	31			37
		11			38
6		33			
①					㊵

★☆☆☆☆

		46		13	12	
49	17					8
		24		44		
		22				
20	21		5			
	28	32			39	
30		34	35	37		1

★★☆☆☆

						44
			39		43	
35		37	18	17		
						12
		30	10	4		
21					7	
24	23				2	1

★★☆☆☆

343

	26	25	23			
				13		
		■	11		15	
	31	■				17
33	46		■			
	47		■			6
48		42	1			

★★☆☆☆

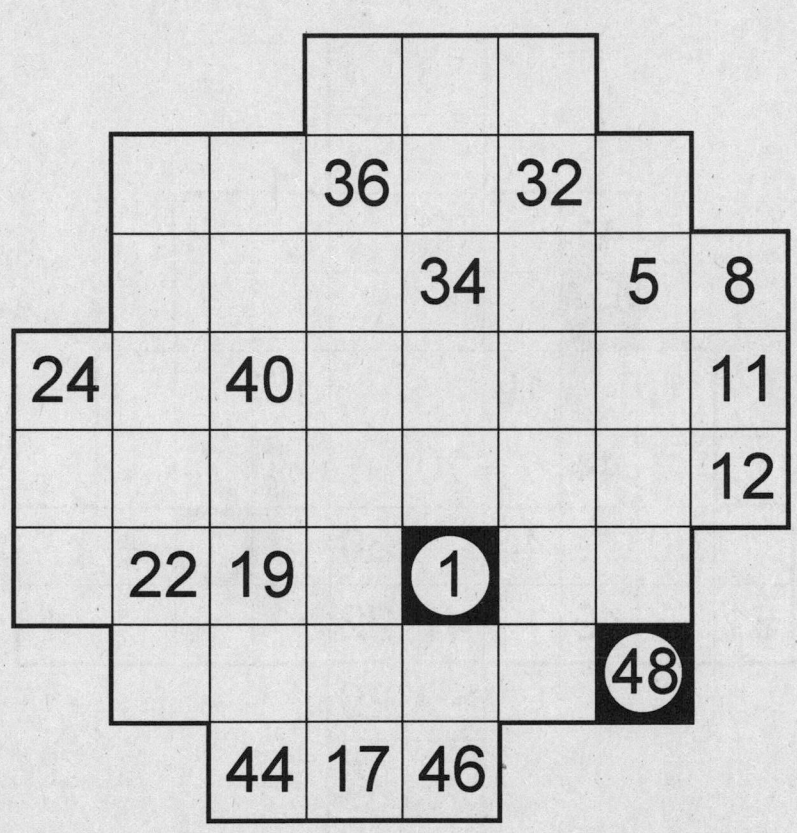

★★☆☆☆

	21	22		16	
		30	33		
28		■	■		
2	4	■	■	12	36
①		5		11	
	7				
㊹		42	41		

★★☆☆☆

				31	
42	44		29		
	40				
		39	22		
	15		36		
	11		6	25	1
12	10				

★★☆☆☆

41						32
	38		㊹		27	
39		■	■	26		30
9		■	■		24	23
	10		12	■		21
	4	①		16		19
		2	14			

★★☆☆☆

		13			
			20		
9		19			41
	2	22		44	40
4	①	㊽			38
26	25		33		
				34	
	31				

★★☆☆☆

	23	22		19	①		
28			18		2		
29			15	14	3		
34	39			12	7		
33	42			10	9		
	43				48		
		45					

★★☆☆☆

354

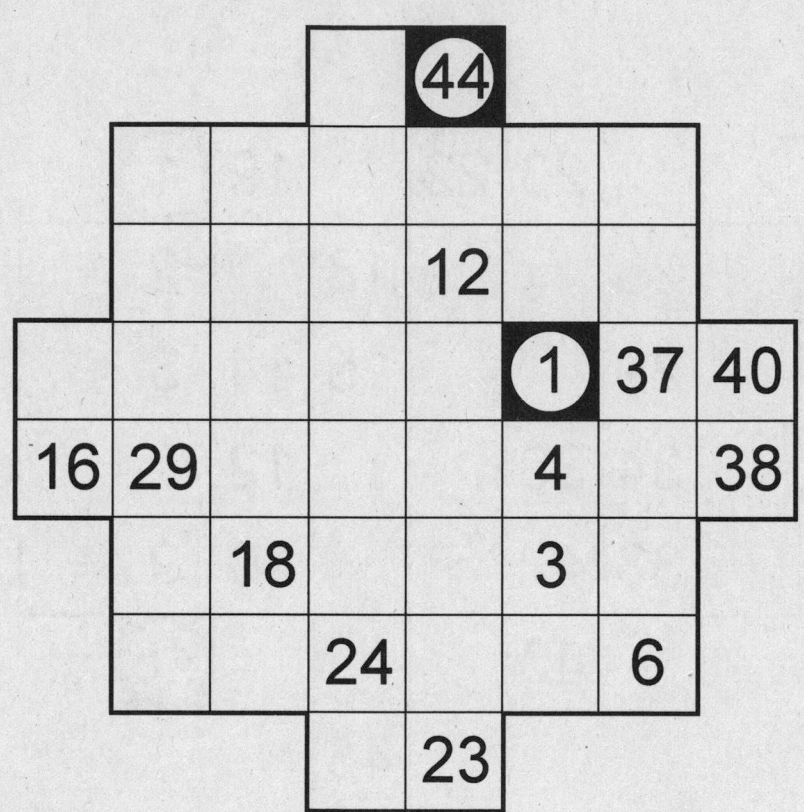

★★☆☆☆

355

★★☆☆☆

		16	17			
3		(1)				
47	2		8		13	25
			10	57		24
45				58		
43	53			35	61	(63)
	54				31	
41						30

★★★☆☆

		26	25		1	
	23			16		3
					5	
		55	■		8	
			■	13		
	34				44	
		35				45
60	36		41	40	50	

★★★☆☆

18		14	13	1	9		
	16			10		7	
20							58
	22		41				
		37		42			56
	27	35					46
	34		30		50		
		31		52			

★★★☆☆

3	5							
2		6		10				
①1	13							
	16	24						
	17		22				32	31	47
		21		38	35	33			48
						44		
							55	
				42				54
				60			52	

★★★☆☆

		1		13		
4				14	37
	10	15			
	19	17			
29	21		40		
65	27	26	22	45	46
	25				
58	56	50	51		
62	59				

★★★☆☆

361

	60				54	52	
5		3	1	57	55		
	4	19					50
		18					
21			17		48		37
	10		12	45	30	39	
				44			
	24		27			41	

★★★☆☆

			58		18	20		
11		59				■		
		9	60	56	55	■		
			6		■	51	24	
65			5	■			25	
	66		■	44		32		
	70	■						
	■		34		36		28	
72	1			39				

★★★☆☆

					1	
	57	7	5	3		
		6		45		
60	9	10		39	41	
	17		49	38		
13	19			27	28	
		24			33	
				31		

★★★☆☆

		27			17
34	32		26		
		29	23	21	15
37				52	
	39			50	
	41		48		7
	44	43	46		
59			9	1	
			65		3

★★★☆☆

365

★★★☆☆

		58			23	21	
65		██			██		
	██	██	26		██	██	
		33				18	
	35		9	8	30		
	53		7				
	██	50	6		██	██	
	43	██	46		██		
						1	

★★★☆☆

60								
	43		37	38				
58		46		36				
56	48							
	52			32	21		17	
	54			31	20			
						23		13
					25		8	
						3		11
						2	1	

★★★☆☆

	52						
		51		44		42	
	56		47		20		
59		57	14	18			
		12		15			
			24	26			34
		6	25		28		
64		5		①1			32
	65					30	

★★★☆☆

43							59
44		39		36		58	60
47							62
	48						
			51			15	
	10		20	19	17	30	
	6			22	24	29	
7	1			23			28

★★★☆☆

53			60				
	52	54					63
			23			65	
48			24	26	28	31	
		45	20		32		
13				18			
	8				37		
		6		42	1	38	

★★★☆☆

			10				①
	46		43	8	6	4	
49		42			16	18	
50	52		13	15			
		40					20
		55		25			
	56			26	33	32	
		62			34		30

★★★☆☆

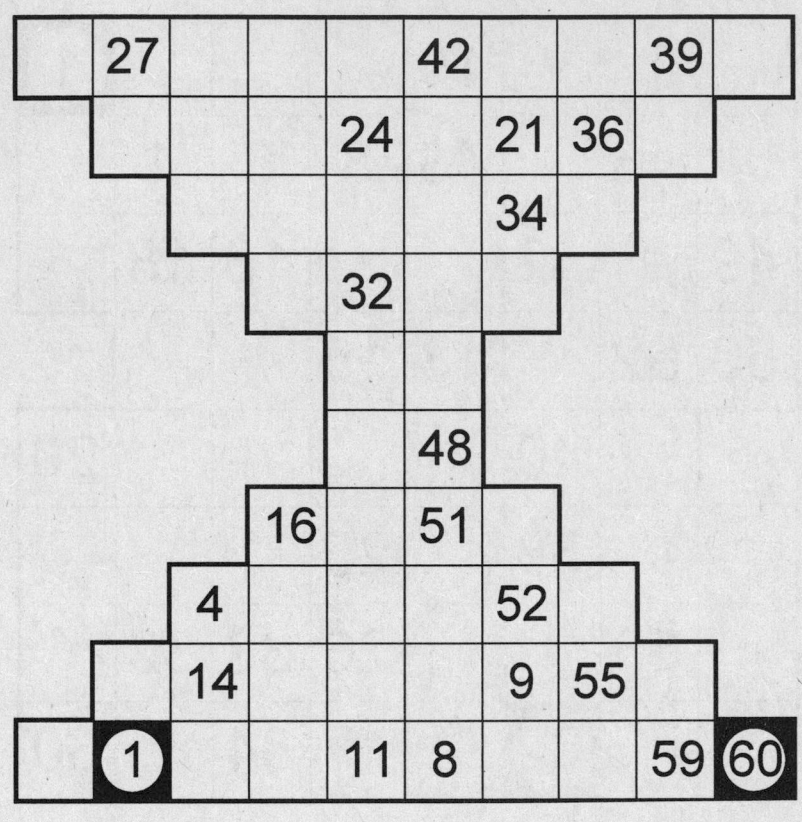

		6		11		
	4	7		12		

58	60	62		(1)		15	23
56		46		(64)			22
49		41	40			18		

		33	27
	34	31	
36		30	

★★★☆☆

		32	30	29	28			
		33			26			
			19					
	36			17	21		5	
41		37				23	6	
42		51				9	7	
			13	14				1
				61				
		54		62				
	56		64					

★★★☆☆

375

		36		38		44	
			37	28		42	
32	22			26	27		46
		24					
	16						62
	17			6	52	54	60
	12	10			56		
			8	1			

★★★☆☆

80	(81)					31	28	
	78		6	8	30			26
	37			9			23	22
76					(1)			20
75		39	40	3	2	13		
67						14	16	
	66				43	51		
63		59	57		44		49	48
64	62				53			

★ ★ ★ ★ ☆

78	12			21		
		13	10	8			23
75	1			18			26
74			3	17		29	
	71				34	
		69			35	
63		65			38	37
	64		66			46
				52		45
	58	56	54		50	48

★★★★☆

	75	76		15		80		6	5
74							2		
	71				9			1	
	65			12	11		19	20	
		64				23			
		62							
				46	44	42		26	
		52	49		40			27	
							28		
54				36	35			33	32

★★★★☆

						31	28	⑧④	
	70		35			30			
		37		33			79		26
	64		■	■	■	■			
		40	■	■	■	■	22		
43		62	■	■	■	■			5
44			■	■	■	■	19		
	50					9		18	
46		51	53		11	10	16		
	48		54					①	

★★★★☆

12				16		19	20	
11			2		17			
			(1)			30		25
46		50	6	■			28	26
	45	■	■	■			74	(76)
44			■	37	73			
	53							
55		61	41		65	68		
	56			66				

★★★★☆

43		⑦⑦					
	41			64	65	66		68
39		45	47			62	69	
38			48	50				
27				53		57		
	25		23	6		8	9	59
				5				13
30		3				17	14	
31		①	20	18		15

★★★★☆

★★★★☆

383

	10			77	78		69	70
	9	2		4				
	16	①1		⑧81	66			
	17		22		64		29	
	18		24		36	32		
	51		47		37		34	
		49	59	45	38			
							39	40

			15				
22	23		19		14	1		
27		25		38	12		5	6
			34		11		
			35		10		
	44						
	45				55		
78	46			56		63	
			52		67	66	65
74	51				

★★★★☆

	34			39	42			
	31		37		40		46	
	30	68			54		47	
		69		56	53			
	70		66					
	22		███	███				
78		73	███	███		61	60	
			███	███			12	
	76	1	19			6		
		17		15				

★★★★☆

				38	37		1		
73			70	40		33	9		
	67	68					13	7	
				42	11				
		63						22	
			59	57	28		24		16
80	46			55	26			20	
			52					19	
		50							

★★★★☆

			57		84			81
	60							80
	66		55	69			79	
65			52	47		73		77	78
			51		71		41	
						39		
9				20		36	30	
	11	14	15		22			31
6	7	1					32
						33

★★★★☆

	69		75					⑧1
		68	63	62	61	78		
		①1			57		35	36
	4		2				33	
			54				32	
	10	9	53	51		30		40
12			21	22		29	46	
	13		20					42
15	16						44	

★★★★☆

		71						
69	64	73	3	5				
63					84			
61	1							13
	58					11		
57						17	15	
46						22		
47				24	23			
48		39		26				
51	50		37		34	33	29	30

					80	78		
52	53					77	10	9
51				1		7		
	57	72		4				
43	48			3			14	13
42	60	59						16
40		63					17	
39		29		65	23			
37		32	27	26			21	
	35	33						

★ ★ ★ ★ ☆

	63						
35				71	3		
	32		67		58	6	(1)
33		40					
			75	74	9		
	23	76				55	
		(77)				53	
25	20	18	12	13		46	
				47	48	50	

★★★★☆

393

	11		68	67				
	9					64		
		2	①	74	73	55	61	60
	14			53				
				㉘				
	16		■					
	18	19	■					
			■		42		44	47
25	24		30			39		46
		28	33	35	36	37		

★★★★☆

						①			
		19			13	11		5	
32		26		21		12	9		7
33	35	25							
39	40			79		74			71
							75	68	
					44				90
						82			
	57	59	50		48	47			
	58			62					

★★★★☆

	12		17		21				
	13	15		19	22	24	25	26	
									32
1			82	80	78				35
	7			70				34	
	6		71	68					38
4								40	
								41	
					50		47	46	43
	62	64		55	51				44

★★★★☆

			65		121			126			
	61	63	49			124					130
	56		48	68	71		119				
	55		47		73	75		108			
		45		77		74		109		1	
			42					106			114
83		81					140		111		
	85					98			112	4	
	39			88							6
	37	30	28	100						9	7
		29		25		21				14	
				24	22				17		12

★ ★ ★ ★ ★

397

		71	75							97
	68	70				85		88	95	
	63	61	73				90	91		
					11	102				
	52				10		108			
	50	54	56		14	104		114		
		46		17			106			
			45		16	123				
	23		44		40			119		117
	24		43	41		38		125		1	3
	29	31		35			130		132		136
		33					131			

★ ★ ★ ★ ★

399

			62	60		53	51	50	47		
				59	54					48	
	65	66			57	43					
1			■	■		41	40			37	36
		70	■	12		22			126		31
			11		13	20	123			29	30
	7	73		10		18					27
		89				17		■			
77	76		90	93			■	■		114	
	79	86		94		102			108	109	111
		81		95		103					
			82								

★★★★★

			100	99							■
	89					65			■		
85			103		96	67	62	61	■	55	
	86	109						■		50	
81			105			■		70		51	
132	79	111				■			46	4	
				75	■			45	7	5	
	129	77		■		41		9			1
127			■	115		28			11		
126		■		117			25	38			17
	■		31		33			24	21	18	
■									22		

★★★★★

Crossword Solutions

1

A	W	A	I	T		T	H	U	D		H	A	S	
C	H	I	D	E		G	E	N	O	A		A	R	K
M	E	D	I	A	C	I	R	C	U	S		L	E	I
E	E	Y	O	R	E		D	A	B	S		F	A	D
			M	O	A	T		P	L	E	A	S		
R	A	J		U	S	A		E	N	L	I	S	T	
E	M	O		T	E	X	A	S		T	A	S	T	Y
A	B	B	A		D	E	P	O	T		S	T	O	P
P	L	O	T	S		D	E	L	H	I		E	V	E
S	E	P	T	E	T		A	R	M		R	E	D	
		E	N	S	U	E		R	I	P	A			
T	A	N		A	N	N	E		C	A	L	L	U	S
O	U	I		M	I	D	D	L	E	C	L	A	S	S
U	R	N		E	C	O	N	O		T	A	K	E	N
R	A	G			S	W	A	T		S	H	E	D	S

2

B	L	A	R	E		L	E	A	P		C	A	R	D
E	A	S	E	L		A	R	I	A		A	L	O	E
D	R	I	V	E	A	P	A	R	T		S	O	M	E
S	A	T		M	U	S	S		T	O	E	T	A	P
			R	E	N	E		D	E	L	I			
	B	L	U	N	T		P	A	R	E	N	T	A	L
F	L	I	N	T		B	O	R	N		P	A	L	O
I	O	T	A		G	L	U	E	S		O	T	I	S
N	O	U	N		R	U	T	S		S	I	E	V	E
E	M	P	E	R	O	R	S		G	E	N	R	E	
			R	O	U	T		W	A	T	T			
B	A	D	R	E	P		C	H	I	P		A	W	E
A	S	I	A		P	I	L	O	T	L	I	G	H	T
Y	A	R	N		I	D	O	L		A	R	E	A	S
S	P	E	D		C	O	D	E		N	A	S	T	Y

3

R	O	A	R		B	E	E		K	Y	R	A		
O	L	D	E		T	O	L	D		S	I	O	U	X
W	I	D	E	A	W	A	K	E		C	A	U	S	E
E	V	O	L	V	E		N	P	R		G	E	L	
D	E	N		R	E	G	S		A	U	T	O		
		S	I	D	E	A	I	R	B	A	G	S		
L	I	B	E	L		N	I	T	S		X	I	N	G
A	M	A	L		B	E	L	L	E		D	R	I	P
S	U	R	F		E	V	I	L		S	A	L	T	S
	P	R	I	D	E	A	N	D	J	O	Y			
		Y	E	A	R		G	O	O	N		S	E	A
D	I	M		T	S	A		N	I	C	K	E	L	
E	R	O	D	E		R	I	D	E	A	L	O	N	G
C	O	R	E	S		I	N	N	S		A	S	I	A
K	N	E	W		A	K	A		W	H	E	E		

4

B	A	D	P	R		G	R	A	Y			G	M	S
E	F	I	L	E		O	H	I	O		B	O	O	T
G	R	O	U	N	D	P	O	R	K		A	L	O	O
	O	N	S	T	A	R		S	O	A	N	D	S	O
				A	T	O	N		B	A	G	E	L	
E	A	S	T	L	A		O	H	W	E	L	L		
T	U	T	U	S		T	W	E	E	T		O	L	E
C	R	A	B		P	A	W	N	S		S	V	E	N
H	A	T		T	E	C	H	S		S	P	E	N	D
			E	X	A	C	T	A		B	L	A	S	T	S
S	E	V	E	R			T	A	L	E				
P	A	I	N	T	E	R		B	U	D	D	H	A	
O	S	S	O		C	O	L	O	R	G	U	A	R	D
R	E	I	N		O	D	O	R		E	E	R	I	E
E	D	T			N	E	X	T		S	T	E	A	L

5

```
A C T S · A R C · · S L U M P
F R A T · B O R E · K O R E A
L U X U R Y B O X · A N G E L
· D I C E S · P A D · G E T S
· · C A S T · M E L T · · · ·
U P T O P · I M S L E E P Y ·
L E E · · P T A · U N R E A L
T E X T B O O K E X A M P L E
A L A R M S · E V E · · S I T
· S N O W T I R E · F R I E S
· · U S E R · R O L E · · · ·
S P A S · R A Y · P E C O S ·
P O R E S · T A X E X E M P T
A S T R O · E R I N · S I R E
M E S S Y · · D I S · S T Y E
```

6

```
· F R A U · A Q U A · · A G O
S L U M P · F U N D · U R L ·
P O L O S · G O O F S · T E A
A R E N T · R O T I · C H E F
M A R G A R E T A T W O O D ·
· · · T A T · · · E A R · · ·
· O N E D A Y A T A T I M E ·
S E D A N · T O X I N · Z O E
O Z O N E · H U L L · D E L L
A R R O W · U N E · A I D E S
R A S · Y A N G · I N C · · ·
· · C O B B · S T A T U T E ·
U N D E R S E L L S · A S I A
S H O O K · R E A M · T E N T
A L E S · · G I V E · E R A S
```

7

```
B E N D S · F L U B · F E S T
A B O U T · L O R I · I D E A
W A T E R S I G N S · F I L M
L Y E · A W E S · C A T T L E
· · · B I A S · R U T H · · ·
B A K I N G · C A I M A N S ·
F L O G S · T E N T · V I C E
F L A B · B R A G S · E G O S
S O L O · L O S E · O N E U P
· T A X R A T E · S C U R R Y
· · S I C S · F E T E · · · ·
T I K T O K · F L E A · F O E
O R E O · C O L O R G U A R D
G O E R · A R E A · O N I C E
A N N E · T E X T · N O L A N
```

8

```
V E R G E · T A M I · P H E W
E X E R T · R O A R · A E R O
N A M E C H A N G E · N A I R
T M I · · O V E N · L I V E D
· S T R I P E · E B O N Y · ·
· · U T I L I T Y B I L L S
S O R T S · C I T E · O I L ·
P R E S · P R I C E · R A K E
E S P · T R E E · B O D E D ·
C O U R S E C R E D I T · · ·
· · G O A P E · Y U C C A S ·
S O N A R · I S E E · L E O ·
E R A S · S P E L L C H E C K
R A N T · E T T E · A O R T A
B L T S · A S S T · B E T S Y
```

9

```
H E A D · T O R E · S I G H S
A M M O · O M E N · A R E A S
R A P T · G A L A · L A T T E
M I L I T A R Y B R A S S · ·
· L E N A · · L E D · G P A ·
· · G R A N T E D · M O A N ·
O W L · T R I O · T A I N T ·
P R E V A I L I N G W I N D S
R O M A N · L I M O · G A Y ·
A T O N · A D S P A C E · · ·
H E N · F O R · A L I E · · ·
· P U L L E D S T R I N G S
T H E R E · D E C O · C A G E
O M E G A · G N A T · I W O N
P O L E S · E Y R E · T E S T
```

10

```
S I L O S · · H E Y · B A L M
A T A R I · N O D E · I S E E
A R T E X H I B I T · G I G S
B Y E · P I V O T · S M A S H
· · S A F E · I D E A · · · ·
· S O C I A L O U T C A S T ·
I M O K · A N T S · M O E ·
L O A N · B E T S Y · M I L E
O W L · T E X T · S O S O · ·
S A L T W A T E R F I S H · ·
· W I N E · A L L S · · · ·
R I S E N · R E N E E · N B A
E D E N · I N D I A N C O R N
B O L T · R A I N · C A R A T
A L L Y · A L E · · E R A S E
```

11

```
CAB   CALM   IBIZA
GILA  ACAI   REVEL
IMOK  FINN   ALIBI
   WINEDECANTERS
SANTA    ELI   SAT
ITSADONEDEAL
TEA  APPS    NOEL
HAVE  TRIPS  ONES
 MEME   GOOP  EVE
   ONLINEDEGREE
ADD  TAN    LUGED
DRONEDELIVERY
MANOR  VOTE  UBER
INUSE  ERIN  SAGE
TOTED  REST   ROD
```

12

```
VAST  PASS  PAINT
IDLE  OCHO  OLDIE
SOON  TAIL  OMENS
APP  CHINACLOSET
STEREO   RUTS
    ILLGO  BOTCH
ONACLEARDAY  OIL
DOSE   RCA   AIDE
EAT  OHBARNACLES
 HIPPO  STOLE
    REDS  CUSTOM
PUTINACLAIM  IPO
ANIME  RING  MATT
DINER  ATTA  ERIE
STARS  PEER  NACL
```

13

```
APPS  GWEN   ALUM
GUAM  LIBYA  LENA
OLGAKORBUT   LAIR
 PERUSE   FIGHTS
    TDS   DINE
ACT  OYSTERKNIFE
SLAYS  TRES  DORA
TAME  ERUPT  EWES
RIPA  TELL  ERASE
OMARKHAYYAM  NHL
   LEAK   BOD
DESIGN   SITARS
UDON  ONSIDEKICK
SING  LATTE  ACAI
KEYS   BYES  RENT
```

14

```
FOAL  SCARS  WASP
ARLO  TAROT  ALAS
DEEPDARKSECRETS
SOX  ODDSARE  VAT
 SAUDI   OLSEN
   NOUN  BILL
OHHI  MOPED  ICON
BOOTS  TEA  SPADE
EMO  ALBERTA  MOM
YEP  LEAPDAY  PRO
  DREAD  SKIED
CLAIMS   ETRADE
RUNG  HITIT  AVIA
ARCH  ERODE  SINS
BEET  SATON  EDGY
```

15

```
LOL  EPS   GRAHAM
ORO  LEAD  REDEYE
RIO  EDGE  ANDYET
DEFICIENCIES
ENACT   ONE   TAG
 THEONION   SATE
   RIRI  EPHRON
NOPLACELIKEHOME
ORIOLE  EVER
ASKS   PREDICTS
HOE  SPA   PHAIR
 STUDIOGHIBLI
CAREER  TRUE  LIP
ARENAS  SCAR  ECO
TEXTME   AMY  TAN
```

16

```
ACID  CHAT  RADAR
TONI  HONE  ACUTE
MOSS  IOTA  GREED
SPECIALISSUE
 STUN  ICEE   PAD
   STAG  TAXCODE
TAP  EBAY  ROSIE
INORGANICMATTER
ANNIE   PLAY  SUE
RECORDS  ACLU
AXE  ALAS  ANDS
 ROYALSUBJECT
GAZED  LOIS  AVIA
AHEAD  ONCE  MIFF
BANDS  MESS  SLIT
```

17

```
ADHOC  AWOL  SLAT
MOOLA  DIME  TONE
POWERSURGE  ROTE
SRS ELLE  CRIMES
    BEAT  SHUN
ABSORB  RAINGEAR
CROWS  WILL  ACRE
TUNA  FINED  LAID
ONIN  ENDS  FORAY
ROADBEDS  KINDLE
    ALLY  RING
SMARTS  MANE  CBS
POUR  BLACKSHEEP
ALTO  AIDE  SONAR
STOW  DEED  ENTRY
```

18

```
SEEM    MIL    SPAR
AMMO  NICE  CLOVE
TUTU  ONES  AILED
    STATESOFMIND
WHOSWHO  EKE  CGI
TOMEI  RANT  BEET
ANN  NOEL  HER
  KINGDOMHEARTS
   BED  AUNT  AWE
SOBA  LAYS  SOLAR
ERA  COP  TRICEPS
WAYOUTOFLINE
ATLAS  LEIS  LUMP
GOOFS  LANE  OGRE
ERRS   ORG   THIN
```

19

```
TARO  SARA  STRUM
ALIA  EWES  PAUSE
TECH  TALK  INLET
 COUNTRYSINGER
    OLD   NAY
 ADORE  OPAL  PBJ
ALIAS  SPAN  AREA
STATEUNIVERSITY
OARS  PINE  HINTS
FRY  METE  MISTY
    KEN   FAN
 LANDDEVELOPER
CAMEL  CANT  ICON
AMPLE  ONCE  THOU
NASTY  NEED  SOFT
```

20

```
PADS    SCAR  ALOE
IMAMS  TATA  LAST
PERON  ASAP  ABCS
EXTRACREDIT  RAY
    ERAS   NIGER
CHOSEN  STONES
RAP  SEACREATURE
AHEM  RAE  SLAM
BANANACREAM  TRI
  FLASHY  RUSSET
 CLERK   PEST
BOA  CAMERACREWS
EMMA  WIDE  LEGAL
AMEN  ALAS  EAGLE
MAST  YAMS  MOLD
```

21

```
GILA  PSST  MWAH
EMUS  OUTIE  PORE
MASSAPPEAL  GRIM
 CHEST  PROS  RAP
  THATSAPITY
BIB  ERR  ENEWS
ECON  TALC  GNATS
LANES  PAL  STREP
TRACT  SWAB  STAR
 EPCOT  SEA  SKY
  POLESAPART
ORE  EXIT  TEEUP
MOTH  ADAMSAPPLE
ASIA  SERUM  ITEM
RATS  DIME  DODO
```

22

```
AGES  SODAS  HARD
CULT  EXERT  EDEN
LALA  MELEE  RUED
 VIRGINIAWOOLF
ASTO        BITS
   ENDS  NEON
GEORGIA  OKEEFFE
OAK  SPRITES  LET
VCRS  ABS  TATA
 HANNAHMONTANA
   OAT   OAR
KERRYWASHINGTON
ABUT  ALIAS  EASY
LANE  RETRY  TILE
EYED   SEE   SLOT
```

23

```
S P I N E · T A R T · C L A P
O R D E R · A L P O · H A L O
F E L T A T H O M E · I S O N
A P E · S O O T · L I F T E D
· · · C U T E · G O L F · · ·
B E F O R E · C O O L O F F
E L A T E · F L O P · N O L A
A B U T · G L A S S · C R A B
N O N O · R I S E · M A G I C
· W A N D E R S · B A K E R S
· · C O A T · C O R E · · · ·
T E A A C T · G A R R · L A P
I R A N · J E R S E Y B O Y S
L A R D · O M I T · M O R E S
E S P Y · B U D S · E X I S T
```

24

```
J O N A S · C O L O R · W E T
U P O N E · A B O V E · I P O
J U S T A R R I V E D · F I G
U S H E R E D · E R O T I C A
· · · · A I D · P S A · · · ·
T E S T A R O S S A · O A K S
I X N A Y · L I S T · C A T
A C A D E M Y · A S A R U L E
R E F · S U E S · P U R E E
A L U M · S T A R T S M A L L
· · · B I T · P E R · · · · ·
P I R A N H A · D O G T A G S
O D E · S A L E S T A R G E T
L E S · E V A D E · S A U N A
E A T · T E S S A · H Y A T T
```

25

```
H E L P · R A R E · B E T A
O R A L · U N I X · S I M O N
T A K E I N T O A C C O U N T
· S E A M S · C H E · S E E
· · T A L C · T A N · · · ·
T M Z · C O M F O R T F O O D
S E E P · W O E · E L I T E
A D L I B · N A S · D E L H I
R I D E R · S K I · D U E T
S C A R E D S T I F F · P R Y
· · · W O O · D O E R · · ·
M A R · S N O · R A I S E
B R E A K S N E W G R O U N D
A L I B I · E C H O · T I V O
S O N S · R O O T · S T Y E
```

26

```
C R E E D · S T U · P A N D A
H A R P O · O O P · A R B Y S
A C R I D · D U H · R A C E S
C H O C O L A T E L A B · · ·
H E R · S I C · L O S · E A R
A L S O · S A N D C A S T L E
· · · P L A N O · K I T T E N
C A C T I · S I P · L E A S T
U P L I F T · S A L S A · · ·
S P A C E O P E R A · M A T T
P S Y · H O E · A M C · W E E
· · S A L A D S P I N N E R
E T H I C · K O I · G A I N S
B R I N K · E M T · A N N I E
B Y T E S · D E E · R A G E R
```

27

```
· T R I O · W I T H · H O P
M O O C H · H O H O · F I R E
B R O A D · I T E M · O P E N
A N K L E B R A C E · U P O N
· · · L A B · W E T N O S E
N U T · R A M P · C U D · · ·
A D A M · L O O S · B A A E D
S O C I A L B U T T E R F L Y
A N T S Y · S T A R · T A M E
· · · P E T · S T U N · R O D
S T I R S U P · L I E · · ·
M I N I · C A N D Y C R U S H
O M A N · K N E E · K O R E A
K E P T · E D E N · E D G E S
E S P · D A D S · L E E K ·
```

28

```
C A R · O N S E T · S W A T
H B O · D E L L A · A R C H
I O W E Y O U B I G T I M E
P R E Y S · G A P E · T E N
S T R E S S · E L S E · · ·
· · · D E T R O I T L I O N S
S O D · Y E A H · O N L O W
O L I N · M E A N S · S A R A
S A F E R · R O A R · Y I N
O F F T H E M A R K E T · · ·
· · · C O C O · S A U D I S
W O O · R U E S · C R E D O
I T S J U S T N O T F A I R
S I T E · E R O D E · L O T
P S S T · S E W E D · S M S
```

29

```
  M O M S   S T A I N   I F S
S O N I A   T E M P O   N O N
E L E C T   E X P A T   F R I
N A S H   B E T   D E F I E D
D R I E S U P     S I N C E
  S E L L S   O F F   V I A L
    L E I   T O O   E T S Y
  A R E W E T H E R E Y E T
B R A Y   S E E   A L E
E R I E   T A R   B L A I R
R A N O N     P I E R C E D
N I C H E S   P U T   P I S A
A G O   S N A R L   S L E E T
R N A   T O N E S   P A S T A
D S T   S W I P E   A N T S
```

30

```
C A D E T   M A L T   T R A M
A L I V E   E R I E   R I L E
N O B E L P R I Z E   I N T O
E T S   L A I D   S H A D O W
    C E N T   P H I L
S A B E R S   P R O S P E R S
T U R N S   P L O T   E X I T
E D I T   A R A B S   R I F E
P I E R   N I N E   A I S L E
S O F A B E D S   E M O T E D
    L A C E   S T U D
S O S P A D   C A T S   O H O
A R E A   O I L P A I N T E R
S E A R   T R A P   N O T M E
H O N K   E S P Y   G R O S S
```

31

```
S P A R   I R O N   P S A L M
N I L E   T A D A   R U L E R
A Q U A   S T E P   E M I T S
R U M M A G E S A L E S
L E S   C O D   O N U S E S
    S T O R A G E S P A C E
I T R I E D   T A B   L A W
D R E A D   A O L   C H O R E
T O P   E L M   G R I N D R
A V E R A G E S P E E D
G E L A T O   I N S   W A S
    P O S T A G E S T A M P
S A T I N   A C E S   O H I O
A S I D E   C H O I   L O G O
C H E S S   T E N S   L O O N
```

32

```
P R I G   W O M B   B O G S
R A V E   M I N E R   E D N A
I D O L   O P E N I N G D A Y
E A R   D U E S   T O A S T S
D R Y R U N S   S T U N
  T E S T   C H A N   P O D
  V O D K A   S I N S   O R E
B O W S   C O P A Y   O W E N
A T E   S O B A   F R O D O
H E R   C M O N   R A Z E
  T R E E   W A T E R E D
S C A R A B   C A N S   B R A
T E L E P A T H I C   P L O T
I D E A   C H O S E   D U D E
R E S T   K E P T   F E E D
```

33

```
O R C A   B A R K   D A B S
D E A D   O P E N S   R U I N
O N T H E L E V E L   I D E A
R E S E N T S   W A R P I N G
  R V S   C O P E D
  H E Y   O F F S C R E E N
D U E   D U O   H A Y L E Y
I P A   S I T   B O P   O L E
S T R E W S   O A T   P S T
H O T S E C O N D   T E E
  C L I N E   B E D
R U D O L P H   S E R I A L S
A F A R   L I F T T I C K E T
F O N T   E G R E T   T I V O
T S K S   H Y P E   S N I P
```

34

```
T I N T   T Y P E   S M O C K
O R E O   R E E L   T I T H E
D O W N Q U A R K   A N T E D
O N S I T E     B R O O M S
  P C S   E S C O R T
  H A S   B R A I N   A K A
L I P   D R A G O N Q U E S T
S T E R E O     E U R E K A
D I R E C T Q U O T E   P I G
  T S A   H U R L S   F I N
  C R E O L E   B L T
D A S H E R     S B A R R O
U N T I E   D R A G Q U E E N
S T U N K   A U N T   T A F T
K I N G S   M E D S   A L S O
```

35

```
STEP   MEAN   ALPS
AHYES  BONA   TARA
BREAKRANKS   EWES
LOGSIN  SLAB   CVS
ENE  PAC  ELM  LEE
SELL  IOS  OPENS
   OCEAN  AVERT
  BATHROOMSINKS
  ALTAR  FILET
ALIAS  KFC  ASHE
USE  ERA  SAP  LOX
RAN  SARA  GEMINI
OMAR  BANJOPICKS
RITE  ATTA  SLEET
ACED  TEEM   ADDS
```

36

```
SALSA  DORA  YELP
IWILL  RIOT  ACAI
TAKEITONTHECHIN
  YEP  WOK  EXHORT
   TEAL  SNIT
  SHORN  FIST  ANA
THENAGAIN  SILOS
HOLI  NSA   NODS
UNITY  THISISFUN
SEX  ITSY  TRUTH
   VERY  PEEL
ATTILA  ORE  ADS
THIRDGENERATION
MENU  IMUP  VENUE
SETS  CUSS  ADOPT
```

37

```
POET  ABBI   TWAS
TULIP  BRAT  HARE
ARENA  HATE  EDGE
  VANGOGHMUSEUM
BRA  ERRS  TIDES
RATTLE  PLUS
IDOL  STEER  HBO
BARCODESCANNERS
ERS  PITAS  ARIA
  TAGS  RATEDG
ASTER  LANE  WEE
SKIRTTHEISSUE
SIBS  ROAD  OHARE
EDIE  ELSE  PORES
TSAR  EYED  HEMP
```

38

```
KALE  SIGN  UPDOS
ERIE  ANNA  NORSE
YELLOWLAB  STALE
SAY  VIEW  COTTON
   DENT  TALE
AIMING  SHUDDERS
SNAPS  PAIL  PLUM
CALL  SHUCK  LISA
ONTO  COCK  LATER
TEAMMATE  HONEST
  AERO  FAST
SEEMLY  ROME  SEW
UPLIT  COOLRANCH
BIBLE  ABLE  LORE
SCALD  WEST  ABUT
```

39

```
MARSH  SOULS  EGG
ELATE  COPES  LOU
HARRYHAMLIN  BUT
  SEE  ALPO  PODS
  ANNEHATHAWAY
PICKED  DEANS
ACHED  DRIES  TAP
SEED  EON   MAXI
TEA  SLANG  PANEL
  TWEED  HURDLE
MICHAELCHANG
AHOY  YOUR  ITS
COD  HASANMINHAJ
APE  EXIST  SAUNA
WES  RENTS  ALDER
```

40

```
SPAR  PSST  SHUI
TAME  REACH  WONT
EPIC  ANGIE  ATMS
PARASITE  FONDUE
  LOS  SIN  ATE
COLLECTORSITEM
DONE  THOSE  NESS
OWED  HIP   NEO
DEN  GEL  RESIDES
ORDOESITEXPLODE
  ROT  EMT  NIX
ASIA  ALLOT  RATE
MISTAKE  VISITED
ITSOPEN  AMUSED
DEAREST  LEEKS
```

41

```
SMITH  ASST    NSA
ROMEO  UTAH   TOWN
SMART  TATA   OBIT
 SCISSORSISTERS
   AUS     HOLLY
 SOPUP  TAME
ANTIC  SANG  TOSS
CORNERTHEMARKET
TWOS  YEOW  NELLY
   MEME  STEAL
ACHOO    LEI
DROPEVERYTHING
LOPE  ACAI  EVIAN
IWIN  THIN  RATIO
BEN   SONG  ONEND
```

42

```
DRAB NOSED  ISEE
RISE AROMA  SHUN
UPINTHEAIR  HERD
MAFIA  OPTIC  DOS
   CRAB  SNOBS
BABE  RAT  GOLAST
EVA  ALOT  PUTTY
TALKABLUESTREAK
AIDED  STAN  ARE
SLEEVE  SKI  IRKS
 ALIVE  EPIC
COG  LIMIT  TEMPE
LOLA  CASTASPELL
OPEN  TILLS  ONUS
PSST  SLEEK  PUMA
```

43

```
EGGS  SRA  SWIRL
PORED  AIM  MONAE
ITALY  LOOSEENDS
CONFAB  TELLS
 NINA  ABIT  SHH
STYE  RECAP  AQUA
AAS  DRAT  SCRUBS
YUMMIER  STOMACH
SNIVEL  WIRY  RAE
HTTP  RAISE  REPS
ISH  HOTS  AHEM
 HALLE  MOWERS
DALAILAMA  GRAIL
ATALL  SEN  SALMA
DEBTS  TNT  PSST
```

44

```
ENDED  LOFTS  DVD
AIOLI  ORION  RAE
RATKANGAROO  ALE
  POOLS  WAGER
LISTENS  ADRATE
EMPIRE  SPRAIN
DEANS  SPICY  DAM
TAC  TALKS  DRE
ONE  CELIE  MERGE
 HORNET  FAROUT
WEELAD  SERAPES
READS  CALMS
ART  HORSEAROUND
TIE  ELATE  ERROR
HER  DEBIT  DENTS
```

45

```
PDFS  FAD  TASTE
ARIE  RIO  NATURE
GONEGIRL  ENAMEL
EVENED  LIPGLOSS
REP  CAL  ROLL
 OAK  AGATE  OUR
EPILOGUE  IDUNNO
RENO  EDITS  SLIP
RETTON  CAMPSITE
SRS  MELON  URN
 RIPE  SAM  ELF
TIMETOGO  CARPAL
ONAUTO  LETSHOPE
TINSEL  AYE  ELSE
STEED  FED  ALES
```

46

```
PDF  PHO  SLURPS
LEAF  IAN  TENURE
EATRIGHT  UTOPIA
ANTES  ODDS  EEL
 YELL  PAINTED
IMADEIT  MEOW
MAC  SVEN  STOPIN
PLIE  EDITH  SADE
SEDAKA  TOAD  POT
 SILO  TRAVELS
 PRESIDE  DIOR
LEO  STEM  LIMOS
INSECT  OKEYDOKE
ANIMAL  JIG  SORE
RENTME  IDO  NAP
```

47

```
PJS   MAST  CASTE
BLOG  CUTE  ACTED
SOAR  EDIT  THONG
   PUTSINREVERSE
 SONIC  GIGI  YES
CAPTCHA  SODA
ARE   ERA   EBBED
PARFORTHECOURSE
SNARL   IDO   ESE
   IDLE  MLBTEAM
OMG  BEAM  DOOZY
 PURSUITOFFAME
ILIED  SOLE  EDNA
NAMED  ISEE  IBET
ENEMY  TEXT   YEA
```

48

```
 CUES  AMP  MOTHS
TANKS  LAD  ANVIL
GREENROOF  RUSTY
IPA  SOUR   FIST
FEST  EDISON  USA
 TEEM    TRENDED
   EMOTION  OILS
 GOTAKICKOUTOF
CODE  FREEWAY
DOORDIE    EELS
CPR  ANSWER  TOTS
 LYRE  ORAL  TRI
PLEAT  GOODGRIEF
AISLE  ODD  BOOST
MUSED  BYE  TONS
```

49

```
TAB   IHOP   TRES
AXIS  MANE  REEVE
ZEROWASTE  EXTOL
OLDSAW  OLAF  ALL
 FORAY  ELUSIVE
SLO  PROWRESTLER
POOH  EWE   SEA
YODA  LED   HEMP
 NAG  DOH   LGBT
HEROWORSHIP  GAS
ATEINTO  ATLAS
ARF  UHUH  HOTAIR
GAUNT  NEROWOLFE
EDGES  DRUM  MASS
NEED   SANE   DOT
```

50

```
JIBE  CLEAN  EDGE
ADAM  HALLE  NILE
YELP  ASKEW  GOAL
 ADOPTS  SOUNDS
  EWE  EARFUL
FARED  SKILIFT
INDRAG  ADA  SAPS
RNA  LAB  ESC  LIU
MESS  TOT  HACKER
 HERETIC  PASSE
  LYCHEE  EMT
PREFER  LASERS
AUDI  ATTIC  LAOS
ISEE  SWINE  OSLO
LENS  HOPES  THEY
```

51

```
SLAM  APES  STORM
LIVE  RATE  THREE
OMIT  IRAN  RESIN
BASEBALLDIAMOND
  RENO   NYE
TOP  GARAGES  BEE
ALIBI  CAP   BRAS
SITINFIRSTCLASS
TVAD  ARE  ATSEA
YES  PLASTER  SLY
   HAS   EATS
PRIORENGAGEMENT
SINUS  ORAL  ARIA
SCONE  NICE  SILL
TENDS  EMTS  HEEL
```

52

```
SALEM  TIER  OVAL
ALINE  ACRE  LAVA
GOLDRECORD  INON
STY  CAIN  RAVINE
   MUST  GOTIT
 SHORE  DISMAYED
STORY  BODES  FAA
NAME  SLEDS  MARY
ARE  QUERY  TAILS
PROCURES  HURRY
 FRIED  HUTS
BEFITS  SOLO  SHE
AVIS  HOTPURSUIT
MICE  OHIO  EVENS
ALES  TORN  DUSTY
```

53

```
ALTOS . ACED . MITE
LEAST . COCO . EDEN
PINCUSHION . DIED
SAGA . EEL . ONION
. . RIG . CREAMS
MOUNTAINLION .
AUTOS . DYED . GOB
GRAD . GILAS . BORE
ISH . ODOR . MINER
. . BRAINSURGEON
. ALCOTT . DIS
. PACTS . AGO . TACO
ANTI . KEVINBACON
REIN . IRON . IGIVE
FANG . NANA . CEDES
```

54

```
CCS . BELT . . FIB
LOO . ARTURO . DICE
ALL . GINGER . AREA
SLATEMAGAZINE
PACE . . ADONISES
. BEANBAG . HEAVE
. SILVERBULLET
WET . GEO . IAM . ERS
ASHWEDNESDAY
STAIR . SEENOTE
PETTIEST . URNS
. CHARCOALGRILL
ACHE . MENTEE . VII
PEER . ANIMAL . ISM
POD . TASK . ATE
```

55

```
IWILL . OHH . SPA
NOKIA . SNOOT . MAW
CONSTANCEWU . ALA
ALOT . LAD . SMARMY
. SWIPER . BLURT
. COCKTAILMENU
COALS . RIFT . NIB
NATE . CHUTE . MUTE
BTW . SHIN . PAPER
CHICKENKATSU
. THEFT . REINED
DJSETS . ABE . AXED
RUE . CHEVYMALIBU
ANN . HALOS . NOTIT
WED . TIN . TASTY
```

56

```
PITS . DELTA . POKY
ACHY . ARIEL . OWIE
DEAR . BREADROLLS
SETUP . SEEALSO
. SPOOF . GRID
BRASSRING . NETS
RAN . TERI . CHOO
APOP . SECTS . KING
NINE . ERAS . SIR
. DOTS . BROWNRICE
. SITE . TSARS
. ARMLOCK . GATES
BREAKRANKS . TRAP
TEAR . SLEEP . EURO
WALT . OMEGA . DENT
```

57

```
. BAMBI . USES . EON
SOLEIL . TORE . SHY
PIPECLEANER . TIC
ALIKE . CHIC . FOG
NUN . PAL . ATTUNED
SPEC . RAS . UNITE
. AUDIT . STRAIN
. BURNERACCOUNT
POPSIN . MOURN
ONSET . PUB . SWIM
DATASET . RAM . ECO
. FAT . ROBS . ATTIC
JIG . TINDERMATCH
ODE . IKEA . ABUELA
YES . EASY . NOTRE
```

58

```
BESTS . PDA . TORE
LECHE . IONS . HAIR
AREAS . ANTI . ETTA
HINTHINT . ETCHES
SEES . POPTRIO
. SEA . OHREALLY
SENOR . OKRA . SEAM
HAILS . REO . ATTIC
UCLA . PATE . VISTA
THESOUTH . TAS
. TUREENS . CLAW
THEYRE . BIKELANE
HOLE . SPEC . AETNA
ISLA . TEAK . SATIN
STAR . IRS . TREES
```

59

```
S E L F . I N C A . E G G S
T R E E . S N O O P . L E A K
R O G E R A N D M E . A N T I
A D A . E L I S E . S T I E S
W E L L S E E . A D I E U . .
. A T M . A G E S . S E T . .
. M E N U . T S A R . A B L E
R O L E P L A Y I N G G A M E
U R L S . O X E N . O A R S .
B E E . D I R T . M E T . . .
. N O R S E . D E S E R T S .
A P P L Y . F A U L T . E A T
B E A D . R O S E T O F A M E
E D G E . B R A T S . R I P A
T I E R . I M P S . O R A L .
```

60

```
O R C A . C U L T . B R I E .
P E R U . R O S I E . L O N G
E V E N . I M A F R A I D S O
R E D T A P E . E M T S . . .
A L I . L E O . P O S T I T .
. T A B . N A S A L . I C U .
S C U B A S . D I P L O M A T
T O N E . P A D R E . N E R O
A S I T W E R E . R A T H E R
I M O . H E E D S . L O O . .
N O N E E D . O L E . N A P .
. . G E R E . N I C E O N E .
W I G G L E R O O M . A R T S
O R E O . A G A M E . S E E K
O A T S . D O R A . E D D Y .
```

61

```
A L I S T . A N T S . R I S E
H E L L O . R O I L . A L T A
I S L A M . B O N O . B I A S
. B A B Y B A B Y B A B Y . .
G E E . T I S . A I D S . . .
R E A S O N . T O G O . . . .
A R G U E . V I S A . S A G A
B I L L S B I L L S B I L L S
S E E K . U N D O . A C T I I
. O B O E . I T S O D D . . .
. P A I N . O O H . S E E . .
T U R N T U R N T U R N . . .
A R E S . B O A T . O U G H T
G E N E . E L S E . B L O O D
S E A T . R E A R . E L V E S
```

62

```
B A B A . E C A R D . I R K .
A M I S H . M A R I A . T E A
J O B S E C U R I T Y . S N L
A S S U R E . E A U . M A T E
. . C E L L . N A S A L . . .
W A S H . L O C A L C O L O R
A L E . J O S H . A R O M A .
L A N C E . S I T . L I V E N
S M A L L . C A K E . E G O .
H O T E L C H A I N . I R A N
. E R O D E . L O N G . . . .
C A S K . R I P . W A L R U S
O N E . C A S E I N P O I N T
E T A . O T T E R . S O F I A
N E T . T E S L A . S E X Y .
```

63

```
L I T . T E A L . H D T V .
A G O G . E A S Y A . A R E A
P U P P E T S H O W . L I N T
C A B A R E T . N A I L E D .
A N I S E . U N I T . D E E .
T A D . C A R P E T S T O R E
. E T H I C . Y O U L L . . .
S A X . A D L I B . S T Y . .
A T L A S . O M E N S . . . .
T R U M P E T S O L O . A O L
L A M . A R I E . H A R P O .
. D I M S U M . P A I N T E D
E D N A . P E T S I T T I N G
G L U T . T R E A D . I S E E
G E M S . S A S S . T D S . .
```

64

```
. M A R I . M A S . C P A S .
C A P E D . I L L . H I V E .
R U R A L . S A L E . A L O E
E V I L E S T . Y E L L O W S
D E L I . T A B . P E L T S .
. . S I E G E . T I A . . . .
. . S T R E E T L I G H T . .
U S A . E L F . U G H . H U M
P E R U . R A S H . M E N U .
S W I P E R I G H T . E R I C
. . A M I G O . P L A T H . .
A C E H I G H . S C O O P . .
D U V E T . T H A T S N I C E
A R E A S . O G R E . S U R .
M E N D . P A L S . T E A . .
```

65

```
A S A   B L O B   T R O Y
G L U E   B R A V O   R E N E
H A R D E A R N E D   Y M C A
A N O I N T   E N Y A   A A H
S T R E A M S   A L A R M
T S A   M A D E A R A C K E T
    C O N C E I T   T O R E
A L T A R   A R M   M O N A E
P A I R   M R I S C A N
P I E R C E D E A R S   L I V
  D R Y E R   T E A T I M E
T B A   O M I T   P L A T E S
R A C E   A N A D E A R M A S
A R K S   I D L E S   T U N E
P E S T   D Y E S   S T L
```

66

```
G L A D E   I D S   F I S T
P E R I L   N E S S   I D L E
S N E A K A P E E K   R E E D
  D A M   S U M   I M S A D
    O R A T E   C U T
C A T N A P   D E A D T R E E
H A R D Y   S N A P   H O L D
I R O N S   P E T   D E B U G
N O P E   S I C S   A B O D E
A N E C D O T E   C R A T E S
    K I D   S P I E D
  P A L E O   S E A   N A S
D O H A   P L A N O T E X A S
A L E C   E A R N   S W E D E
D O M E   D Y E   A S S E T
```

67

```
T U F T S   A V I D   A F R O
I G L O O   C A M O   C R I B
C H U P A C H U P S   H E N S
    S P O O L S   G E E S E
T E N   L O T   P A S S E S
A G A T H A   L U V   A D S
G O T Y A   I S U R E A M
  S U P P O R T G R O U P S
  R E P L A Y S   U N L I T
A R E   I A N   O T T E R S
L E T F L Y   B O D   S I A
U V R A Y   G O P O O F
M E A L   S U P E R D U P E R
N A I L   E R I N   D R A M A
I L L S   C U T S   S Y R U P
```

68

```
B L I P   S I T E   L E A N
R O T O R   O D E S   A X L E
B A L L E T F L A T   S T O W
  F L Y A W A Y   E X E R T S
    C A R   T E R R A
T O A S T S   P U M A   S P A
A B L E   M O N E Y   H E N
M O L E   P O S E D   W A T T
P E T   C R O S S   E R A S
A S H   H O N E   D E E P L Y
  E M I T S   D A M
S H R I N E   M U R M U R S
H E E D   S T I C K Y N O T E
U R S A   T A L K   S I D E S
T A T S   S U D S   T E M P
```

69

```
G A M E   I M P E L   T W O
A P O P   C A I R O   H O O P
L E T S B E R E A L   E Y R E
A S H   E M I T S   B I P E D
    S T O N Y   H E R O
  S T A T U E   D O E   O R S
W O O L E N   M O P P E D U P
R I O T   T E R S E   A L S O
A L L S T A R S   D I V E S T
P S A   A I R   L I K E S O
    R A I N   D E A N S
T R O L L   C O S M O   W A S
R E U P   P I L L O W T A L K
I N N S   A T E I N   A C T I
P O D   W I S E D   G O O P
```

70

```
M A T T   S H A D E   W R A P
O B O E   R O D I N   E O N S
V O W E L S O U N D   B O N A
E V I T A   F L E E   S T A T
D E T E R S   T R A G I C
    R A I L   R O T A T E
O P T S   R U S T   R E N A L
R E V   S I C K B A Y   A R M
C A C A O   K I S S   A L T O
A T H E N S   P I N T
  A R G U E S   N E L S O N
O H N O   B R A Y   S A M B A
D E N S   L I V E S T R E A M
O R E O   E C O L I   G A M E
R O L L   T A R P S   E R A S
```

71

```
ASSET  BRAND  WAG
RHINO  ROTOR  HUE
MUDDYWATERS  ART
STEREO  IOU  PTAS
    UDON  USTED
CLAN  FILTHYRICH
LES  ISLE  PIDAY
AMPED  EVA  OLIVE
NURSE  EMUS  DEN
GROSSSALES  CODA
   METER  NEMO
TRIX  CTR  BOUNCE
HAS  GREASYSPOON
EVE  AERIE  SLEET
MED  STYLE  YELLS
```

72

```
HAW  HEAD  RISK
MINI  OASIS  ERIE
EGGS  PRINT  BODY
WHEELOFFORTUNE
EEL  INU  ANSWER
DRAWL  LEAPT  AYE
  OAF  SIS  OREO
INKCARTRIDGES
ACES  NEE  NOR
PAW  MEMES  NEARS
ENSUED  PIN  COO
WISHINGONASTAR
GATE  TOONS  HIRE
PIER  SURGE  OVER
ATMS  NYET  WED
```

73

```
PUB  EMMA  KNEW
ONUS  MOON  BOISE
BAIT  PLOT  IRATE
LILYALDRIDGE
ART  DOS  ADAGES
NETPAY  AIDE  AGO
ODOR  ENDS  AFROS
  LAURAASHLEY
GRAYS  SPAY  RIBS
DIS  SLAT  DANNON
POTATO  SRI  DUE
  LAURENALAINA
HITIT  OBIT  RACK
USAGE  TAPE  KNEE
THIN  EYED  ADD
```

74

```
LAMP  CHIRP  ADD
CAMEO  RADIO  TOE
OVERTHEMOON  LOT
RILESUP  GLARE
PSI  BEBOP  ENDS
SHAFT  SAVE  ATIT
  INC  TAS  PIES
  INTHECLOUDS
NICE  ALA  SPA
AMES  RSVP  SYRIA
MACS  TEEUP  ANG
EGRET  RESPITE
TIE  UNDERTHESUN
ANA  GAUGE  ARENT
GEM  STOOD  MUSE
```

75

```
BOPIT  UPDO  TBSP
EARTH  SHIA  HOPE
THOSE  HEARMEOUT
HUM  CHEWS  INTRA
  POLAR  PAL  SNL
 TONAL  LOCKS
ROSES  HORA  UGGS
HEATHROWAIRPORT
OSLO  OURS  AILEY
  NOISY  WINDY
MAP  ALE  MELEE
ALLOT  MOODY  NIT
HEADSTART  AWAKE
AVID  UTAH  RAGER
LENS  GELS  DREAM
```

76

```
LARK  SLIT  BLIP
OBIE  COORS  ZINC
PEPPERONIPIZZAS
 TETRA  STILT
  OOPS  ICK  TAR
POUNDPUPPY  CASA
ERR  EYRE  OILS
DEGAS  EPA  COPES
AGED  ULTA  EEL
NONO  COPPERPIPE
TNT  MAP  OAHU
  COMET  POLKA
JALAPENOPOPPERS
OWES  LINDT  INTO
BEAK  TIAS  TOSS
```

77

```
BATHE HEMS FRET
BROOM AXEL LAVA
STYLE NENE ODES
  BARBECUEJOINT
PHO GMS  PERUSE
TEXMEX TOLL SOS
AREA   OPALS
 SAVINGSBOND
   MEDIA  OOPS
APP NATS PAWNEE
SAILOR FIN TAX
INCOMEBRACKET
DENS YEAR ADAGE
ERIE OGRE RELAY
SACS USES ANKLE
```

78

```
ENTRY STRAW OPS
MARIE AIOLI KAT
THINSKINNED FLY
   SEND  TRIAL
LOVESONGS HENCE
AMI  BOOED SEED
MANGA  ACUTE
BREATHOFTHEWILD
  LEAPT  ANNIE
RASP SEERS  TEL
ONTAP CRIEDFOUL
AGILE   PAUL
MEN PEPPERPOTTS
ELK SARAN ERASE
DAY ITEMS DANKE
```

79

```
MISO  SLABS
AMPUP THELIKE
SAUTE SAVETIME
AGREEDPRICE ILL
LENAPE EEK ERIE
ASST ADDS EXACT
   PROB GRATIS
 PHYSICALLIMIT
PLEASE TOON
LEAPT WHOO TARA
OATS FOR MAILER
PTS MEMORYSPACE
 SUPERBOY ITSON
 PENNAME NOKIA
 GUSTS   PALS
```

80

```
FALSE REED TADA
ATEIN ERGO IMIN
JOANDIDION MANY
INKS DEEM PERON
TEE DOE ALLRISE
ADDLE MONEY LAW
 ALA VIA PLUS
 CHRISTIANDIOR
WOOD TIN SAN
ALT DEREK ISSUE
ROTHIRA ADS EPA
BROOM MARE MEDS
LAPS KIRANDESAI
EDIT ISIT ORATE
DOCS DUDE SEWER
```

Logic Solutions

81. Going Green

Peter's ball is number 4 (clue 2). Ball 1 cannot be Henry's (clue 5). Nor, since ball 2 had only been struck once (clue 3), can ball 1 belong to Martin, whose ball was next counterclockwise from the one with which Mr. Bunker had taken four shots to reach the green (clue 1), so it must be Gerry who was using ball 1, with which he reached the green in two (clue 4). We know ball 2, which was hit directly from the tee, is not Mr. Bunker's, nor, since it was Gerry who had taken two shots, can it be Mr. Rough's (clue 2). Nor does it belong to Mr. Tees (clue 3), so it must be Mr. Green's. So, from clue 5, Henry, whose ball we know is not number 4, must be using ball 3, leaving ball 2 as Martin's. So, from clue 1, Mr. Bunker must be Henry Bunker, who took four shots, leaving Peter taking three strokes to reach the green. Finally, from clue 2, Mr. Rough must be Gerry Rough, leaving Peter as Peter Tees.

Ball 1, Gerry Rough, 2.
Ball 2, Martin Green, 1.
Ball 3, Henry Bunker, 4.
Ball 4, Peter Tees, 3.

82. Getting the Point

The person with the 9:40 time wasn't Gary, Fifi, Bess, Carl, or Hugo (clue 1), or Alan or Iris (clue 2), and so must be Dora. The 9:05 appointee wasn't Alan, Bess, Hugo or Iris (clue 1), or Fifi (clue 3). Nor, since Alan's time can't have been 9:20 and Iris' time can't have been 9:10 (clue 2), can the 9:05 time be for Gary or Evan, so it must be Carl's. So, from clue 3, Fifi must have had the 9:00 time and, from clue 1, Bess must have had the 9:15 time. The 9:10 time can't be Alan's or Iris' (clue 2), or Hugo's or Evan's (clue 1), and so must be Gary's, with, from clue 1, Alan's time being 9:25 and Evan's 9:20. Finally, from clue 1, Hugo must have had the 9:30 time and Iris the 9:35 appointment.

9:00 Fifi; 9:05 Carl; 9:10 Gary; 9:15 Bess; 9:20 Evan; 9:25 Alan; 9:30 Hugo; 9:35 Iris; 9:40 Dora.

83. Pigeon Holes

The head of department is Professor Spriggs (clue 1), so, from clue 3, Chubb must be the senior lecturer, pigeon hole D must belong to the lecturer, and the junior lecturer must be Arabella. Darby is male (clue 2), so he cannot be the junior lecturer, Arabella, and must be the lecturer whose pigeon hole is D. So, from clue 2, Melissa's pigeon hole must be C and Arabella must be Arabella Howlett. She does not have pigeon hole A (clue 4), so it must be B and Graham's is pigeon hole A (clue 4), leaving Darby, the lecturer, whose pigeon hole is D, as Jolyon Darby. Finally, from clue 3, Graham is not Chubb, so he must be Professor Graham Spriggs, leaving Chubb, the senior lecturer, as Melissa Chubb with pigeon hole C.

A, Graham Spriggs, professor.
B, Arabella Howlett, junior lecturer.
C, Melissa Chubb, senior lecturer.
D, Jolyon Darby, lecturer.

84. Chicken Run

The china chicken must have an even number (clue 3), but it cannot be no.2 since Daniel's gift, right of the teapot, cannot be no.1. Nor for the same reason can Daniel have supplied chicken no.4, so the china chicken cannot be no.8. No.6 is an egg cup (clue 3), so the china ornament must be no.4, Daniel must have given no.2 and no.1 must be the teapot. Now, Nadine's felt present, numbered twice that of Roger (clue 2), must be no.8, with Roger contributing the china chicken in position 4 and Ethel's gift at no.5. The dog toy cannot be on the bottom row (clue 1), and there is now no room for it on the middle row, so it must be on the top row. We have placed Daniel's and Melanie's gifts, so the teapot at no.1 must be from Albert and Daniel must have given the dog toy, so Ethel's chicken in position 5 must be made of wood. Caroline's gift must now be on the bottom row (clue 2) so Melanie must have contributed the robot chicken at no.3 and Caroline's present must be at no.7. From clue 4, it must be the jug, and the bronze chicken must be at no.9. By elimination, it must have been given to Henrietta by Paul, leaving Bridget as the giver of the egg cup in position 6.

1, teapot, Albert; 2, dog toy, Daniel; 3, robot, Melanie.
4, china ornament, Roger; 5, wood ornament, Ethel;
6, egg cup, Bridget.
7, jug, Caroline; 8, felt ornament, Nadine;
9, bronze ornament, Paul.

85. Gas Giants

Planet 8 can't be Juno, Vesta, or Fauna (clue 1), Nemesis, Diana, or Flora (clue 2), or Aurora or Fauna (clue 3), and so must be Minerva. Planet 1 can't be Vesta or Fauna (clue 1), Diana, Flora, or Juno (clue 2), or Aurora (clue 3), so must be Nemesis. So planet 2 can't be Fauna (clue 1), Diana, Flora, or Juno (clue 2), or Aurora (clue 3), and so must be Vesta. So Fauna's non-ringed planet can't be number 3 (clue 1) or 7 (clue 3), must be 6 and, from clue 3, Aurora must be planet 7. Finally, from clue 2, Juno can't be planet 3, so must be one of the ringed planets 4 and 5, so Diana must be the non-ringed planet 3, with Flora being planet 4 and Juno planet 5.

1 Nemesis; 2 Vesta; 3 Diana; 4 Flora; 5 Juno; 6 Fauna; 7 Aurora; 8 Minerva.

86. Soap Box Derby

The Mercedes came third (clue 1), so, from clue 3, the cart driven by Jenny Hillman and co-driven by Hassan Riley can't have been fourth. From clue 4, the fourth-placed cart wasn't co-driven by Gemma Lanchester, and clue 2 rules out Mandy Austin, so the co-driver of the fourth cart must have been Peter Humber. The cart he co-drove wasn't the Jaguar (clue 3) or the Porsche (clue 4), so it must have been the Ferrari, which was driven by Aisha Morris (clue 2). So, from clue 2, Mandy Austin must have been co-driver of the third-placed Mercedes. Now, from clue 3, Jenny Hillman and Hassan Riley must have crewed the second-placed cart and the Jaguar must have been first, leaving the cart which came second as the Porsche. The driver of the third-placed Mercedes wasn't Roy Jowett (clue 1), so must have been John Singer, leaving Roy Jowett as driver of the winning Jaguar. By elimination, his co-driver must have been Gemma Lanchester.

First, Roy Jowett, Gemma Lanchester, Jaguar.
Second, Jenny Hillman, Hassan Riley, Porsche.
Third, John Singer, Mandy Austin, Mercedes.
Fourth, Aisha Morris, Peter Humber, Ferrari.

87. Hair Today

Hopelus was trying to impress his girlfriend (clue 3), and the servant hoping to disguise himself managed 3 days (clue 4), so Branelus' eight-day regimen, which was too long for him to be the servant imitating his gladiator-hero (clue 5) and wasn't intended as a rebel statement (clue 1) must have been hoping to make himself look more distinguished. Cluelus grew his sideburns (clue 3) and the servant visiting the hair-plucker gave up after day (clue 2), so Branelus' regimen, which didn't involve growing his hair long or a beard (clue 1), must have been to cultivate a mustache. So, from clue 1, the servant growing his hair long as a rebel statement must have continued for at least 3 days. The disguise idea lasted exactly 3 days (clue 4), so the rebel must have gone without a hair cut for 6 days before the experiment was, quite literally, cut short. The servant involved wasn't Euselus (clue 5), so it must have been Gormlus. Euselus wasn't trying to copy his gladiator hero (clue 5), so must have been the servant with the 3 day disguise, leaving the star-struck servant as Cluelus. Euselus' disguise didn't involve the "body-wax," so he must have hoped to fool Prefect Crassus with a beard, leaving Hopelus visiting—very briefly—the hair-plucker to impress his girl and Cluelus' sideburn growth lasting 2 days before he decided they didn't suit him.

Branelus, mustache, 8 days, distinguished.
Cluelus, sideburns, 2 days, copy hero.
Euselus, beard, 3 days, disguise.
Gormlus, long hair, 6 days, rebel statement.
Hopelus, body wax, 1 day, impress girlfriend.

88. Logi-5

B	A	E	D	C
D	E	A	C	B
A	C	B	E	D
C	B	D	A	E
E	D	C	B	A

89. Sign In

4	2	3	1	5	6
6	3	2	4	1	5
5	4	1	3	6	2
1	5	4	6	2	3
3	6	5	2	4	1
2	1	6	5	3	4

90. Logi-5

C	E	A	D	B
D	C	B	E	A
A	B	D	C	E
E	A	C	B	D
B	D	E	A	C

91. Sign In

3	4	1	5	2	6
1	6	4	2	5	3
6	5	2	3	1	4
5	2	6	4	3	1
4	3	5	1	6	2
2	1	3	6	4	5

92. Having Designs

The 2017 project cost $14 million (clue 6) and the firm that won in 2010 had a name without an "and" (clue 2), so Steele and Klaas, who won the award for their sports arena before the 2018 theater win (clue 1), must have won in 2016. Their building was not the $50 million offices (clue 1), Hightower's offices (clue 1), or, from clue 2, the bridge, so Steele and Klaas must have designed the sports arena. The $50 million offices did not win the prize in 2015 (clue 2), so they must have been 2019, and so L.E. Vashun must have won the prize for their $14 million design in 2017 (clue 6) which must have been the bridge. By elimination, Hightower must have won the award in 2015. Now, from clue 3, Cinder and Bloch must have won the award in 2018 and Brickman in 2019. The cost of the offices was less than Cinder and Bloch's project (clue 2), so it must have been $30 million, and Cinder and Bloch's theater must have cost $36 million.

2015, Hightower, offices, $30m.
2016, Steele and Klaas, sports arena, $24m.
2017, L.E. Vashun, bridge, $14m.
2018, Cinder and Bloch, theater, $36m.
2019, Brickman, apartments, $50m.

93. Very Cross Runners

The fourth runner home tore his shorts on barbed wire (clue 4). The fifth man to finish had not tripped in a pothole (clue 3), nor can he be Doome, who lost a shoe in the mud (clue 1), or the man attacked by a goat, who finished ahead of Rudolf Plite (clue 2), so, by elimination, he must have slipped into the ditch, and is therefore Manfred (clue 5). Klanger finished first (clue 7), so he cannot be Manfred, or Karl, who took third place (clue 6). Clue 1 rules out Johann, and clue 2, Rudolf, so, by elimination, Klanger must be Emil. We now know Doome is neither Emil nor Rudolf, nor is he Johann (clue 1). His mishap rules him out as Manfred, so he must be Karl, who finished third. So, from clue 1, Johann, who we know was not fifth, must have been fourth. So he is the runner whose shorts were torn. This leaves Rudolf as the man who finished second. Johann is not Scurge (clue

4), so he must be Grief, leaving Scurge as Manfred. It is now clear, from clue 2, that Emil, who finished first, was attacked by the goat, which leaves Rudolf's mishap as tripping in the pothole.

Emil Klanger, attacked by goat, first.
Johann Grief, tore shorts on barbed wire, fourth.
Karl Doome, lost shoe in mud, third.
Manfred Scurge, slipped into ditch, fifth.
Rudolf Plite, tripped in pothole, second.

94. Couples in Photos

Picture 3 was taken at Washington (clue 1), so, from clue 6, picture 4 must have been taken at Arlington, and Dean and Alison must be the pair in photo 2. So Kirsty, who was married at Sunnyside (clue 4), must be in picture 1 and picture 2 must have been taken at Daisy Fields. Kirsty did not marry William Marshall, so, from clue 4, he must be in picture 3 and Jason must be the groom in picture 4. So, by elimination, Kirsty's new husband, in picture 1, must be Neville. We know his surname is not Marshall, nor is he Mr. Wilde (clue 2) and clue 5 rules him out as Mr. Gregson, so he must be Neville Smith. Sonia Holland is not the bride in picture 4 (clue 7) and we know that she is not in photo 1 or photo 2, so she must be William Marshall's bride in picture 3. Miss Rowley is not Kirsty (clue 2) and the same clue rules out Alison, who we know was married at Daisy Fields, so she must be Vicky, and she must be the bride in photo 4. Kirsty is not Miss Sowter (clue 3), so she must be Miss Parsons, leaving Miss Sowter as Alison. Finally, from clue 5, Jason is not Mr. Gregson, so he must be Mr. Wilde, leaving Mr. Gregson as Dean.

1, Kirsty Parsons and Neville Smith, Sunnyside.
2, Alison Sowter and Dean Gregson, Daisy Fields.
3, Sonia Holland and William Marshall, Washington.
4, Vicky Rowley and Jason Wilde, Arlington.

95. Impresso Investigations

The Ugandan blend tastes malty (clue 3) and the floral coffee is packaged in red (clue 2) so the Cambodian coffee in the cream pod, which doesn't have woody or peppery notes (clue 1), must taste of cereal. So it's not Green Mountain (clue 4), Bourbonia (clue 1), Rainforest Blend (clue 2), or the blue-packaged Monsoon Coast (clue 3) and must be Robust Arabic. The malty coffee from Uganda isn't called Monsoon Coast (clue 3) or Bourbonia (clue 1) and Rainforest Blend comes from Guatemala (clue 2), so the Ugandan coffee must be Green Mountain. It's not in a purple pod (clue 4), or a red one (clue 2), so must be packaged in olive-green. We know the colors of three of the named coffees, so the woody Bourbonia, which doesn't come in a red pod (clue 2), must come in purple, leaving the Rainforest Blend from Guatemala in red pods and tasting flowery, and the blue pods containing the peppery coffee. It isn't from Mauritius (clue 1), so must be from Sri Lanka and called Monsoon Coast, leaving the purple pods containing the woody Bourbonia blend coming from Mauritius.

Bourbonia, Mauritius, woody, purple.
Green Mountain, Uganda, malty, olive green.
Monsoon Coast, Sri Lanka, peppery, blue.
Rainforest Blend, Guatemala, floral, red.
Robust Arabic, Cambodia, cereal, cream.

96. Knights Off

From clue 4, Antonia's request to Sir Spyneless cannot have been made on Monday or Friday, while Sir Coward declined the Wednesday request (clue 6) and Elaine required help on Tuesday (clue 3), so it

must have been on Thursday that Sir Spyneless said his sword was blunt (clue 5). Clue 4 now tells us it was on Friday that one knight claimed to have an upset stomach. Sir Sorely, who used the loose visor excuse, was not called upon on Monday (clue 1), so he must have made his excuse to Elaine on Tuesday. So, from clue 1, it was Gertrude who made the Monday request. We have now matched four days with a damsel or an excuse, so the knight who turned down Diana's request because it was his day off (clue 2) must have been Sir Coward on Wednesday. Now, by elimination, Estella must have requested help on Friday and Gertrude's reluctant Monday knight must have used the lame horse excuse. This was not Sir Timid (clue 6), so it must have been Sir Poltroon, leaving Sir Timid as the alleged victim of an upset stomach on Friday.

Monday, Sir Poltroon à Ghaste, Gertrude, horse lame.
Tuesday, Sir Sorely à Frayde, Elaine, loose visor.
Wednesday, Sir Coward de Custarde, Diana, day off.
Thursday, Sir Spyneless de Feete, Antonia, sword blunt.
Friday, Sir Timid de Shayke, Estella, stomach upset.

97. Logi-5

A	D	E	C	B
C	B	A	D	E
B	D	C	E	A
D	A	E	B	C
E	C	B	A	D

98. Sign In

6	1	3	4	2	5
5	3	1	6	4	2
4	2	5	1	3	6
3	5	6	2	1	4
2	6	4	3	5	1
1	4	2	5	6	3

99. Logi-5

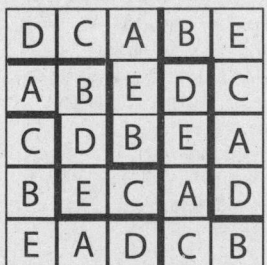

D	C	A	B	E
A	B	E	D	C
C	D	B	E	A
B	E	C	A	D
E	A	D	C	B

100. Sign In

4	1	5	3	2	6
6	4	2	1	3	5
1	5	4	2	6	3
5	3	6	4	1	2
3	2	1	6	5	4
2	6	3	5	4	1

101. Going Batty

The Shoe bat appears in episode 3 (clue 6). So episode 1, which doesn't feature the Baseball bat (clue 3), the Sher bat courting (clue 1), or the Alfa bat (clue 5), must feature the Akro bat from Senegal and the Alfa bat must be in episode 2 (clue 5). Episode 4 shows a bat giving birth (clue 4), so the courting sequence must be in the fifth episode, showing the Sher bat. By elimination, the Baseball bat must be in the fourth episode and the Malaysian bat eating must be in episode 3 (clue 3). The film from Ukraine is not featured in episode 2 or episode 4 (clue 2), so it must be the courting Sher bat in episode 5. The giving birth sequence was not filmed in India (clue 4), so it must have been Venezuela, leaving the Indian bat as the Alfa in episode 2. It was not filmed flying (clue 6), so it must be mating, which leaves the flying bat as the Akro from Senegal.

1, Akro, Senegal, flying.
2, Alfa, India, mating.
3, Shoe, Malaysia, eating.
4, Baseball, Venezuela, giving birth.
5, Sher, Ukraine, courting.

102. Comic Relief

The yard sale buy was Clark Stark's and the comic bought at the thrift shop was rated fine (clue3), so Peter Kent, who didn't acquire his comic in fair condition from an auction site (clue 1), and its condition rules out the comic fair (clue 4), must have filled his gap by trading with a fellow collector. So it wasn't *Mercury Man* (clue 2) or *The Bulk* (clue 1). Dick Parker bought *Groovy Girl* (clue 2) and *Dr. Weird* was in mint condition (clue 4), so Peter's mag must have been *Beetle Boy*. From clue 2, neither *Groovy Girl* nor *Mercury Man* was rated very fine, so this must have been the condition of *The Bulk*, acquired through the online auction (clue 1). The fine condition comic came from the thrift shop and the mag bought at the comic fair must have been rated higher than good (clue 4), so this was the mint condition copy of *Dr. Weird*. It wasn't bought by Bruce Grayson (clue 4), so *Dr. Weird* must have been acquired by Tony Wayne, leaving Clark's yard sale find rated good. We now know either the condition or the collector for four issues, so the very fine copy of *The Bulk* must have been bought by Bruce, leaving Clark as the collector of *Mercury Man* and Dick's *Groovy Girl* as the fine condition magazine found at the thrift shop.

Bruce Grayson, *The Bulk*, very fine, auction site.
Clark Stark, *Mercury Man*, good, yard sale.
Dick Parker, *Groovy Girl*, fine, thrift shop.
Peter Kent, *Beetle Boy*, fair, traded with collector.
Tony Wayne, *Dr. Weird*, mint, comic fair.

103. AI, AI, Oh!

One AI won the Gold Star (clue 3) and Rob O'Tick received the Ounsley award (clue 4), so Otto Maton's Cup, which was not the Partington prize for Journalism (clue 2) or the Hurlbut prize (clue 4), must have been the Sorenson Cup. Cal Q. Later won the Math prize and the Statuette was the prize for Fiction (clue 1), so Otto Maton's Sorenson Cup must be awarded for Music (clue 4). We now know the name of the winner or the prize for three fields, so Rob O'Tick's Ounsley prize, which isn't for Science (clue 4) must be the Ounsley Statuette for Fiction. Cal Q. Later's Mathematics prize wasn't the Gold Star (clue 3), so must have been the prize awarded by the Hurlbut Academy. Ann Droid did not win the Science prize (clue 4), so that must have been AI Gorithm, leaving Ann with the prize for Journalism. It wasn't the Trophy (clue 4), so Ann Droid must have won the Partington Medal for journalism, leaving Cal Q. Later picking up the Hurlbut Trophy for Mathematics and AI Gorithm receiving the Gold Star for Science.

AI Gorithm, Gold Star for Science.
Ann Droid, Partington Medal for Journalism.
Cal Q. Later, Hurlbut Trophy for Mathematics.
Otto Maton, Sorenson Cup for Music.
Rob O'Tick, Ounsley Statuette for Fiction.

104. Fancy-Dress Party

Max collected Captain Hook (clue 2) and Aladdin went home at 1:25 a.m. (clue 6), so Ernie, who collected his fares at 2:15 a.m. but who didn't pick up the Cheshire Cat (clue 6) or the Big Bad Wolf (clue 1), must have had Mother Goose and Pinocchio (clue 5) in his cab. So, from clue 6, Ali Baba, who left the party later than 1:25 a.m., must have gone home at 1:45 a.m. Humpty Dumpty climbed into a taxi at 1 a.m. (clue 4), so the Ugly Sister, who wasn't the first to leave the party (clue 2), must have left at 1:25 a.m. with Aladdin, leaving Robin Hood being driven home by Babs (clue 3) at 12:30 a.m. So Max, who picked up his fares before the Ugly Sister left at 1:25 a.m., must have collected Humpty Dumpty at 1 a.m., who squeezed into the taxi with Captain Hook. Antonio didn't pick up Aladdin (clue 6), so it must have been Heather who collected Aladdin and an Ugly Sister at 1:25 a.m., leaving Antonio collecting Ali Baba at 1:45 a.m. So he didn't also chauffeur the Cheshire Cat (clue 6) and must have collected the Big Bad Wolf, leaving Babs collecting Robin Hood and the Cheshire Cat at 12:30 a.m.

Antonio, 1:45 a.m., Ali Baba, Big Bad Wolf.
Babs, 12:30 a.m., Robin Hood, Cheshire Cat.
Ernie, 2:15 a.m., Pinocchio, Mother Goose.
Heather, 1:25 a.m., ugly sister, Aladdin.
Max, 1 a.m., Humpty Dumpty, Captain Hook.

105. Logi-5

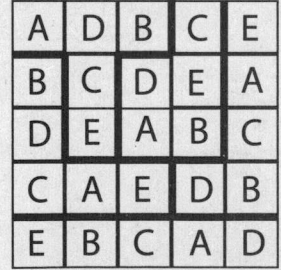

106. Sign In

4	5	3	2	6	1
1	6	4	3	5	2
3	1	6	4	2	5
6	2	5	1	3	4
5	4	2	6	1	3
2	3	1	5	4	6

107. Logi-5

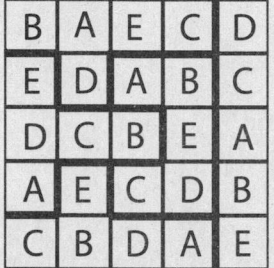

B	A	E	C	D
E	D	A	B	C
D	C	B	E	A
A	E	C	D	B
C	B	D	A	E

108. Sign In

4	2	3	1	6	5
2	6	1	5	3	4
3	1	5	4	2	6
1	5	2	6	4	3
5	4	6	3	1	2
6	3	4	2	5	1

109. Electric Dreams

The game featuring Caz, next left to the one featuring Kez (clue 1) was not at E and, since Daz was in the game at D (clue 2), she was not at D or C either (clue 1). Game B had a male character (clue 2), so Caz must have been in the game on machine A and was cleaning her keyboard (clue 3). From clue 1, Kez must have been in the game at B and the game character at C must have been installing a hard drive. Pacman, playing a character updating a database, was not any of these three, nor was he at E (clue 3), so he must have been at D, controlling Daz, and Jez must have been the character at E, leaving Baz on machine C. His player was not Mario or Lara Croft (clue 2), so must have been Sonic the Hedgehog. Jez was not the character amending the website (clue 3), so she must have been debugging a program, leaving Kez amending the website. Jez's player wasn't Mario (clue 3), so must have been Lara Croft, leaving Mario enjoying the game on machine A in which Caz cleans her keyboard.

A, Mario, Caz, cleaning keyboard.
B, Donkey Kong, Kez, amending website.
C, Sonic the Hedgehog, Baz, installing drive.
D, Pacman, Daz, updating database.
E, Lara Croft, Jez, debugging program.

110. On Reflection

The flat top is the style being attempted at mirror 5 (clue 3) and mirror 2 is being used by Gracula (clue 3), so Tracula, left of the quiff maker but right of Bracula (clue 2), must be at mirror 3. So, from clue 2, Bracula must be spiking her hair at mirror 1 and mirror 4 must be being used by the quiffer. Fracula is standing next to the side-parting maker (clue 1), so can't be at mirror 5 and must be at mirror 4, struggling with the quiff, and Tracula at mirror 3 must be trying the side parting. By elimination, Gracula at mirror 2 must be attempting a mop top and the flat-top arranger in mirror 5 must be Pracula.

1 Bracula, spikes; 2 Gracula, mop top; 3 Tracula, side parting; 4 Fracula, quiff; 5 Pracula, flat top.

111. Full Timetable

Pam's in the hockey team (clue 2), so the student who is studying organic chemistry and belongs to the Debating Society, who must have a four- or five-letter first name (clue 4), must be Tess Parker (clue 5). Diana is studying geology (clue 1), so Ms. Steele, the English literature student, who isn't Caroline or Pam (clue 1), must be Laura. Caroline isn't studying medicine (clue 2), so must be studying law, and Pam must be studying medicine. Caroline doesn't belong to the Choral Society (clue 2) or the Drama Club (clue 3), so she must belong to the environmentalists group and she must be Caroline Riordan (clue 5). Ms. Hardy has a five-letter first name (clue 4), so must be Diana Hardy and Pam must be Pam Bellamy. Finally, Laura doesn't belong to the Drama Club (clue 3), so she must belong to the Choral Society and it must be Diana Hardy who belongs to the Drama Club.

Caroline Riordan, law, environmentalists.
Diana Hardy, geology, Drama Club.
Laura Steele, English literature, Choral Society.
Pam Bellamy, medicine, hockey team.
Tess Parker, organic chemistry, Debating Society.

112. The Bard Who Borrowed?

The date of Ralph Varney's play, which was (perhaps) a source for *The Winter's Tale*, must have been either 1545 or 1560 (clue 6). 1560 is the date for *Tragedy of Shadrach the Gypsy*, which is the source of either *Coriolanus* or *Hamlet* (clue 4), so the Varney play must date from 1545 and Cedric Amoury's *History of Duke Reuben* must date from 1540 (clue 6). Now, the date of Magnus Peacock's play, which ends in a 5 (clue 3), must be 1555. The *Tragedy of Shadrach the Gypsy*, dating from 1560, wasn't by Jesse Lilburne (clue 4), so it must be by Solomon Twysden, leaving Jesse Lilburne's play dating from 1570. We know that the date of *A Sicilian Tragedy*, the proposed source for *Romeo and Juliet* (clue 2), wasn't 1545, nor, from its title, was it 1540 or 1560. Clue 2 rules out 1570, so it must date from 1555 and was by Magnus Peacock. The source for *The Winter's Tale*, the Ralph Varney play dated 1545, isn't *Hassan the Persian* (clue 1), so it must be *Gelais and Medora*, and *Hassan the Persian* must have been written by Jesse Lilburne and date from 1570. It's not the source for Macbeth (clue 1), and its date rules it out as the source for *Hamlet*, which is a play older than the source of *Coriolanus*, so *Hassan the Persian* must be the source for *Coriolanus*. So the source for *Hamlet* must be *Tragedy of Shadrach the Gypsy* (clue 4), leaving *History of Duke Reuben* by Cedric Amoury, dating from 1540, as the source for Macbeth.

Coriolanus, *Hassan the Persian*, Jesse Lilburne, 1570.
Hamlet, *Tragedy of Shadrach the Gypsy*, Solomon Twysden, 1560.
Macbeth, *History of Duke Reuben*, Cedric Amoury, 1540.
Romeo and Juliet, *A Sicilian Tragedy*, Magnus Peacock, 1555.
The Winter's Tale, *Gelais and Medora*, Ralph Varney, 1545.

113. Knit Wits

Betty is Betty Cable (clue 1) and Jo shopped at 2 p.m. (clue 3), so the last customer of the day, Ms. Stitch (clue 4), who wasn't Gemma (clue 2) or Anna (clue 4), must have been Helen Stitch. The first customer wasn't either Gemma (clue 2) or Anna (clue 4), and so must have been Betty Cable. So Gemma, who visited Knit Wits later than Ms. Woolley (clue 2) and can't have been the 11:15 a.m. customer, must have dropped in at 3:15 p.m., leaving Anna as the 11:15 a.m. shopper. Since Gemma was the 3:15 p.m. shopper, from clue 2, Helen Stitch's 4:30 purchase must have been the chunky wool. Gemma's purchase wasn't a zip or buttons (clue 2), and the double-knit wool was bought in the morning (clue 5), so Gemma's 3:15 purchase must have been the needles. So she isn't Ms. Kneedle (clue 6) or Ms. Woolley (clue 2) and so she must be Gemma Cotton. So Ms. Kneedle didn't shop at 2 p.m. and must have been the 11:15 a.m. shopper Anna Kneedle. By elimination, Jo must be Jo Woolley. She didn't buy the double-knit wool (clue 3) and couldn't have bought the zip (clue 2) and so must have bought the buttons. Finally, the zip wasn't bought at 11:15 a.m. (clue 2) and so must have been bought by Betty Cable at 10:30 a.m., leaving Anna Kneedle's 11:15 a.m. purchase as the double knit wool.

Anna Kneedle, 11:15 a.m., double-knit wool.
Betty Cable, 10:30 a.m., zip.
Gemma Cotton, 3:15 p.m., needles.
Jo Woolley, 2 p.m., buttons.
Helen Stitch, 4:30 p.m., chunky wool.

114. Logi-5

A	B	D	C	E
B	C	A	E	D
D	A	E	B	C
E	D	C	A	B
C	E	B	D	A

115. Sign In

2	1	6	4	5	3
4	5	2	6	3	1
5	4	3	1	2	6
6	2	4	3	1	5
3	6	1	5	4	2
1	3	5	2	6	4

116. Logi-5

B	D	E	A	C
D	A	B	C	E
E	C	A	B	D
A	E	C	D	B
C	B	D	E	A

117. Sign In

1	5	4	2	6	3
3	6	2	5	1	4
4	2	1	6	3	5
2	3	5	1	4	6
5	4	6	3	2	1
6	1	3	4	5	2

118. Happy Losers

Natasha began her new regimen as a dress size 20 (clue 1), and the woman who was once a size 18 is now a 14 (clue 3), so Sam, whose new size is 16 (clue 2), so who didn't begin as a size 16 (intro) or 22 (clue 2), must have been a size 24 at the beginning. Emily rewarded herself with a burger (clue 3), the new size 10 lady had a cream cake (clue 4), and the woman who began as a size 16 had the chocolates (clue 5), so Sam, moving from a size 24 to a size 16, who didn't have the Chinese meal (clue 2), must have had the ice cream sundae. We now know either the name or the treat for three starting dress sizes, so Emily with her burger, who didn't start as a size 18 (clue 3), must have been a size 22, leaving the lady who reduced from an 18 to a 14 (clue 3), undoing some of the good work with a Chinese meal and the new size 10 lady with the cream cake as former size 20 Natasha. From the intro, the woman who was once a size 16 is not now a 16 or 18, so must be a 12, leaving Emily slimming down from a size 22 to a size 18. Finally, from clue 5, Trudi wasn't originally a size 16, so must have been a size 18, leaving Olivia as the lady who began as a size 16.

Emily, size 22, size 18, burger.
Natasha, size 20, size 10, cream cake.
Olivia, size 16, size 12, box of chocolates.
Sam, size 24, size 16, ice cream sundae.
Trudi, size 18, size 14, Chinese meal.

119. Moons of Juno

Ophelia is being explored for life forms (clue 1) and Portia is being visited by *Daedalus* (clue 5), so the moon being assessed as a refuse center by the *Achilles*, which isn't Cordelia or Desdemona (clue 4), must be Viola. It isn't the rocky desert world (clue 2). Desdemona is covered in ice (clue 4), the boiling seas are being explored by *Bellerophon* (clue 3) and the gas giant is being assessed as an energy provider (clue 5), so Viola must be volcanic. We know either the environments or potential uses of three other moons, so the energy-rich gas giant, which isn't Portia (clue 5) must be Cordelia. So, by elimination, the boiling seas investigated by *Bellerophon* must be on Ophelia, and perhaps the home of new life forms, leaving the rocky desert world as Portia. It's not being considered for human habitation (clue 2), so there must be hopes of mining it for minerals, leaving the icy Desdemona as the potential spot for habitation. It isn't being assessed by *Jason* (clue 2), so must be being orbited by *Perseus*; leaving *Jason* exploring the energy-rich gas-giant Cordelia.

Cordelia, *Jason*, gas giant, energy.
Desdemona, *Perseus*, ice world, habitation.
Ophelia, *Bellerophon*, boiling seas, new life forms.
Portia, *Daedalus*, rocky desert, minerals.
Viola, *Achilles*, volcanic, refuse center.

120. Market Mismatch

Branelus brought back tripe (clue 2) and the Falernian wine was replaced with Grappa's finest (clue 1), so Euselus, who didn't come home with chickpeas or a cabbage (clue 3), must have replaced the garum he was meant to be finding with the sausages, and so did his shopping in the Argiletum (clue 6). Cluelus went to the Macellum of Nero (clue 7), so Gormlus, who didn't visit either Forum (clue 2), must have visited the Macellum of Livia, looking for venison (clue 4). Hopelus didn't visit the Forum Holitorium (clue 5), so must have gone to the Forum Boarium, leaving Branelus buying his tripe at the Forum Holitorium. So he wasn't looking for capons and neither was Hopelus (clue 5), so the capons must have been Cluelus' quest. Their substitute wasn't the cabbage (clue 5), so must have been the chickpeas. We now know either the intended purchase or the replacements for four s, so the one who was hoping that no one would tell the difference between Grappa's wine and the fine Falernian must have been Hopelus. By final elimination, Branelus must have been looking for a turbot in the Forum Holitorium but had to settle for tripe and Gormlus had to replace the juicy venison with a cabbage.

Branelus, Forum Holitorium, turbot, tripe.
Cluelus, Macellum of Nero, capons, chickpeas.
Euselus, Argiletum, garum, sausages.
Gormlus, Macellum of Livia, venison, cabbage.
Hopelus, Forum Boarium, Falernian wine, house wine.

121. Gourmet Gannets

The Gannets are planning boeuf bourguignon on the 9th (clue 4), while the main course when Margaret and Jim are guests will be roast lamb (clue 5), and paella will be on the menu later than when Sue and Tony are present (clue 3), so when Jane and Paul will be dining, and the dish won't be poached salmon (clue 1), they must be making baked pasta, so the second couple must be Jan and Andy (clue 6). Therefore Heather and Alan, who are coming the week after Pat and Ray (clue 2), will not be guests on the 9th or the 23rd (clue 1). Annie and Tom are coming on the 23rd, so Heather and Alan won't be with the Gannets on the 30th either, so they must be coming on the 6th. Therefore Pat and Ray must be joining the Gannets for dinner on the 30th. As Sheila and Peter and Jane and Richard are invited for the same evening (clue 2), it is neither the 23rd nor the 30th, so it must be the 9th, when the Gannets will be serving the boeuf bourguignon. They won't be dishing up the paella to Sue and Tony (clue 3), so it must be on the menu for Heather and Alan on the 6th, and, by elimination, they'll be doing the poached salmon for Sue and Tony. This reveals that they'll be sharing the dinner table with Annie and Tom on the 23rd (clue 1), and Pat and Ray on the 30th will be enjoying roast lamb with Margaret and Jim, leaving Elaine and Robert as the second couple with Heather and Alan on the 6th.

2nd, Jane and Paul, Jan and Andy, baked pasta.
6th, Heather and Alan, Elaine and Robert, paella.
9th, Sheila and Peter, Jane and Richard, boeuf bourguignon.
23rd, Sue and Tony, Annie and Tom, poached salmon.
30th, Margaret and Jim, Pat and Ray, roast lamb.

122. Logi-5

D	A	B	E	C
C	E	D	B	A
A	C	E	D	B
B	D	C	A	E
E	B	A	C	D

123. Sign In

5	6	4	3	2	1
6	1	2	4	5	3
1	4	5	2	3	6
3	5	6	1	4	2
2	3	1	5	6	4
4	2	3	6	1	5

124. Logi-5

E	C	D	A	B
B	D	A	E	C
A	B	E	C	D
D	E	C	B	A
C	A	B	D	E

125. Sign In

2	6	5	3	1	4
4	3	1	6	2	5
3	5	4	2	6	1
1	4	6	5	3	2
5	2	3	1	4	6
6	1	2	4	5	3

126. Recovery Positions

Mr. Evans was owed $19.25 (clue 1) and Miss Blair was owed money by Northern Water (clue 3), so the $25 owed by Consume Energy, which wasn't due to be paid to Mr. Armitage or Mrs. Dawkins (clue

4), must have been owed to Mr. Courtney, who was eventually paid after 21 days (clue 2. Mr. Evans wasn't owed his $19.25 by the rent company J.D. Housing or the gardeners T.G. Gardening (clue 1), so must have been owed the money by H.J. Phone Co. T.G. Gardening took 33 days to refund their customer (clue 5), so the $18 refunded after 15 days, which wasn't owed by J.D. Housing (clue 6) must have been paid to Miss Blair by Northern Water. Mrs. Dawkins wasn't owed $23.37 (clue 4), so must have been waiting for a refund of $21.50. So she wasn't T.G. Gardening's customer (clue 5) and must have been expecting the refund from J.D. Housing, leaving Mr. Armitage waiting for a refund of $23.37 from T.G. Gardening, who paid up after 33 days. Finally, Mr. Evans didn't have to wait 44 days for his refund (clue 1), so must have waited 38 days for his $19.25 from H.J. Phone Co, leaving Mrs. Dawkins finally receiving $21.50 from J.D. Housing after 44 days.

Mr. Armitage, $23.37, T.G. Gardening, 33 days.
Miss Blair, $18, Northern Water Co, 15 days.
Mr. Courtney, $25, Consume Energy, 21 days.
Mrs. Dawkins, $21.50, J.D. Housing, 44 days.
Mr. Evans, $19.25, H.J. Phone Co, 38 days.

127. Lab Report

Bungler is the uranium chemist (clue 3) and the Dean is Dean Numskerle (clue 2), so the Doctor who is the platinum expert but isn't Patter (clue 5) or Botcher (clue 1) must be Doctor Flunkitt. Bungler is not the Principal or the Professor (clue 3), so he must be Reader Bungler. The Principal filled the lab with gas (clue 3), so he is not Botcher, who burned his notes (clue 1), and must be Principal Patter, leaving Botcher as Professor Botcher. Doctor Flunkitt didn't drop a bottle of acid or flood the lab (clue 5), so he must have broken the test tubes. Dean Numskerle also didn't drop a bottle of acid (clue 2), so he must have flooded the lab, leaving Reader Bungler as the scientist who dropped a bottle of acid and ruined his shoes. Dean Numskerle is not the sodium chemist (clue 2) or the fluorine expert (clue 4), so his specialism must be sulphur. Finally, Professor Botcher does not specialize in sodium (clue 1) and must be the fluorine expert who burnt his notes, leaving Principal Patter as the sodium specialist who filled the lab with gas.

Dean Numskerle, sulphur, flooded lab.
Doctor Flunkitt, platinum, broke test tubes.
Principal Patter, sodium, fill lab with gas.
Professor Botcher, fluorine, burned notes.
Reader Bungler, uranium, dropped acid.

128. Ladd's Map

The 50 paces have to be made toward the rocky outcrop, but not in a south-easterly or south-westerly direction (clue 2), or to the north, which is the 70 paces (clue 3), or to the east, which is heading towards the dead tree (clue 4), so it must be 50 paces to the north east. The third instruction is to walk to the south west (clue 5), so the 30 paces is not the fifth instruction leading to the treasure (clue 6), and that final walk is also not of 40 (clue 6), 70 paces (clue 3), or 50 paces, so it must be 60 paces. By elimination, the 60 paces must be on a south-easterly bearing. The 70 paces are not to be made towards the waterfall (clue 3) or the dead tree, so it must be the cavern, leaving the waterfall destination as the third, south-westerly, instruction. From clue 1, the second instruction must involve walking toward the cavern, the third must involve the 30 paces and the first is to the north-east. By elimination, the easterly walk toward the dead tree must involve the 40 paces, and be the fourth instruction.

1, 50 paces NE toward a rocky outcrop.
2, 70 paces N toward a cavern.
3, 30 paces SW toward a waterfall.
4, 40 paces E toward a dead tree.
5, 60 paces SE toward the treasure.

129. Shoes Who?

The Mithras product is in position 7 (clue 3), so, from clue 7, the Rondo product, which is also in the left-hand column, but can't be in position 4, must be in position 1, and, from the same clue, the Mithras product in position 7 must be the tennis shoes. So, from clue 3, the footwear in position 6 must be the running shoes. Clue 6 now places the Libbra product in position 2, so it is the beach sandals (clue 4), and the Ensign product, which we know isn't in position 1, must be in position 3 and the boat shoes must be the Rondo product in position 1 (clue 6). The cycling shoes can't be in position 9 (clue 5), so they must be in position 5 and the football boots must be in position 4. We have now identified the type of footwear in positions 2, 4, and 6, so, from clue 2, the hiking boots made by Bowman must be in position 8. The baseball shoes can't be in position 9 (clue 1), so they must be in position 3 and, from clue 1, the running shoes in position 6 must be a Muntjac product. By elimination, the footwear in position 9 must be golf shoes, which, from clue 5, must be an Emery product. Finally, the football boots in position 4 weren't made by Eagle (clue 5), so they must have been made by Maxim, and Eagle must have made the cycling shoes in position 5.

1 boat shoes, Rondo; 2 beach sandals, Libbra; 3 baseball shoes, Ensign 4 football boots, Maxim; 5 cycling shoes, Eagle; 6 running shoes; Muntjac 7 tennis shoes, Mithras; 8 hiking boots, Bowman; 9 golf shoes, Emery.

130. Get the Picture

Picture no.1, *No.1*, is not the work of Jez (clue 1), Caz (clue 3), Baz or Kez (clue 2), so must be Daz's finger painting (clue 1). Now, from clue 3, Caz's artwork cannot be no.2 and must be no.4, and no.2 must be the collage. Caz's effort is not the photo (clue 2) or print (clue 3), so must be the oil painting and, from clue 1, Jez must be the creator of no.3. No.2 is not Baz's photograph (clue 2) so must be Kez's *Composition in Green and Silver* and Baz must be the photographer of no.5, which must be *Degas at the Bar* (a photo of a completely flat glass of beer, degassed in an ultrasonic bath), leaving Jez as the printer of *After Renoir* and Caz as the creator of *Hipster Telephone*.

1, Daz, *No.1*, finger painting.
2, Kez, *Composition in Green and Silver*, collage.
3, Jez, *After Renoir*, print.
4, Caz, *Hipster Telephone*, oil painting.
5, Baz, *Degas at the Bar*, photograph.

131. Sunday Ceremonies

Alex lives at number 7 (clue 1). Todd does not live at number 5 (clue 4) and, since Alex did not start washing his automobile at 8:30 (clue 1), clue 2 also rules out number 5 for Dennis, the Porsche owner, so Martin must live there. The Toyota owner lives at number 9 (clue 5), so this is not Alex or Martin, and we know Dennis owns the Porsche, so Todd must drive the Toyota, leaving Dennis living at number 11 and, from clue 2, Todd beginning his washing ceremony at 8:30. Alex's automobile is not the Ford (clue 1), so it must be the Mercedes, leaving the Ford as Martin's vehicle. He did not start washing it at 10:30 (clue

3), so clue 1 rules out both 9:30 and 11:30 for Alex, who must have begun washing the Mercedes at 10:30. So, from clue 1, Martin must have made the 9:30 start, leaving 11:30 as the time Dennis began washing his Porsche.

No.5, Martin, Ford, 9:30.
No.7, Alex, Mercedes, 10:30.
No.9, Todd, Toyota, 8:30.
No.11, Dennis, Porsche, 11:30.

132. Absent People

Polly sat at table 4 (clue 1), and Roxy and Mandy conversed with the server wearing a green apron (clue 2), so table 2, where the photo of the server in the blue apron was taken (clue 3) but wasn't where Anthea and Joey (clue 2) or Marie (clue 3) sat, must have been where Natasha and Phil sat. Heather took a photo of Marie (clue 3) and Ben took one of people at table 3 (clue 4), so table 4, which wasn't where Glen or Jack took a photo (clue 1) but must have been where Chrissy took a photo of the server in the maroon apron with Polly. The photo of Natasha and Phil and a navy-clad server at table 2 wasn't taken by Glen (clue 3), so it must have been taken by Jack. Heather also didn't take a photo at table 5 (clue 3), so must have snapped Marie at table 6, leaving Glen who took his picture at table 5. We now know the guests at tables 2, 4, and 6, so, from clue 2, Anthea and Joey must have been at table 5 and Roxy and Mandy at table 3 having their photo taken with a green-aproned server by Ben. Finally, the waiter wearing the white apron didn't serve at table 6, so must have appeared at table 5 with Anthea and Joey when Glen took the picture, leaving Heather taking a picture of Marie at table 6 with a server in a beige apron.

Anthea/Joey, table 5, Glen, white.
Marie, table 6, Heather, beige.
Natasha/Phil, table 2, Jack, navy.
Polly, table 4, Chrissy, maroon.
Roxy/Mandy, table 3, Ben, green.

133. Rooms for Improvement

A wall in the primary bedroom had cork tiles (clue 2), the cladding was replaced with ivory color paint (clue 4), and the flocked wallpaper was the first thing to be replaced (clue 3), so the dining room, recently painted in apple white but which wasn't the first to be dealt with and didn't have the striped wallpaper (clue 1), must have had purple painted walls. The ivory paint wasn't used in either of the guest bedrooms (clue 4), so must have been used to replace the cladding in the sitting room. Guest bedroom 2 was tackled second (clue 4), so the room that was decorated, first, which was the one with flocked wallpaper (clue 3), must have been guest bedroom 1, leaving guest bedroom 2 with the striped wallpaper. Magnolia was used for the third room decorated (clue 5), so the first room decorated which didn't get the nougat paint, must have been painted almond, leaving the nougat for the second room decorated and the magnolia used to replace the cork in the primary bedroom. Finally, from clue 6, the sitting room wasn't painted last, so must have been dealt with fourth, leaving the dining room last to be painted.

First, guest bedroom 1, flocked wallpaper, almond.
Second, guest bedroom 2, striped wallpaper, nougat.
Third, primary bedroom, cork tiles, magnolia.
Fourth, sitting room, cladding, ivory.
Fifth, dining room, purple painted walls, apple white.

134. In the Bag

Each bag is touching 2, 3, 4, or 5 other bags. The lunchbox, in the bag numbered half that of Stan Bull's bag (clue 3), must be one of 1, 2, 3, or 4. It's touching more bags than is Frank Fort's (clue 3), so it can't be bag 1, which is touching only two others, and fewer than Sandy Aygo's, so it can't be bag 4 which is touching 5 others. Bag 3 contains the suspicious computer components (clue 6), so the lunchbox must be in bag 2 and Stan Bull's bag must be number 4. So the lunch box is in a bag that is touching 3 others and, from clue 3, Frank Fort's bag must be number 1, the only one that is touching only 2. So, from clue 1, Oz Lowe's bag must be touching three other bags, and so the bag with the flour must be touching 5 others and so must be Stan Bull's bag 4. This bag isn't touching Ali Canté's bag (clue 1), so Ali's bag can't be 2, 3, 5, 6, or 7, and we know it isn't 1, so Ali Canté's bag must be number 8. So Oz Lowe's bag, touching 3 others, which now can't be number 7 (clue 4), must be number 2, with the heavy lunchbox. Jo Berg's even-numbered bag must now be number 6. Bag 7, touching 3 other bags, doesn't belong to Moss Coe, whose bag must be touching 4 (clue 1), or Sandy Aygo, whose bag must also be touching 4 others (clue 3), so must be Mel Borne's with her suspect alarm clock. So, from clue 4, Ali Canté's bag must have the cine camera film. Sandy Aygo's bag isn't number 5 (clue 3), so must be bag 3 with its computer bits, leaving bag 5 belonging to Moss Coe. So, from clue 5, Jo Berg's bag 6 must contain the kitchen spatula. Finally, Frank Fort's bag doesn't have the toy water pistol (clue 3), so it must have the ornament, leaving the toy pistol in Moss Coe's bag 5.

1 Frank Fort, ornament; 2 Oz Lowe, lunchbox; 3 Sandy Aygo, computer components; 4 Stan Bull, bag of flour.
5 Moss Coe, toy; 6 Jo Berg, spatula; 7 Mel Borne, clock;
8 Ali Canté, camera film.

135. Logi-5

A	E	B	D	C
C	D	A	B	E
E	B	D	C	A
B	C	E	A	D
D	A	C	E	B

136. Sign In

3	1	5	2	6	4
2	6	1	3	4	5
6	4	3	1	5	2
1	3	4	5	2	6
4	5	2	6	1	3
5	2	6	4	3	1

137. Logi-5

B	D	E	A	C
D	B	C	E	A
E	C	A	B	D
A	E	D	C	B
C	A	B	D	E

138. Sign In

4	5	1	6	2	3
6	1	5	2	3	4
5	2	4	3	6	1
2	3	6	1	4	5
3	4	2	5	1	6
1	6	3	4	5	2

139. Going Nuts

Clue 1 tells us each vertical column must contain just one of the four nuts. Squares C1 and C3 both contain letters (clue 3), so the hazelnut must be in square C2 (clue 2) and be the only nut in that column. So, clue 1 rules out the R immediately to the right of the chestnut from both column A and column D. Nor can R be the letter in either C1 or C3 (clue 3), so it must be in column B. The nut in this column cannot be in B2 (clue 1) and clue 3 rules out B1, so it must be in B3, with the L in B2 (clue 3). So the first R referred to in clue 2 must be in B1 and the chestnut must be in A1 (clue 2). From clue 5, the beechnut cannot be in column D, and we have placed nuts in A1 and C2, so, by elimination, the beechnut must be the one in B3, and C3 contains the I (clue 3). So, from clue 1, the acorn must be the nut in column D. It cannot be in D1 (clue 2), or D2 (clue 1), so it must be in D3. Nor can the E be in D2, next horizontally to the hazelnut (clue 2), so it must be in D1. So, from clue 3, and having placed both the E and the I, the U must be the vowel in C1. Finally, the Q above the second R (clue 2), must now be in A2 with the R in A3, leaving the letter in D2 as the S.

chestnut	R	U	E
Q	L	hazelnut	S
R	beechnut	I	acorn

140. Minnie's Taxi

The person who hailed the taxi in the main street in Arlington, Minnie's first fare of the day (intro), wasn't Fran or Cher (clue 1), Dana (clue 2), Bess (clue 3), Gail or Alma (clue 4), and so must have been Emma. The last fare of the day wasn't Fran or Cher (clue 1), Bess (clue 3), or Gail or Alma (clue 4), and so must have been Dana. So, from clue 2, the sixth fare must have been to the theater. Now, from clue 1, the restaurant was three destinations after the law courts, so must have been the fourth, fifth, or seventh. The fourth fare needed to go to the airport (clue 5), so the restaurant can't have been the fourth or the seventh fare and must have been the fifth with, from clue 1, Cher being the fourth fare going to the airport, Fran being the third fare and the law courts being the destination of Minnie's second customer of the day. Gail was immediately replaced in the taxi by Alma (clue 4), so Gail can now only have been the fifth fare going to the restaurant and Alma must have been the sixth fare from the restaurant to the theater, where Dana got in and asked to be taken to the sports stadium. This leaves Bess climbing into the taxi second at the railway station (clue 3), when Emma, the first fare, got out and going to the law court and Fran, Minnie's third passenger, going from the law courts to the museum.

First, Emma, railway station; Second, Bess, law courts; Third, Fran, museum; Fourth, Cher, airport; Fifth, Gail, restaurant; Sixth, Alma, theater; Seventh, Dana, sports stadium.

141. Aristo Caughts

The Vicomte had a second-floor cell (clue 3), so Reynaud's cell was on neither the first floor nor the fourth floor (clue 1). The third-floor prisoner was Maxim (clue 4), so Reynaud must have had the second-floor cell and is the Vicomte. So, from clue 1, the Comte de Petits-Pois must be Maxim on the third floor and, from clue 2, Adolphe must have been the fourth-floor prisoner with the Marquis on the ground floor. Now, by elimination, Adolphe must have been the Baron and the Marquis must have been Celestin. From clue 2, neither of them is de l'Epinard, so that must have been Reynaud's family name. Finally, from clue 5, Celestin, who is not de la Basse-Cour, must be the Marquis du Verger, leaving Adolphe as the Baron de la Basse-Cour.

First floor, Celestin, Marquis du Verger.
Second floor, Reynaud, Vicomte de l'Epinard.
Third floor, Maxim, Comte de Petits-Pois.
Fourth floor, Adolphe, Baron de la Basse-Cour.

142. Splish Splash

The fish in position 1 isn't Ben, Dot, Hal, or Eva (clue 1), or Amy, Col, or Fay (clue 2), and so must be Gus. So, from clue 2, Col must be fish 2. Fish 8 isn't Ben, Dot, or Hal (clue 1), or Amy or Fay (clue 2), and so must be Eva. Now Fay, two places left of a fish facing right (clue 2), must be either fish 3 or fish 5. But she's facing the same was as Gus (clue 2), so can't be fish 3 and must be fish 5. So right-facing Amy can't be fish 7 (clue 2) and must be fish 4, and right-facing Ben (clue 1) must be fish 7. Finally, Hal isn't next to Amy (clue 2), so must be fish 6, leaving Dot as fish 3.

1 Gus; 2 Col; 3 Dot; 4 Amy; 5 Fay; 6 Hal; 7 Ben; 8 Eva

143. Belling the Cat

Dinner is gray and her collar isn't gold (clue 1) or red (clue 2) and Candy's collar is green (clue 2), so Dinner's collar must be blue. She hasn't been chasing a pigeon (clue 1), mouse, or skink (clue 2), so must have been stalking a sparrow. The cat in the red collar isn't tabby (clue 1) or ginger (clue 2) so must be black. So this isn't Candy in the green collar (clue 2), who can't be tabby either (clue 1), so must be the ginger cat who has been hunting the skink (clue 2). Alfie didn't chase the mouse (clue 2), so must have pursued the pigeon. So he isn't the tabby cat with the gold collar (clue 1) and must be the black cat with the red collar, leaving Buttons as the gold-collared tabby cat who chased the mouse.

Alfie, black, red, pigeon.
Buttons, tabby, gold, mouse.
Candy, ginger, green, skink.
Dinner, gray, blue, sparrow.

144. Capital Dogs

The dog formerly known as Kingston Kid is number 5 (clue 2), so the racing name of dog 4, which isn't Luanda Lad (clue 1), Belgrade Boy (clue 3), or Dakar Dude (clue 2), must be Freetown Fellow. So, from clue 3, Kingston Lad in position 5 must now be known as Archie. Charlie raced as Belgrade Boy (clue 3), so Luanda Lad, who isn't now known as Eddie or Donny (clue 1), must be Benny. So he's not dog 1 and must be dog 2 (clue 1). So, from cue 1, Freetown Fellow in position 4 must be Donny and, from clue 2, Dakar Dude must be dog 1. This leaves Charlie, aka Belgrade Boy, in position 3 and Dakar Dude in position 1 as Eddie.

3 Charlie, Belgrade Boy; 4 Donny, Freetown Fellow;
5 Archie, Kingston Kid 1 Eddie, Dakar Dude;
2 Benny, Luanda Lad.

145. Candler's Folly

Vehicle 5 is a bus (clue 2) and vehicle 6 was made by Norcross (clue 4), so, from clue 1, the Farway ambulance must be vehicle 4. The Holdridge vehicle dates from 1908 (clue 7). It is not a tow truck (clue 7) and we know it is not an ambulance. It can't be a dump truck (clue 3) or a fire truck (clue 4), and the gas tanker dates from 1923 (clue 6), so the Holdridge must be a bus and is therefore vehicle 5. The Wilgreve isn't vehicle 3 (clue 5), nor can vehicle 3 be the Jamison (clue 3), so it must be the Rudderford. We know that the Norcross, vehicle 6, doesn't date from 1908, nor can it date from 1953 (clue 4). Vehicle 1 dates from 1936 (clue 8) and we know the gas tanker dates from 1923, so clue 4 rules out 1919 for the Norcross, while the 1949 vehicle is in the back row (clue 1), so the Norcross must date from 1923, and so is the gas tanker. So vehicle 1, dated 1936, must be the fire truck (clue 4). Vehicle 3, the Rudderford, can't date from 1919 (clue 5), so must date from 1949 or 1953. So the Wilgreve must date from 1923 or 1936 (clue 5). But we know it's the Norcross that dates from 1923, so the Wilgreve must be a 1936 model, and is vehicle 1. This leaves the Jamison as vehicle 2. From clue 5, vehicle 3, the Rudderford, must date from 1953, and, from clue 3, it must be the dump truck. From clue 1, vehicle 2, the Jamison, must date from 1949, and it must be a tow truck, leaving vehicle 4, the Farway ambulance, dating from 1919.

1, Wilgreve fire truck, 1936.
2, Jamison tow truck, 1949.
3, Rudderford dump truck, 1953.
4, Farway ambulance, 1919.
5, Holdridge bus, 1908.
6, Norcross gas tanker, 1923.

146. Dog With a Bone

Oscar received his bone on Monday and the spaniel got his on Tuesday (clue 3), so Romeo the terrier, who wasn't the last of these four to get their bone (clue 2), must have got his on Wednesday. So the dog at No.9 got his bone on Thursday (clue 2). If Charlie lived at No.9, No.7, and No.11 would each be either Romeo the terrier or the bulldog (clue 1). But the dog at No.11 is the lurcher (clue 4), so Charlie can't live at No.9 and must live at No.7, with Romeo the terrier and his Wednesday bone at No.5 and the bulldog at No.9. We now know the breed of dog or day for three addresses, so the spaniel who got his bone on Tuesday (clue 3), must be Charlie at No.7, leaving the lurcher at No.11 getting his bone on Monday. So he is Oscar (clue 3), leaving Victor as the bulldog at No.9 getting his bone on Thursday.

No.5, Romeo, terrier, Wednesday.
No.7, Charlie, spaniel, Tuesday.
No.9, Victor, bulldog, Thursday.
No.11, Oscar, lurcher, Monday.

147. The Fallen Crown

The vowel in D4 (clue 4) isn't E or I (clue 3) and the three Os are in diagonal alignment (clue 1), none of the possibilities for which includes D4, so it must be an A. So, from clue 2, D3 is G and D5 is N. So C5 doesn't have an O (clue 1) and the three Os must be in D2, C3, and B4. The I in row C is not next to a vowel in any direction (clue 3), so isn't in C1, 2, 4, or 5. Nor is it in C7 (clue 3), so it must be in C6. So the E above the K (clue 3) isn't in B7 or C7 (clue 3) and must be in column 1. It's not in C1 (clue 3), so must be in B1 with K in C1. Now the only places left for both Rs to be immediately left of Ms. are Rs in C4 and D6 and Ms. in C5 and D7. The D is in a column numbered one higher than the F so the F must be in D1 and the D in C2. The H isn't in the same column as an M, so can't be in column 7 and must be in A4. Finally, the S isn't above the Y, so the Y must be in B7 and the S in C7.

		H				
E		O				Y
K	D	O	R	M	I	S
F	O	G	A	N	R	M

148. Towel Rail

With no two men's towels being adjacent and one pair of towels belonging to women (clue 1), the two towels at the ends of the rail must both belong to men and so, towels 2 and 9 must both belong to women. Towel 1 doesn't belong to Gus or Don (clue 2), or Ben or Gus (clue 3), and so must be Hal's. The woman who owns towel 2 isn't Joy or Eva (clue 3), or Cyd or Fay (clue 2), and so must belong to Ivy. The woman who owns towel 9 doesn't belong to Joy or Fay (clue 2) or Eva (clue 3) and so must be Cyd's. So, from clue 2, Don's towel must be number 6. So the owner of towel 3 isn't Joy (clue 2). Nor is it Eva's (clue 3), so must belong to Fay, and Alf's towel must be number 4. Now, from clue 3, Joy's towel must be number 5 and Gus' number 10, leaving Eva's to the left of Ben's (clue 3) in position 7 and Ben in position 8.

1 Hal; 2 Ivy; 3 Fay; 4 Alf; 5 Joy; 6 Don; 7 Eva; 8 Ben; 9 Cyd; 10 Gus.

149. Trade Winds

Umbrella 4 belongs to the employee at the jewelry store (clue 3), so umbrella 1 which isn't being hung on to by the psychiatrist's assistant (clue 1) or the interior design employee (clue 2), must belong to Gary Gayle, the clothes boutique assistant (clue 2). Now, from clue 1, psychiatrist Dr. Freemantle's assistant must own umbrella 3 and Scott Skwall must have broken umbrella 2 on the way to his job at Miss Tralle, which, by elimination, must be the interior design company. Bonnie Bries doesn't own umbrella 3, so she must be the watch repairer at the jewelry store, leaving Dr. Freemantle's assistant as Gwen Gussed. Finally, the jewelry store is not Harry Caine Ltd (clue 3), so must be Willie Willie and Winned, leaving Harry Caine Ltd as the clothes boutique where Gary Gayle works.

1, Gary Gayle, Harry Caine Ltd, clothes boutique.
2, Scott Skwall, Miss Tralle, interior design.
3, Gwen Gussed, Dr. Freemantle, psychiatrist.
4, Bonnie Bries, Willie Willie and Winned, jewelry store.

150. Up in Arms

Neither of shield 1 nor 4 has a bear (clue 4). They can't both have lions (clue 2) and can't both have dragons (clue 2), so they must each have either a dragon or a lion. The two dragons are numbered two apart (clue 2), so they can't be on shields 1 and 3 (clue 1), and so shield 1 must have a lion and shields 4 and 2 must have dragons and, from clue 2, shield 2 must have a dragon sejant. By elimination, shield 3 must have a bear, and the dragon statant (clue 2) must be on shield 4. Now, from clue 2, the lion to the right of the dormant pose must be on shield 6 and shield 5 must have the dormant animal which must be a bear dormant. The courant animal is to the right of the couchant, so shield 1 must have a lion couchant. Finally, the bear on shield 3 doesn't have a rampant pose so must be a bear courant, leaving shield 6 with the lion rampant.

1 lion couchant; 2 dragon sejant; 3 bear courant.
4 dragon statant; 5 bear dormant; 6 lion rampant.

151. Parnoica Dates

The agent in position 5 isn't carrying the yo-yo (clue 1), the bicycle pump, the pineapple or the table tennis bat (clue 2), the butterfly net (clue 3), or any of the roller skate, the shoe, or the top hat (clue 4), so must have the spanner and, from clue 1, agent 4 must have the yo-yo. The agent with the table tennis bat isn't agent 1 (clue 2), so the one with the pineapple can't be number 2. Nor, since the yo-yo holding agent is in position 4 can the one with the pineapple be agent 8, so he must be agent 6 with the agent holding the bat in position 3. The agents with the skate and the top hat are separated by one other agent (clue 4), so, from the agents we have left to encumber, each must be either agent 7 or 9. So the agent with the shoe can't be agent 8 (clue 4) or agent 2 (clue 1) and must be agent 1, with, from clue 2, agent 2 having the bicycle pump and leaving agent 8 holding the butterfly net. So, from clue 3, agent 9 must have the roller skate and agent 7 the top hat.

1 shoe; 2 bicycle pump; 3 table tennis bat; 4 yo-yo; 5 spanner; 6 pineapple; 7 top hat; 8 butterfly net; 9 roller skate.

152. Suite of Carts

Marketing matters are being discussed in the Excelsior Suite and the cream pastries are being delivered to the Royal Suite (clue 3), so the discussions about new products, the cart for which is immediately left of the one carrying the pain au chocolat for Reddy Willing and Abel (clue 2), must be in the Premier Suite, and Reddy Willing and Abel must be discussing marketing ploys in the Excelsior Suite fuelled by pain au chocolat. Information International are talking about expanding their overseas offices (clue 1), so The Goode Company, who aren't talking about a merger (clue 4) must be discussing new products in the Premier Suite. They haven't ordered the doughnuts (clue 4), so must be having cookies, leaving the doughnuts being delivered to the Imperial Suite. The merger discussions aren't in the Imperial Suite, so they must be in the Royal Suite, leaving Information International discussing overseas expansion with doughnuts in the Imperial Suite and Finance Solutions talking mergers in the Royal Suite.

Premier Suite, The Goode Co, new products, cookies.
Excelsior Suite, Reddy, Willing, and Abel, marketing, pain au chocolat.
Imperial Suite, Information International, overseas expansion, doughnuts.
Royal Suite, Finance Solutions, merger, cream pastries.

153. *Sloth and Slander*

Abigail is wooed by Mr. Farcey and Mr. Barcey is accused of fraud, so Cordelia's betrothed who is accused of bigamy (clue 3), must be Mr. Larcey, leaving Mr. Barcey as the prospective husband of Beatrice and Abigail's suitor, Mr. Farcey, as the soldier unjustly accused of cowardice. Beatrice's Mr. Barcey isn't the banker (clue 2), so he must be the mill owner accused of fraud, leaving Cordelia's Mr. Larcey as the banker accused of bigamy.

Abigail, Mr. Farcey, soldier, cowardice.
Beatrice, Mr. Barcey, mill owner, fraud.
Cordelia, Mr. Larcey, banker, bigamy.

154. Music Makers

Andy Minor is half of Twin Set (clue 2), so Sandi Scayl and Ralph Riffe, who aren't Duo Decimal (clue 1); must be Two of Us. They didn't perform on Sunday (clue 3), or Friday (clue 1), and must have been Saturday's band, with Duo Decimal playing Friday (clue 1) and Twin Set on Sunday. Karen Keah didn't play on Friday (clue 3), so she must be Andy Minor's partner in Twin Set playing on Sunday, leaving Friday's pairing as Carrie Cored and Stan Stave as Duo Decimal.

Friday, Carrie Cored and Stan Stave, Duo Decimal.
Saturday, Sandi Scayl and Ralph Riff, Two of Us.
Sunday, Karen Keah and Andy Minor, Twin Set.

155. Cold Hard Cashless

Piers' surname is Broak (clue 2), so Lynn and Nigel, who are not the Strapts (clue 1), must be Lynn and Nigel Penylus, leaving Oliver as Oliver Strapt. The couple whose heating comes on at 7 p.m. isn't the Broaks (clue 2) or the Strapts (clue 1), so Lynn and Nigel Penylus must have heat between 7 p.m. and 9 p.m. So, from clue 1, the Strapts' boiler must fire up at 6 p.m., leaving the Broaks' boiler in action between 5 p.m. and 7 p.m. So Mrs. Broak isn't Kate (clue 3) and must be Mary, leaving Mrs. Strapt as Kate.

Kate and Oliver Strapt, 6 p.m.–8 p.m.
Lynn and Nigel Penylus, 7 p.m.–9 p.m.
Mary and Piers Broak, 5 p.m.–7 p.m.

156. Sunny Afternoon

The oval pool is home to the blow-up shark (clue 2), so the square pool, which doesn't have the dinosaur (clue 1), must have a floating crocodile, and the round pool owned by the Brites (clue 1) must be home to the dinosaur. It's not at No.11 (clue 1) and the Heatons live at No.9 (clue 3), so the Brites with their round pool and dinosaur must be at No.7. By elimination, the Clements live at No.11. They don't own an inflatable croc (clue 3), so must have the blow up shark in the oval pool, leaving the Heatons at No.9 with the square pool and crocodile.

No.7, Brite, round, dinosaur.
No.9, Heaton, square, crocodile.
No.11, Clement, oval, shark.

157. Odd Jobs

The fence was mended on Monday (clue 3), so Mrs. Green's sticky door, which wasn't unstuck on Wednesday (clue 1), must have been dealt with on Tuesday, leaving the shelves being put up on Wednesday. The shelves weren't Mr. Brown's job (clue 2), so must have been wanted by Mrs. Scarlett, leaving Mrs. Brown's fence needing fixing. Mrs. Scarlett's shelves didn't take 4 hours (clue 2) or, since they were the Wednesday job, 2 hours (clue 1), so must have taken 3 hours. So, from clue 1, Mr. Green's door must have taken 2 hours, leaving Mrs. Brown's fence taking 4 hours.

Monday, Mrs. Brown, fence, 4 hours.
Tuesday, Mr. Green, door, 2 hours.
Wednesday, Mrs. Scarlett, shelves, 3 hours.

158. Timber

Mrs Copse's cherry tree had been blown down and the birch tree had hit a greenhouse (clue 2), so Mr. Forester's tree that had ended up filling his pond (clue 3) must have been the apple tree. So he didn't call at 9:15 (clue 1) and it was Mrs. Bower who made the first call (clue 1), so Mr. Forester must have called at 9:30. We know Mrs. Bower didn't ring about the cherry tree, so she must have called at 9:00 about the birch in her greenhouse, leaving Mrs. Copse calling at 9:15 about the cherry tree that had been blown onto her shed.

9:00, Mrs. Bower, birch, greenhouse.
9:15, Mrs. Copse, cherry, shed.
9:30, Mr. Forester, apple, pond.

159. Logi-5

B	D	A	E	C
D	E	C	B	A
A	B	E	C	D
C	A	B	D	E
E	C	D	A	B

160. Sign In

2	6	4	5	3	1
6	2	5	4	1	3
1	4	6	3	2	5
4	5	3	1	6	2
5	3	1	2	4	6
3	1	2	6	5	4

Sudoku Solutions

161

9	6	5	1	2	8	7	4	3
4	2	7	9	5	3	6	1	8
3	1	8	7	6	4	5	2	9
8	9	3	6	1	5	4	7	2
6	4	2	8	3	7	9	5	1
5	7	1	2	4	9	8	3	6
7	8	4	3	9	2	1	6	5
1	3	9	5	7	6	2	8	4
2	5	6	4	8	1	3	9	7

162

7	3	8	4	9	1	5	6	2
9	2	4	3	5	6	7	8	1
1	5	6	2	8	7	9	3	4
4	1	7	5	6	9	8	2	3
6	9	3	7	2	8	1	4	5
5	8	2	1	4	3	6	9	7
3	7	9	6	1	4	2	5	8
2	6	1	8	3	5	4	7	9
8	4	5	9	7	2	3	1	6

163

1	2	3	8	5	9	7	6	4
5	9	7	6	2	4	8	1	3
4	8	6	7	1	3	5	9	2
6	4	8	1	7	2	9	3	5
3	7	2	4	9	5	6	8	1
9	1	5	3	6	8	4	2	7
8	6	1	5	3	7	2	4	9
7	3	9	2	4	6	1	5	8
2	5	4	9	8	1	3	7	6

164

4	3	6	7	1	2	8	9	5
9	5	7	8	3	6	2	4	1
2	1	8	9	4	5	3	6	7
5	4	9	3	8	7	6	1	2
8	6	3	4	2	1	7	5	9
1	7	2	5	6	9	4	3	8
3	9	1	2	7	4	5	8	6
6	2	4	1	5	8	9	7	3
7	8	5	6	9	3	1	2	4

165

9	6	5	2	1	4	8	3	7
1	8	7	5	9	3	6	4	2
3	2	4	8	6	7	5	9	1
8	9	2	6	3	1	7	5	4
6	5	1	4	7	2	3	8	9
7	4	3	9	5	8	1	2	6
2	1	9	3	8	6	4	7	5
5	3	6	7	4	9	2	1	8
4	7	8	1	2	5	9	6	3

166

6	2	5	7	3	1	4	9	8
4	1	7	5	9	8	2	6	3
9	8	3	2	6	4	7	1	5
2	6	9	8	1	7	3	5	4
8	7	4	6	5	3	9	2	1
5	3	1	4	2	9	6	8	7
3	5	2	1	4	6	8	7	9
1	4	8	9	7	2	5	3	6
7	9	6	3	8	5	1	4	2

167

5	6	2	1	8	3	9	4	7
3	4	7	6	5	9	8	2	1
8	1	9	4	7	2	3	6	5
7	2	8	9	4	6	1	5	3
4	3	5	2	1	8	7	9	6
6	9	1	7	3	5	2	8	4
2	5	3	8	6	1	4	7	9
1	8	4	5	9	7	6	3	2
9	7	6	3	2	4	5	1	8

168

6	8	7	4	5	1	2	9	3
2	3	1	7	9	8	5	4	6
4	5	9	2	3	6	7	1	8
1	2	3	5	6	9	4	8	7
8	7	6	1	2	4	9	3	5
5	9	4	3	8	7	1	6	2
7	6	5	9	1	3	8	2	4
9	4	8	6	7	2	3	5	1
3	1	2	8	4	5	6	7	9

169

8	4	9	2	6	1	7	5	3
3	2	5	9	8	7	6	4	1
1	7	6	4	3	5	9	2	8
9	8	1	6	5	3	2	7	4
6	3	4	7	9	2	8	1	5
2	5	7	1	4	8	3	6	9
5	9	2	3	7	4	1	8	6
4	1	3	8	2	6	5	9	7
7	6	8	5	1	9	4	3	2

170

9	3	7	4	2	5	8	6	1
8	5	2	9	6	1	7	4	3
6	4	1	3	7	8	2	9	5
7	1	3	8	9	6	4	5	2
5	6	9	2	1	4	3	7	8
4	2	8	5	3	7	6	1	9
2	8	6	1	4	9	5	3	7
3	9	4	7	5	2	1	8	6
1	7	5	6	8	3	9	2	4

171

9	4	8	1	6	3	7	2	5
5	7	1	8	9	2	6	3	4
3	2	6	7	4	5	1	8	9
7	3	2	9	5	6	8	4	1
8	1	5	2	7	4	3	9	6
6	9	4	3	1	8	2	5	7
4	8	9	6	2	1	5	7	3
1	5	3	4	8	7	9	6	2
2	6	7	5	3	9	4	1	8

172

6	1	2	4	8	9	3	7	5
5	3	8	7	1	2	6	9	4
7	4	9	5	6	3	1	8	2
8	6	5	1	4	7	2	3	9
9	2	4	3	5	8	7	6	1
3	7	1	2	9	6	4	5	8
2	8	7	9	3	1	5	4	6
1	5	6	8	7	4	9	2	3
4	9	3	6	2	5	8	1	7

173

8	5	6	7	1	9	2	3	4
1	2	4	8	6	3	5	9	7
9	3	7	2	5	4	6	1	8
4	8	5	6	7	1	3	2	9
7	6	2	9	3	5	4	8	1
3	1	9	4	2	8	7	6	5
6	7	1	5	8	2	9	4	3
2	4	8	3	9	7	1	5	6
5	9	3	1	4	6	8	7	2

174

2	4	6	9	5	1	3	7	8
9	3	8	4	6	7	2	1	5
5	7	1	2	3	8	6	4	9
6	8	4	3	9	5	1	2	7
7	1	5	8	2	6	9	3	4
3	2	9	7	1	4	8	5	6
1	9	7	6	4	3	5	8	2
4	5	2	1	8	9	7	6	3
8	6	3	5	7	2	4	9	1

175

2	3	7	8	1	6	5	4	9
1	8	6	5	9	4	3	7	2
9	4	5	7	2	3	1	6	8
8	1	9	3	4	7	2	5	6
6	7	2	1	8	5	9	3	4
4	5	3	9	6	2	7	8	1
7	6	1	2	5	8	4	9	3
5	2	4	6	3	9	8	1	7
3	9	8	4	7	1	6	2	5

176

6	8	9	2	7	3	4	5	1
5	3	7	9	1	4	8	2	6
4	1	2	8	6	5	3	7	9
7	5	8	1	3	2	6	9	4
9	2	6	5	4	8	7	1	3
3	4	1	7	9	6	5	8	2
1	7	3	6	8	9	2	4	5
8	6	5	4	2	1	9	3	7
2	9	4	3	5	7	1	6	8

177

4	3	8	7	5	9	1	2	6
7	9	1	4	2	6	8	5	3
6	2	5	1	3	8	4	9	7
1	6	7	8	9	3	5	4	2
2	5	9	6	7	4	3	8	1
3	8	4	2	1	5	7	6	9
8	7	3	5	6	2	9	1	4
9	4	2	3	8	1	6	7	5
5	1	6	9	4	7	2	3	8

178

1	7	8	9	5	6	2	3	4
6	3	9	2	8	4	7	1	5
2	4	5	7	1	3	8	6	9
5	1	7	4	6	2	3	9	8
9	2	3	5	7	8	1	4	6
4	8	6	1	3	9	5	2	7
3	5	4	6	2	7	9	8	1
8	9	1	3	4	5	6	7	2
7	6	2	8	9	1	4	5	3

179

9	2	1	3	8	5	7	4	6
3	5	4	7	9	6	1	2	8
8	6	7	2	1	4	3	5	9
1	3	8	4	6	9	2	7	5
7	4	6	8	5	2	9	3	1
2	9	5	1	7	3	8	6	4
5	8	9	6	3	7	4	1	2
4	1	3	5	2	8	6	9	7
6	7	2	9	4	1	5	8	3

180

6	1	8	4	9	2	3	7	5
3	7	2	1	5	8	6	4	9
4	5	9	7	6	3	1	8	2
7	2	6	8	1	9	4	5	3
1	9	5	2	3	4	8	6	7
8	3	4	6	7	5	2	9	1
2	6	3	9	4	7	5	1	8
5	4	7	3	8	1	9	2	6
9	8	1	5	2	6	7	3	4

181

7	8	4	2	5	6	9	1	3
5	9	3	8	1	7	4	2	6
6	2	1	9	3	4	8	7	5
8	4	9	3	2	1	5	6	7
2	6	5	7	4	9	1	3	8
1	3	7	6	8	5	2	4	9
9	5	6	4	7	2	3	8	1
4	1	8	5	6	3	7	9	2
3	7	2	1	9	8	6	5	4

182

5	4	7	8	3	6	9	1	2
1	9	8	5	7	2	4	3	6
2	3	6	4	1	9	7	8	5
4	6	9	1	5	7	3	2	8
3	5	2	6	4	8	1	9	7
8	7	1	2	9	3	6	5	4
6	2	3	9	8	4	5	7	1
9	1	4	7	2	5	8	6	3
7	8	5	3	6	1	2	4	9

183

1	3	8	9	2	7	6	5	4
9	4	2	5	8	6	7	1	3
5	6	7	1	3	4	9	2	8
8	2	9	6	1	5	3	4	7
6	1	5	4	7	3	8	9	2
3	7	4	2	9	8	5	6	1
7	9	1	8	5	2	4	3	6
4	5	3	7	6	1	2	8	9
2	8	6	3	4	9	1	7	5

184

1	2	4	3	6	7	8	9	5
9	3	8	5	1	4	6	7	2
5	6	7	9	2	8	4	1	3
6	9	1	4	8	3	2	5	7
7	8	2	1	5	9	3	4	6
4	5	3	2	7	6	1	8	9
3	1	6	8	9	5	7	2	4
8	4	9	7	3	2	5	6	1
2	7	5	6	4	1	9	3	8

185

8	6	5	3	2	4	1	7	9
1	9	3	6	5	7	8	4	2
4	7	2	8	9	1	5	6	3
2	3	7	5	1	9	6	8	4
9	8	4	2	7	6	3	5	1
5	1	6	4	3	8	9	2	7
3	4	1	7	6	5	2	9	8
6	2	8	9	4	3	7	1	5
7	5	9	1	8	2	4	3	6

186

3	9	6	1	8	2	4	5	7
7	5	2	9	6	4	1	8	3
1	8	4	5	3	7	9	6	2
2	7	3	6	5	9	8	1	4
9	4	1	3	2	8	5	7	6
5	6	8	7	4	1	3	2	9
8	1	7	2	9	3	6	4	5
6	2	9	4	1	5	7	3	8
4	3	5	8	7	6	2	9	1

187

6	7	5	2	8	9	4	3	1
1	4	3	7	6	5	9	2	8
8	2	9	3	4	1	6	7	5
5	6	1	8	3	2	7	4	9
4	9	7	5	1	6	3	8	2
2	3	8	9	7	4	1	5	6
3	8	2	6	9	7	5	1	4
9	5	4	1	2	3	8	6	7
7	1	6	4	5	8	2	9	3

188

5	6	9	2	3	1	4	7	8
8	4	2	7	5	6	1	9	3
3	1	7	4	8	9	6	2	5
9	2	1	6	7	5	8	3	4
6	8	4	3	1	2	9	5	7
7	3	5	9	4	8	2	6	1
2	5	3	1	6	4	7	8	9
4	7	6	8	9	3	5	1	2
1	9	8	5	2	7	3	4	6

189

1	6	5	3	9	4	7	8	2
8	7	2	6	5	1	4	3	9
4	9	3	2	8	7	6	5	1
2	3	9	7	6	5	1	4	8
6	8	7	4	1	2	3	9	5
5	1	4	8	3	9	2	7	6
7	5	8	1	2	3	9	6	4
9	4	1	5	7	6	8	2	3
3	2	6	9	4	8	5	1	7

190

2	9	8	7	6	5	4	3	1
1	7	5	9	3	4	8	2	6
3	6	4	1	2	8	9	5	7
8	5	2	4	1	7	6	9	3
9	3	1	6	5	2	7	4	8
6	4	7	3	8	9	5	1	2
5	2	6	8	4	3	1	7	9
4	1	9	2	7	6	3	8	5
7	8	3	5	9	1	2	6	4

191

4	8	3	2	7	9	1	5	6
9	1	2	6	4	5	3	7	8
5	7	6	1	8	3	2	4	9
1	5	7	9	3	6	8	2	4
2	4	8	5	1	7	9	6	3
3	6	9	8	2	4	5	1	7
7	9	4	3	5	1	6	8	2
6	2	5	4	9	8	7	3	1
8	3	1	7	6	2	4	9	5

192

3	7	6	8	9	2	1	4	5
4	9	2	6	1	5	8	3	7
5	1	8	4	7	3	9	2	6
6	2	4	7	3	8	5	9	1
8	3	7	9	5	1	4	6	2
9	5	1	2	6	4	7	8	3
7	6	3	5	8	9	2	1	4
1	4	9	3	2	7	6	5	8
2	8	5	1	4	6	3	7	9

193

2	8	4	7	6	3	1	5	9
7	5	1	4	8	9	2	3	6
9	6	3	1	2	5	8	4	7
1	4	6	8	9	7	3	2	5
8	7	9	3	5	2	4	6	1
3	2	5	6	4	1	9	7	8
6	9	8	2	7	4	5	1	3
4	3	7	5	1	8	6	9	2
5	1	2	9	3	6	7	8	4

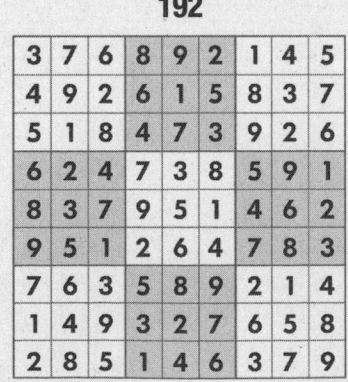

194

7	2	8	9	4	1	6	5	3
1	6	5	2	3	7	9	4	8
3	9	4	5	6	8	2	1	7
5	3	9	4	2	6	8	7	1
2	7	1	8	9	3	4	6	5
8	4	6	7	1	5	3	2	9
6	1	2	3	5	9	7	8	4
9	5	7	6	8	4	1	3	2
4	8	3	1	7	2	5	9	6

195

5	6	3	2	1	4	9	8	7
2	4	1	9	8	7	5	3	6
7	9	8	5	3	6	2	4	1
1	8	2	6	4	9	3	7	5
6	3	4	1	7	5	8	9	2
9	5	7	8	2	3	6	1	4
3	7	6	4	5	8	1	2	9
4	2	5	3	9	1	7	6	8
8	1	9	7	6	2	4	5	3

196

2	9	6	1	4	8	3	7	5
7	4	8	2	5	3	1	6	9
1	5	3	6	7	9	4	2	8
6	2	7	9	3	1	8	5	4
4	1	5	8	2	7	6	9	3
8	3	9	4	6	5	7	1	2
3	6	4	7	9	2	5	8	1
5	8	2	3	1	6	9	4	7
9	7	1	5	8	4	2	3	6

197

4	9	5	3	8	7	6	1	2
3	7	1	5	2	6	4	8	9
8	6	2	9	4	1	7	3	5
2	8	4	6	5	9	3	7	1
7	3	6	4	1	2	5	9	8
1	5	9	8	7	3	2	4	6
6	2	8	7	9	4	1	5	3
9	4	3	1	6	5	8	2	7
5	1	7	2	3	8	9	6	4

198

6	1	7	3	2	8	4	5	9
8	3	9	1	4	5	2	7	6
2	4	5	9	6	7	8	3	1
9	2	8	7	1	6	5	4	3
1	5	4	8	9	3	7	6	2
3	7	6	4	5	2	1	9	8
5	6	1	2	3	4	9	8	7
7	9	3	5	8	1	6	2	4
4	8	2	6	7	9	3	1	5

199

3	4	7	6	1	2	5	9	8
1	6	9	3	5	8	2	7	4
5	2	8	7	4	9	1	3	6
9	8	5	4	2	3	6	1	7
6	1	3	8	7	5	4	2	9
2	7	4	9	6	1	8	5	3
4	9	2	5	8	7	3	6	1
8	3	1	2	9	6	7	4	5
7	5	6	1	3	4	9	8	2

200

6	5	3	1	9	2	4	7	8
4	1	2	7	3	8	6	5	9
7	9	8	5	4	6	2	3	1
1	4	9	2	8	7	3	6	5
2	8	5	9	6	3	1	4	7
3	6	7	4	1	5	9	8	2
5	7	4	6	2	9	8	1	3
8	2	1	3	7	4	5	9	6
9	3	6	8	5	1	7	2	4

201

1	7	8	5	2	4	3	9	6
5	9	4	3	7	6	2	8	1
3	2	6	9	1	8	5	7	4
2	1	5	7	3	9	6	4	8
8	4	7	6	5	1	9	2	3
6	3	9	8	4	2	1	5	7
4	5	2	1	6	7	8	3	9
7	8	1	2	9	3	4	6	5
9	6	3	4	8	5	7	1	2

202

6	7	8	3	5	1	9	4	2
3	1	5	2	4	9	7	8	6
2	9	4	7	6	8	1	5	3
9	3	6	8	7	5	4	2	1
5	8	7	1	2	4	6	3	9
4	2	1	6	9	3	8	7	5
1	6	2	5	8	7	3	9	4
7	5	9	4	3	6	2	1	8
8	4	3	9	1	2	5	6	7

203

3	1	8	4	2	6	9	7	5
6	4	7	3	5	9	1	8	2
2	9	5	1	8	7	6	4	3
5	3	4	7	6	2	8	9	1
8	6	9	5	3	1	4	2	7
1	7	2	8	9	4	3	5	6
7	5	3	6	4	8	2	1	9
4	2	1	9	7	3	5	6	8
9	8	6	2	1	5	7	3	4

204

4	2	7	3	5	9	1	6	8
1	9	6	8	7	2	5	4	3
5	3	8	1	4	6	2	7	9
9	1	4	5	3	8	6	2	7
8	6	3	4	2	7	9	5	1
7	5	2	9	6	1	8	3	4
2	7	9	6	1	3	4	8	5
3	4	1	2	8	5	7	9	6
6	8	5	7	9	4	3	1	2

205

3	6	5	7	8	1	4	9	2
8	7	9	3	2	4	6	5	1
2	1	4	6	5	9	3	8	7
9	5	2	4	1	6	8	7	3
7	8	3	5	9	2	1	6	4
1	4	6	8	7	3	9	2	5
5	9	8	1	4	7	2	3	6
6	2	1	9	3	5	7	4	8
4	3	7	2	6	8	5	1	9

206

5	7	3	2	1	6	8	4	9
1	6	4	5	8	9	2	3	7
8	9	2	4	3	7	5	1	6
6	5	9	1	7	8	4	2	3
2	3	7	9	4	5	1	6	8
4	8	1	3	6	2	7	9	5
3	2	5	7	9	1	6	8	4
9	1	6	8	5	4	3	7	2
7	4	8	6	2	3	9	5	1

207

4	3	8	7	6	5	9	2	1
5	7	1	4	9	2	6	3	8
6	9	2	8	1	3	7	4	5
7	4	6	5	3	8	1	9	2
3	1	9	2	4	6	8	5	7
2	8	5	1	7	9	3	6	4
9	2	7	3	5	1	4	8	6
8	6	4	9	2	7	5	1	3
1	5	3	6	8	4	2	7	9

208

7	4	5	6	2	8	3	1	9
9	2	8	3	7	1	6	4	5
1	6	3	5	9	4	8	7	2
4	5	6	2	1	3	7	9	8
8	1	2	9	5	7	4	6	3
3	7	9	4	8	6	2	5	1
6	8	7	1	3	9	5	2	4
5	3	1	7	4	2	9	8	6
2	9	4	8	6	5	1	3	7

209

6	4	1	8	3	5	2	9	7
5	8	3	7	9	2	4	6	1
9	2	7	1	4	6	3	8	5
8	6	9	4	7	3	1	5	2
1	5	4	6	2	9	8	7	3
3	7	2	5	1	8	9	4	6
7	9	5	3	8	1	6	2	4
4	1	8	2	6	7	5	3	9
2	3	6	9	5	4	7	1	8

210

7	8	1	9	4	5	3	6	2
3	6	9	2	8	1	4	7	5
4	2	5	6	3	7	8	9	1
1	7	4	3	2	9	6	5	8
5	3	6	7	1	8	2	4	9
2	9	8	5	6	4	7	1	3
8	5	3	1	7	6	9	2	4
9	4	7	8	5	2	1	3	6
6	1	2	4	9	3	5	8	7

211

2	4	9	1	5	3	6	8	7
1	3	7	9	6	8	5	4	2
5	8	6	2	4	7	9	1	3
6	1	3	8	2	5	7	9	4
4	7	8	3	9	6	1	2	5
9	2	5	4	7	1	3	6	8
7	6	4	5	8	9	2	3	1
3	9	2	7	1	4	8	5	6
8	5	1	6	3	2	4	7	9

212

6	1	3	2	7	4	5	9	8
4	5	7	6	8	9	2	1	3
9	2	8	5	3	1	7	6	4
8	4	5	1	9	7	6	3	2
1	6	2	4	5	3	8	7	9
7	3	9	8	6	2	4	5	1
5	8	1	3	4	6	9	2	7
2	9	4	7	1	5	3	8	6
3	7	6	9	2	8	1	4	5

213

5	2	6	9	7	4	3	8	1
4	1	9	3	5	8	6	7	2
7	8	3	1	2	6	4	9	5
1	6	8	2	4	5	7	3	9
3	7	4	8	9	1	2	5	6
9	5	2	6	3	7	8	1	4
2	9	5	7	6	3	1	4	8
8	4	7	5	1	2	9	6	3
6	3	1	4	8	9	5	2	7

214

1	9	7	4	6	3	8	2	5
4	8	3	7	5	2	1	6	9
6	5	2	8	1	9	3	7	4
8	6	4	3	2	5	7	9	1
9	2	1	6	4	7	5	8	3
3	7	5	1	9	8	2	4	6
5	4	6	2	7	1	9	3	8
7	3	9	5	8	4	6	1	2
2	1	8	9	3	6	4	5	7

215

1	7	6	4	8	9	5	2	3
2	5	9	7	6	3	1	4	8
3	4	8	2	5	1	7	6	9
5	1	3	9	7	6	2	8	4
7	8	2	1	3	4	6	9	5
9	6	4	5	2	8	3	1	7
8	3	7	6	9	2	4	5	1
6	9	1	3	4	5	8	7	2
4	2	5	8	1	7	9	3	6

216

6	1	7	4	9	3	2	5	8
5	3	2	6	7	8	4	1	9
8	9	4	2	5	1	6	7	3
4	2	5	9	1	7	3	8	6
1	7	9	8	3	6	5	4	2
3	6	8	5	2	4	1	9	7
2	4	6	1	8	9	7	3	5
9	5	3	7	4	2	8	6	1
7	8	1	3	6	5	9	2	4

217

8	1	4	7	9	5	6	3	2
9	2	3	4	8	6	5	7	1
6	5	7	3	2	1	9	4	8
3	6	1	5	7	4	8	2	9
4	9	5	8	3	2	1	6	7
2	7	8	6	1	9	4	5	3
1	8	6	2	4	3	7	9	5
5	3	9	1	6	7	2	8	4
7	4	2	9	5	8	3	1	6

218

6	9	2	4	8	5	3	1	7
8	5	1	9	7	3	4	6	2
7	4	3	6	1	2	8	9	5
9	2	6	5	4	8	1	7	3
3	7	4	1	9	6	2	5	8
5	1	8	3	2	7	6	4	9
4	8	5	2	6	9	7	3	1
1	3	7	8	5	4	9	2	6
2	6	9	7	3	1	5	8	4

219

7	5	3	8	2	6	4	9	1
4	1	9	7	3	5	2	6	8
2	6	8	1	4	9	7	5	3
5	7	6	4	8	1	3	2	9
1	8	2	3	9	7	6	4	5
3	9	4	6	5	2	8	1	7
8	4	1	5	6	3	9	7	2
9	3	7	2	1	4	5	8	6
6	2	5	9	7	8	1	3	4

220

7	3	5	2	6	4	8	1	9
4	1	9	8	7	5	6	2	3
8	2	6	9	1	3	5	7	4
5	9	3	7	4	2	1	6	8
1	7	2	3	8	6	9	4	5
6	8	4	5	9	1	2	3	7
2	6	7	4	5	9	3	8	1
9	4	1	6	3	8	7	5	2
3	5	8	1	2	7	4	9	6

221

7	3	1	8	6	9	2	4	5
9	6	4	5	3	2	1	7	8
5	8	2	1	4	7	9	6	3
8	5	6	3	2	4	7	1	9
1	7	3	6	9	5	8	2	4
4	2	9	7	8	1	5	3	6
3	4	7	2	5	8	6	9	1
6	1	8	9	7	3	4	5	2
2	9	5	4	1	6	3	8	7

222

4	2	5	3	6	9	1	8	7
6	3	8	4	7	1	9	5	2
1	7	9	8	2	5	4	3	6
7	6	2	9	4	8	3	1	5
5	1	4	7	3	2	8	6	9
8	9	3	5	1	6	7	2	4
3	4	6	1	5	7	2	9	8
2	8	1	6	9	4	5	7	3
9	5	7	2	8	3	6	4	1

223

4	7	8	9	5	1	2	3	6
5	6	9	4	3	2	7	8	1
2	3	1	8	7	6	4	5	9
3	5	4	1	2	8	9	6	7
6	1	7	5	9	4	3	2	8
8	9	2	3	6	7	5	1	4
9	4	5	6	1	3	8	7	2
1	2	3	7	8	9	6	4	5
7	8	6	2	4	5	1	9	3

224

1	6	8	5	9	3	7	4	2
5	9	4	8	2	7	6	3	1
3	2	7	1	6	4	5	9	8
4	7	3	9	1	5	2	8	6
8	1	9	6	4	2	3	5	7
2	5	6	3	7	8	4	1	9
6	4	5	7	8	1	9	2	3
9	8	2	4	3	6	1	7	5
7	3	1	2	5	9	8	6	4

225

3	6	8	2	4	5	9	1	7
4	9	5	1	7	6	2	3	8
1	2	7	9	3	8	4	6	5
2	8	4	3	6	9	5	7	1
6	5	9	8	1	7	3	2	4
7	3	1	5	2	4	8	9	6
5	7	6	4	9	2	1	8	3
8	1	2	6	5	3	7	4	9
9	4	3	7	8	1	6	5	2

226

7	5	4	1	6	8	2	3	9
6	2	8	7	3	9	4	5	1
3	1	9	2	4	5	6	8	7
9	8	5	3	2	6	7	1	4
4	3	2	5	1	7	9	6	8
1	7	6	9	8	4	3	2	5
8	6	7	4	5	2	1	9	3
2	4	1	8	9	3	5	7	6
5	9	3	6	7	1	8	4	2

227

4	6	9	8	2	3	1	5	7
8	1	2	4	5	7	9	3	6
7	5	3	9	6	1	4	2	8
6	3	5	1	8	4	2	7	9
1	8	7	2	9	6	5	4	3
2	9	4	7	3	5	8	6	1
3	7	8	5	4	9	6	1	2
9	4	1	6	7	2	3	8	5
5	2	6	3	1	8	7	9	4

228

6	3	8	1	9	7	5	2	4
2	1	9	3	5	4	8	6	7
7	4	5	6	2	8	1	9	3
4	5	2	7	1	9	3	8	6
8	9	7	5	3	6	2	4	1
1	6	3	4	8	2	7	5	9
5	8	1	9	6	3	4	7	2
9	2	4	8	7	1	6	3	5
3	7	6	2	4	5	9	1	8

229

5	8	2	4	9	7	3	1	6
3	1	7	8	6	5	9	2	4
4	6	9	3	1	2	7	8	5
7	9	8	1	3	4	6	5	2
6	5	3	9	2	8	1	4	7
2	4	1	7	5	6	8	3	9
9	3	5	6	4	1	2	7	8
1	7	4	2	8	9	5	6	3
8	2	6	5	7	3	4	9	1

230

7	9	5	1	8	3	2	6	4
8	4	3	9	6	2	5	1	7
6	1	2	7	4	5	9	8	3
9	6	8	3	5	1	7	4	2
5	2	4	6	9	7	8	3	1
3	7	1	4	2	8	6	5	9
4	5	9	2	3	6	1	7	8
1	3	6	8	7	9	4	2	5
2	8	7	5	1	4	3	9	6

231

2	7	1	4	5	6	9	8	3
6	4	3	9	8	2	5	1	7
8	9	5	1	3	7	2	6	4
1	3	9	6	4	8	7	2	5
4	5	6	7	2	1	8	3	9
7	8	2	3	9	5	1	4	6
3	1	8	5	7	4	6	9	2
9	6	7	2	1	3	4	5	8
5	2	4	8	6	9	3	7	1

232

9	3	4	6	8	1	7	5	2
8	7	1	3	5	2	4	9	6
5	6	2	4	7	9	1	3	8
6	2	3	8	1	5	9	7	4
4	1	8	9	3	7	2	6	5
7	5	9	2	4	6	8	1	3
1	8	5	7	6	4	3	2	9
3	9	6	1	2	8	5	4	7
2	4	7	5	9	3	6	8	1

233

3	6	9	5	7	2	4	1	8
4	8	2	9	1	3	5	7	6
5	7	1	8	6	4	3	9	2
9	3	5	2	8	1	6	4	7
6	1	4	3	9	7	8	2	5
8	2	7	4	5	6	9	3	1
1	5	3	7	4	8	2	6	9
2	9	6	1	3	5	7	8	4
7	4	8	6	2	9	1	5	3

234

4	9	2	5	7	1	6	8	3
1	8	6	9	4	3	7	5	2
7	3	5	8	6	2	1	9	4
8	1	4	2	5	7	9	3	6
5	6	9	4	3	8	2	1	7
3	2	7	1	9	6	5	4	8
2	7	1	3	8	5	4	6	9
9	5	8	6	2	4	3	7	1
6	4	3	7	1	9	8	2	5

235

4	2	1	5	9	7	8	6	3
7	3	6	2	4	8	9	5	1
5	9	8	6	1	3	7	4	2
3	6	9	4	8	5	1	2	7
8	1	4	9	7	2	5	3	6
2	7	5	3	6	1	4	8	9
6	4	3	1	5	9	2	7	8
1	8	2	7	3	4	6	9	5
9	5	7	8	2	6	3	1	4

236

7	6	4	2	1	5	8	9	3
9	8	2	3	6	7	5	4	1
5	3	1	9	8	4	2	6	7
6	7	8	5	9	1	4	3	2
4	1	9	7	3	2	6	8	5
3	2	5	6	4	8	1	7	9
1	9	7	4	2	6	3	5	8
8	4	3	1	5	9	7	2	6
2	5	6	8	7	3	9	1	4

237

5	6	3	7	8	9	4	1	2
8	2	7	1	5	4	9	3	6
9	4	1	6	2	3	5	7	8
7	3	5	2	6	1	8	4	9
6	8	9	3	4	5	1	2	7
4	1	2	9	7	8	6	5	3
1	7	4	8	9	2	3	6	5
3	9	6	5	1	7	2	8	4
2	5	8	4	3	6	7	9	1

238

1	5	6	9	7	4	8	3	2
8	7	4	1	2	3	9	6	5
9	3	2	8	6	5	7	4	1
2	1	7	5	8	6	4	9	3
4	6	5	7	3	9	2	1	8
3	9	8	2	4	1	5	7	6
7	4	3	6	5	2	1	8	9
5	8	9	3	1	7	6	2	4
6	2	1	4	9	8	3	5	7

239

3	9	1	7	5	8	4	2	6
4	7	6	9	1	2	3	8	5
8	5	2	6	3	4	7	9	1
5	8	4	1	7	6	2	3	9
9	6	7	2	4	3	1	5	8
2	1	3	5	8	9	6	4	7
6	2	8	3	9	7	5	1	4
1	3	9	4	6	5	8	7	2
7	4	5	8	2	1	9	6	3

240

3	8	6	2	4	7	1	9	5
5	4	1	3	8	9	7	6	2
7	2	9	1	6	5	3	8	4
2	6	4	7	9	8	5	3	1
1	9	3	6	5	2	8	4	7
8	5	7	4	1	3	9	2	6
4	7	2	9	3	1	6	5	8
6	3	8	5	7	4	2	1	9
9	1	5	8	2	6	4	7	3

241

4	7	5	9	3	6	1	2	8
3	1	6	4	8	2	7	9	5
2	9	8	1	7	5	6	4	3
9	3	1	6	4	8	2	5	7
7	6	4	5	2	1	8	3	9
8	5	2	7	9	3	4	1	6
1	8	3	2	6	9	5	7	4
5	4	9	8	1	7	3	6	2
6	2	7	3	5	4	9	8	1

242

3	7	5	8	1	2	9	6	4
8	1	4	3	6	9	7	5	2
6	9	2	7	4	5	3	1	8
5	8	3	2	9	4	6	7	1
2	6	1	5	7	3	8	4	9
9	4	7	6	8	1	2	3	5
7	3	9	4	5	8	1	2	6
4	2	8	1	3	6	5	9	7
1	5	6	9	2	7	4	8	3

243

6	5	9	8	2	1	4	7	3
1	7	4	5	9	3	8	2	6
2	3	8	6	7	4	5	9	1
4	9	5	1	8	2	6	3	7
3	1	7	9	6	5	2	4	8
8	6	2	3	4	7	1	5	9
7	2	3	4	1	8	9	6	5
9	4	1	7	5	6	3	8	2
5	8	6	2	3	9	7	1	4

244

6	9	5	1	2	7	4	3	8
7	8	2	5	3	4	6	9	1
4	3	1	8	9	6	2	7	5
2	7	9	6	5	1	8	4	3
8	6	3	2	4	9	5	1	7
5	1	4	3	7	8	9	6	2
3	5	6	9	1	2	7	8	4
1	4	8	7	6	5	3	2	9
9	2	7	4	8	3	1	5	6

245

4	6	5	7	3	1	8	9	2
8	3	1	2	9	5	6	7	4
9	7	2	6	4	8	1	5	3
2	8	7	3	1	9	5	4	6
5	4	3	8	6	7	2	1	9
6	1	9	5	2	4	3	8	7
3	5	8	9	7	6	4	2	1
7	2	4	1	8	3	9	6	5
1	9	6	4	5	2	7	3	8

246

9	3	2	5	1	4	8	7	6
6	4	1	2	8	7	9	3	5
8	5	7	3	6	9	2	1	4
2	6	4	7	3	5	1	9	8
3	8	9	1	2	6	4	5	7
7	1	5	9	4	8	6	2	3
1	9	6	8	5	3	7	4	2
5	7	8	4	9	2	3	6	1
4	2	3	6	7	1	5	8	9

247

2	4	8	9	6	7	1	5	3
6	3	1	5	8	4	2	9	7
5	7	9	2	3	1	6	8	4
3	6	7	1	2	8	5	4	9
1	8	2	4	9	5	7	3	6
9	5	4	3	7	6	8	1	2
8	1	6	7	4	3	9	2	5
7	9	3	8	5	2	4	6	1
4	2	5	6	1	9	3	7	8

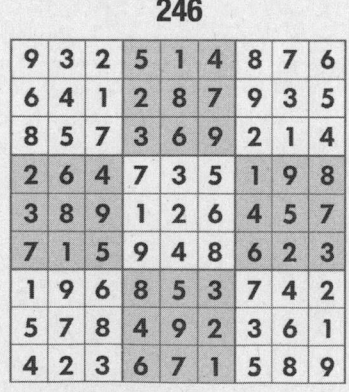

248

3	5	9	2	1	4	7	6	8
1	8	4	7	6	5	3	9	2
7	2	6	8	3	9	1	4	5
4	7	1	3	5	6	2	8	9
5	3	8	9	2	1	4	7	6
6	9	2	4	7	8	5	1	3
8	6	7	5	4	2	9	3	1
9	4	5	1	8	3	6	2	7
2	1	3	6	9	7	8	5	4

249

6	2	9	7	1	8	3	5	4
3	8	5	4	9	6	7	2	1
1	4	7	2	5	3	6	9	8
2	3	1	9	8	4	5	6	7
8	7	6	5	2	1	4	3	9
5	9	4	3	6	7	8	1	2
4	5	2	8	3	9	1	7	6
9	1	8	6	7	5	2	4	3
7	6	3	1	4	2	9	8	5

250

4	2	5	1	9	3	7	6	8
9	3	6	2	8	7	4	5	1
8	7	1	4	5	6	2	3	9
3	5	2	8	7	4	9	1	6
7	8	9	6	3	1	5	2	4
6	1	4	5	2	9	3	8	7
1	4	3	9	6	2	8	7	5
5	6	7	3	4	8	1	9	2
2	9	8	7	1	5	6	4	3

Word Roundup Solutions

251. CLARINET, TRUMPET, GUITAR, PIANO, BANJO, DRUM, HARP, OBOE, TUBA, LUTE—GIVING, GOING—VENUS, MARS—JUNE, JULY—BOB

252. PLUME, BOOM, ROOM, DOOM, ZOOM—ACCURATE, IDEOLOGY, ABRUPTLY, LOCATION—WHITE, BLACK, BROWN, BEIGE—TURTLE, SNAKE—EAST

253. PANTHER, LEOPARD, COUGAR, TIGER, PUMA, LION, LYNX—CLINTON, REAGAN, CARTER, OBAMA, FORD—GREECE, FRANCE—ARMY, NAVY—DAVID

254. FLAMINGO, PELICAN, GOOSE, DUCK, SWAN—RAINY, SNOWY, WINDY, SUNNY—CUBA, LAOS, PERU—PITCHER, CATCHER—TOM, SELLECK

255. HISTORY, SCIENCE, MATH—SNACKING, SOYBEANS, POINTING—ENGLAND, GERMANY, BELGIUM—GOLD, PINK, GRAY—JOHN, PAUL

256. BASKETBALL, FOOTBALL, BASEBALL, SOCCER, HOCKEY, RUGBY, POLO—KAYAK, FERRY, BARGE, CANOE—VERB, NOUN—FLEX, HOAX—ISLAND

257. DRUM, OBOE, LUTE, TUBA, HARP—NATIONAL, DICTATOR, NICOTINE, PACIFIER—MOOSE, MOLE, MULE—GEORGE, CLOONEY—MARK, TWAIN

258. GRIMACE, FROWN, SMILE, SMIRK, SNEER, GRIN—APOSTROPHE, HYPHEN, PERIOD, COLON, COMMA—CANADA, CUBA—JAMES, KIRK—WORM

259. LAGOON, OCEAN, LAKE, GULF, POND, COVE, SEA, BAY—SCIENCE, HISTORY, MATH—MOVIE, FLICK, FILM—SPADES, CLUBS—GRAY, GOLD

260. MANATEE, DOLPHIN, WALRUS, WHALE, SEAL—TANGERINE, ORANGE, LEMON, LIME—TOYOTA, HONDA, MAZDA—MILAN, ROME—FIVE

261. RETINA, CORNEA, PUPIL, LENS, IRIS—SATURN, EARTH, VENUS, MARS—PATIENTS, DOCTORS, NURSES—RUSSIA, ZAMBIA, INDIA—EAST, WEST

262. INCH, FOOT, YARD, MILE—ABSOLUTE, COMPRESS, CONTINUE, SPECIFIC—EGRET, ROBIN, GOOSE—GENERAL, MAJOR—MOAT

263. YOGURT, BUTTER, CHEESE, CREAM, MILK—SMELT, SHARK, PERCH, TROUT—PACIFIC, EASTERN, CENTRAL—TIGER—WORF

264. ANTARCTICA, AUSTRALIA, EUROPE, AFRICA, ASIA—ARMSTRONG, COLLINS, ALDRIN—BERLIN, BOGOTA, BERN—MILES, PER, HOUR—NICKNAME

265. SEPTEMBER, DECEMBER, OCTOBER, MARCH, APRIL, JUNE, JULY, MAY—SALAMI, TURKEY, HAM—KNIFE, SPOON, FORK—BLUE, GRAY—FROST

266. CHAIR, TABLE, DESK, SOFA, BED—SPORADIC, SPRINKLE, SOLUTION, POSITION—DRIVE, PUTT, CHIP—CANADA, MEXICO—JACK, KING

267. KNAPSACK, KNACK, KAYAK, KOOK, KINK, KICK—BANANA, PAPAYA, ORANGE, CHERRY—SOCK, SHOE, BOOT—ACROSS, DOWN—LUTE, HARP

268. MADAGASCAR, SINGAPORE, JAMAICA, ICELAND, CUBA—OSTRICH, PENGUIN, EMU—WHITE, BLUE, RED—OLIVER, STONE—HOTEL, MOTEL

269. BRUSSELS, WARSAW, ATHENS, LISBON, BERLIN, PARIS, ROME—MAMBO, TANGO, WALTZ, SALSA—PENN, TELLER—AHEAD—SHEEP

270. BEND, LEND, MEND, SEND, TEND, VEND—TEAL, BLUE, PINK, GRAY, GOLD—ZEBRA, ZILCH, ZESTY—GOPHER, GERBIL—WORLD, CUP

271. MINUTE, SECOND, DECADE, MONTH, WEEK, HOUR, YEAR—NATIONAL, HOCKEY, LEAGUE—ELECTRON, PROTON—TOM, HANKS—YAHOO

272. NICARAGUA, GUATEMALA, COLOMBIA, ECUADOR, CHILE, PERU—VANCOUVER, MONTREAL, TORONTO—UNCLE, AUNT—EAST, WEST—PORK

273. VIRGINIA, FLORIDA, ALASKA, HAWAII, TEXAS, OHIO—COUSIN, SISTER, MOTHER, FATHER—SMALL, MEDIUM, LARGE—DOCK—NINE

274. DOVE, CROW, DUCK, LARK, LOON, HAWK, TERN, WREN—RECEPTION, ATTENTION, INSPECTOR—GANDHI—FINGER—GECKO

275. MANDOLIN, VIOLIN, GUITAR, BANJO, VIOLA, CELLO, LUTE, HARP—ATLANTIC, PACIFIC, ARCTIC, INDIAN—JAZZ, FIZZ—PONTIAC—CIDER

276. WOLF, PUMA, LION, DEER, MULE, MOLE, GOAT, BEAR—REVERSE, NEUTRAL, DRIVE—ORANGE, LEMON, LIME—GEORGE, LUCAS—SEVEN

277. DAUGHTER, MOTHER, SISTER, NIECE, AUNT—BROWN, BEIGE, BLACK, BLUE—WALRUS, DONKEY, RABBIT—JULY, JUNE, MAY—FORTY

278. ONE, THREE, FIVE, SEVEN, NINE, ELEVEN, THIRTEEN, FIFTEEN—CEILING, FLOOR, WALL—MIDNIGHT, NOON—CANARY, CROW—STOP

279. FIRESTARTER, CHRISTINE, THINNER, MISERY, CARRIE, CUJO—MATCH, COURT, SERVE, DEUCE, FAULT—SATURDAY, SUNDAY—VERB, NOUN—ASIA

280. JUPITER, NEPTUNE, MERCURY, VENUS, MARS—NORTH, SOUTH, EAST, WEST—SUGAR, CREAM—STEVE, JOBS—FAMILY

281. SING, RING, WING, DING, KING—INDONESIA, TUNISIA, CHINA, INDIA, CUBA—MOVIE, FLICK, FILM—BRUCE, WILLIS—BEEF

282. SEPTEMBER, OCTOBER, MARCH, APRIL, JULY, MAY—TWENTY, THIRTY, FORTY, FIFTY—RAIN, SNOW—ANTARCTICA—WAFFLE

283. MULE, MOLE, DEER, BEAR, HARE, GOAT, LION, LYNX, SEAL—BUSINESS, MACHINES—GUITAR, CELLO—WILMA, FRED—COMMA

284. ALUMINUM, LITHIUM, NICKEL, COPPER, SILVER, GOLD, LEAD, IRON, TIN—OSTRICH, PENGUIN—ICELAND, CUBA—CANOE, OCEAN—WEST

285. KNAPSACK, KNOCK, KNACK, KAYAK, KICK, KINK—UNITED, ARAB, EMIRATES—HOME, BOX, OFFICE—MULE, MOLE—LAMB

286. RETINA, CORNEA, PUPIL, LENS, IRIS—CALIFORNIA, ALASKA, HAWAII—LAKE, POND, GULF—STEPHEN, KING—LISBON, ROME

287. APRICOT, AVOCADO, BANANA, ORANGE, CHERRY, APPLE, LEMON, PEACH, MANGO, PEAR—DETROIT, DALLAS, DENVER—MINK—STOP—SINK

288. KNUCKLE, ELBOW, ANKLE, KNEE—TRIUMPHS, HOSPITAL, STANDING, SIMPLEST—GREEN, BROWN, BEIGE, BLACK—JOHN, JOAN—PONY

289. VULTURE, CONDOR, FALCON, HAWK, OWL—PINK, TEAL, BLUE, GRAY, GOLD—RUSSIA, CANADA, ANGOLA—RINGO, STARR—STUMP

290. PREPOSITION, ADJECTIVE, NOUN, VERB—COLOMBIA, BRAZIL, CHILE, PERU—BOXING, RUGBY, POLO—JOHN, PAUL—JACK, KING

291. TWELVE, TWENTY, THIRTY, EIGHT, FORTY, FOUR, TWO, SIX, TEN—EVOLVE, SAVVY, VALVE, VIVID—YARD, MILE—BREAD—TRUE

292. ONE, THREE, FIVE, SEVEN, NINE, ELEVEN, THIRTEEN, FIFTEEN—SCORE, SPARE, FRAME—WINDY, RAINY—FOOT, ROOF—PIG

293. COLOMBIA, CAMBODIA, CANADA, CHINA, CHILE, CHAD, CUBA—SCIENCE, HISTORY, MATH—JAMES, KIRK—MARY—VERB

294. DOLPHIN, MANATEE, WALRUS, WHALE, OTTER, SEAL—MARINES, ARMY, NAVY—BOEING, AIRBUS—BEIGE, BLUE—HOPKINS

295. CHANNEL, PUDDLE, LAGOON, OCEAN, GULF, POND, LAKE, SEA, BAY—TENDER, GENDER, BENDER, SENDER—GOLD, LEAD—BACON—FOX

296. CENTURY, SECOND, MINUTE, DECADE, MONTH, WEEK, HOUR, YEAR—ATLANTIC, PACIFIC, ARCTIC, INDIAN—HOCKEY—TRUNK—NORTH

297. DAUGHTER, MOTHER, SISTER, NIECE, AUNT—WHIPSAW, WINDOW, WILLOW, WALLOW, WOW—GREEN, WHITE, RED—KAYAK, RADAR—EAST, WEST

298. DRUM, LUTE, HARP, OBOE—ADJUSTED, ALUMINUM, PLEASING, THANKFUL—POLISH, GERMAN, LATIN, GREEK—LEMON, LIME—GHOST

299. MICHIGAN, SUPERIOR, ONTARIO, HURON, ERIE—MARMOSET, RABBIT, GOAT, BAT, CAT—GREEN, GRAY, GOLD—KINGDOM—FARM

300. FURLONG, METER, INCH, FOOT, YARD, MILE—CRANE, STORK, ROBIN, GOOSE, EAGLE—CUBA, PERU, IRAN—PAUL, NEWMAN—COBALT

301. CLOUDY, STORMY, WINDY, RAINY, SNOWY, FOGGY, SUNNY, HAZY—FUCHSIA, MAGENTA—OFFENSE, DEFENSE—NOODLE, DOODLE—LONG

302. CENTURY, DECADE, MINUTE, MONTH, WEEK, YEAR, DAY—SINGLE, DOUBLE, TRIPLE—JUMP, JUST, JAIL—STAMP—FULL

303. SEPTEMBER, NOVEMBER, AUGUST, JUNE, JULY, MAY—HORROR, COMEDY, ACTION, DRAMA—BLUE, TEAL, GRAY—CANADA, MEXICO—CENTER

304. ARGENTINA, INDONESIA, ARMENIA, URUGUAY, UGANDA, INDIA, ITALY, IRAN—HYDROGEN, OXYGEN—DUCK, CROW—EAST, WEST—FAST

305. GROWING, GLOWING, GIVING, GONG, GIG—FIRST, SECOND, THIRD, FOURTH—GEORGE, JUDY, JANE—PETER, BENCHLEY—DISNEY, WORLD

306. ANTARCTICA, AUSTRALIA, AFRICA, EUROPE, ASIA—BEIGE, BROWN, BLUE—BEARS, BULLS, CUBS—WILL, SHORTZ—IRIS, LENS

307. PREPOSITION, ADJECTIVE, NOUN, VERB—NESMITH, DOLENZ, JONES, TORK—IRAN, CHAD, LAOS, PERU—KEVIN, COSTNER—SOLID, GAS

308. FOOL, GOOD, BOOM, MOON, FOOD, LOOK—MOTHER, FATHER, SISTER, COUSIN—POND, LAKE, GULF, COVE—SUMMER, WINTER, SPRING—CAT, DOG

309. TWILIGHT, TRUANT, TARGET, TAINT, TILT, TENT—VIOLIN, BANJO, CELLO, HARP—HEART, LIVER, BRAIN—COOLER—DRINK

310. SWEATER, PAJAMAS, JACKET, PANTS, SHIRT, SHOE, SOCK, HAT—FATHER, MOTHER—JERRY, SEINFELD—JOHN, ADAMS—HOME, BOX

311. LEND, TEND, VEND, MEND, BEND, SEND—LISBON, BERLIN, MADRID, ATHENS, ROME—OXYGEN, HELIUM—MOUSE, RAT—RAIN, SNOW

312. ENGLISH, SPANISH, RUSSIAN, FRENCH, GERMAN, POLISH, LATIN, THAI—STREAM, CREEK—BRIDE, GROOM—BUBBLE—SKUNK

313. THIRTEEN, ELEVEN, THREE, SEVEN, FIVE, NINE—HISTORY, SCIENCE, MATH—STEVEN, SPIELBERG—GREEN, WHITE—JOHN, PAUL

314. PENGUIN, PELICAN, PUFFIN, FALCON, RAVEN, WREN, SWAN, TERN—BACON, LETTUCE, TOMATO—SUGAR, CREAM—KING, JACK—BOB

315. STORMY, RAINY, SNOWY, WINDY, SUNNY, HAZY—GULF, POND, LAKE, COVE—INCH, FOOT, MILE, YARD—ROBIN, WILLIAMS—PEPSI, COKE

316. SCALLOP, OCTOPUS, OYSTER, SLUG, CLAM—WALRUS, MONKEY, RABBIT, JAGUAR, DONKEY—MITTEN, GLOVE—CHILE, CUBA—DEUCE

317. GIRAFFE, GAZELLE, ZEBRA, HORSE, CAMEL, SHEEP, DEER, COW, PIG—BUTTER, CHEESE—ARMY, NAVY—LEWIS—CIVIC

318. GRIMACE, SMILE, FROWN, SNEER, SMIRK, GRIN—SALSA, SAMBA, WALTZ, TANGO, MAMBO—EASTERN—JERSEY—DICE

319. WALLABY, WALRUS, WEASEL, WHALE, WOLF—THAILAND, TUNISIA, TURKEY—GENERAL, MAJOR—ALPHA, BETA—GRAY, GOLD

320. SPOON, KNIFE, FORK—NICARAGUA, GUATEMALA, PANAMA—PARTIAL, LUNAR, SOLAR—FISHER, HAMILL, FORD—RUSSELL, CROWE

321. MICHIGAN, MONTANA, FLORIDA, ALASKA, HAWAII, TEXAS, OHIO—WHITE, BROWN, BEIGE, GREEN—GOOSE, HERON—UNICORN—RIDLEY

322. PORPOISE, DOLPHIN, MANATEE, WALRUS, WHALE, SEAL—PATIENTS, DOCTORS, NURSES—ELVIS, PRESLEY—LEMON, LIME—FOOT

323. KNIGHT, BISHOP, KING, ROOK, PAWN—MERCURY, NEPTUNE, SATURN, VENUS—SHARK, PERCH, TROUT—RICHARD, STARKEY—TURKEY, PIGEON

324. TALL, CALL, WALL, BALL, HALL, MALL—APPLE, GUAVA, PEACH, MANGO, LEMON—BARRIER, CARRIER, TERRIER—TOM, HANKS—CHILD

325. COLOMBIA, JAMAICA, ECUADOR, MEXICO, BRAZIL, CHILE, CUBA, PERU—ORANGE, GREEN, WHITE—GOOSE, DUCK—CENTIPEDE—WAVE

Hidato Solutions

326

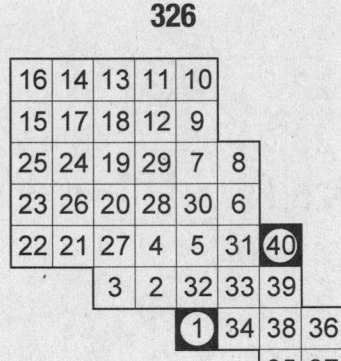

16	14	13	11	10		
15	17	18	12	9		
25	24	19	29	7	8	
23	26	20	28	30	6	
22	21	27	4	5	31	40
	3	2	32	33	39	
		1	34	38	36	
			35	37		

327

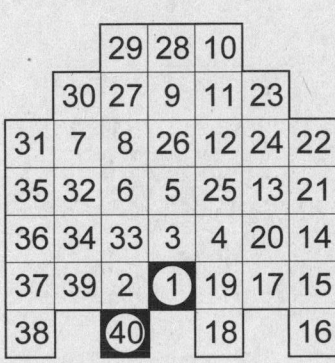

	29	28	10			
	30	27	9	11	23	
31	7	8	26	12	24	22
35	32	6	5	25	13	21
36	34	33	3	4	20	14
37	39	2	1	19	17	15
38		40		18		16

328

23	25	26	27	35	34
24	22	28	29	33	36
21	19	12	30	31	32
20	13	18	11	5	6
14	17	1	4	10	7
15	16	2	3	9	8

329

11	10	40	39	38	37	36
12	8	9	41	32	31	35
7	13	42		33	34	30
14	6				29	27
5	15				28	26
1	4	16	18	19	25	24
2	3	17	20	21	22	23

330

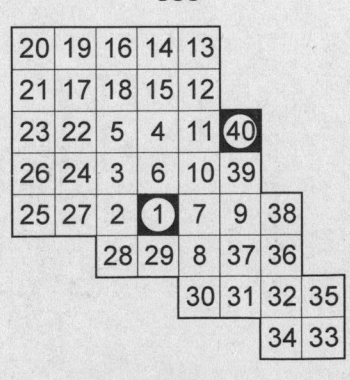

20	19	16	14	13		
21	17	18	15	12		
23	22	5	4	11	40	
26	24	3	6	10	39	
25	27	2	1	7	9	38
	28	29	8	37	36	
		30	31	32	35	
				34	33	

331

		38	40	36	35	34
		39	37	7	32	33
	3	4	8	6	26	31
	2	9	5	25	27	30
1	11	10	24	22	28	29
	18	19	12	21	23	
15	17	13	20			
16	14					

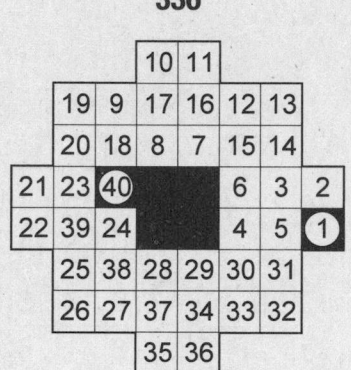

332

	15	13	8	7	5	4
16	■	14	12	9	6	3
17	32	■	11	10	2	38
31	18	33	■	(1)	37	39
19	30	29	34	■	36	40
20	21	28	25	35	■	41
22	23	24	27	26	(42)	

333

	17	19	28			
	16	18	29	20	27	
15	14	13	30	21	23	26
(40)	32	31	12	22	24	25
39	33	11	10	(1)	2	3
38	36	34	9	7	6	4
37		35		8		5

334

21	22	23	6	5		
20	16	8	7	24	4	3
19	17	15	9	25	26	2
18		14	10	27		(1)
		11	13	28		
	36	35	12	29	32	
(39)	38	37	34	33	30	31

335

	6	7	8	16	17	
5	4	9	15	18	23	22
(1)	3	14	10	24	19	21
2		11	13	25		20
		36	12	26		
	35	37	27	28	29	
(39)	38	34	33	32	31	30

336

	10	11					
19	9	17	16	12	13		
20	18	8	7	15	14		
21	23	(40)	■	■	6	3	2
22	39	24	■	■	4	5	(1)
	25	38	28	29	30	31	
	26	27	37	34	33	32	
		35	36				

337

22	21	20	(36)	18	17
23	24	35	19	16	15
25	32	34	(1)	14	12
31	26	33	2	13	11
30	27	3	6	8	10
28	29	5	4	7	9

338

(36)	35	5	20	21	22
3	4	34	6	19	23
(1)	2	7	33	18	24
10	8	32	31	17	25
9	11	14	16	30	26
12	13	15	29	28	27

339

	8	7	5			
	16	9	6	4	(40)	
15	13	17	10	3	(1)	39
14	18	12	11	31	2	38
21	20	19	30	33	32	37
22	24	26	27	29	34	36
23		25		28		35

340

	21	22	19			
	27	26	20	23	18	
28	29	30	25	24	36	17
8	9	10	31	35	16	37
7	5	32	11	34	15	38
6	2	4	33	12	14	39
(1)		3		13		(40)

341

48	47	46	14	13	12	9
(49)	17	15	45	11	10	8
18	16	24	25	44	7	42
19	23	22	26	6	43	41
20	21	27	5	4	3	40
29	28	32	33	36	39	2
30	31	34	35	37	38	(1)

342

					41	(44)	
34	36	38	39	40	43	42	
35	33	37	18	17	14	13	
	32	19	16	15	11	12	
	20	31	30	10	4	5	
	21	22	29	9	3	7	6
	24	23	27	28	8	2	(1)
	25	26					

343

	37	36	39	41			
34	35	38	9	40	42		
33	31	■		8	10	45	43
30	32	■	12	11	7	(46)	44
29	18	13	14	15	■	6	5
19	28	17	16	■		2	4
	20	27	22	23	(1)	3	
	21	26	25	24			

344

	26	25	23	22	21	20
	28	27	24	13	14	19
30	29	■	■	11	12	15	18
32	31	■	■	10	9	16	17
33	46	45	44	■	■	8	7
34	47	43	41	■	■	5	6
(48)	35	42	(1)	40	4
36	37	38	39	2	3

345

	29	30	31				
27	28	36	33	32	7		
26	37	35	34	6	5	8	
24	25	40	38	3	4	9	11
23	41	21	39	2	14	10	12
42	22	19	20	(1)	15	13	
43	18	45	16	47	(48)		
44	17	46					

346

		38	37						
		39	36						
	41	40	34	35	13	12			
	(56)	42	33	16	14	11			
55	43	19	17	32	15	9	10		
54	44	18	20	31	8	7	6		
53	50	45	46	21	30	29	(1)	2	5
51	52	49	48	47	22	27	28	3	4
		23	26						
		24	25						

347

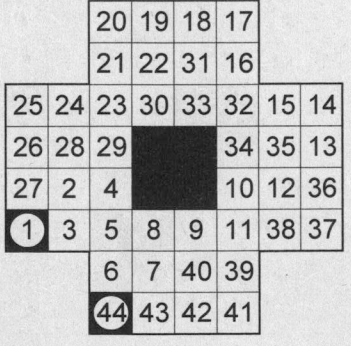

	20	19	18	17			
	21	22	31	16			
25	24	23	30	33	32	15	14
26	28	29	■	34	35	13	
27	2	4	■	10	12	36	
(1)	3	5	8	9	11	38	37
	6	7	40	39			
	(44)	43	42	41			

348

				31	32		
42	(44)	19	20	29	30	33	
43	41	40	18	21	28	34	
	16	17	39	22	35	27	
	14	15	38	36	23	26	
	13	11	37	6	25	24	(1)
	12	10	7	5	4	3	2
	9	8					

349

41	42	43	35	34	33	32
40	38	36	(44)	28	27	31
39	37	■	■	26	29	30
9	8	■	■	25	24	23
7	10	11	12	■	22	21
6	4	(1)	13	16	20	19
5	3	2	14	15	17	18

350 **351** **352**

353 **354** **355**

356 **357** **358**

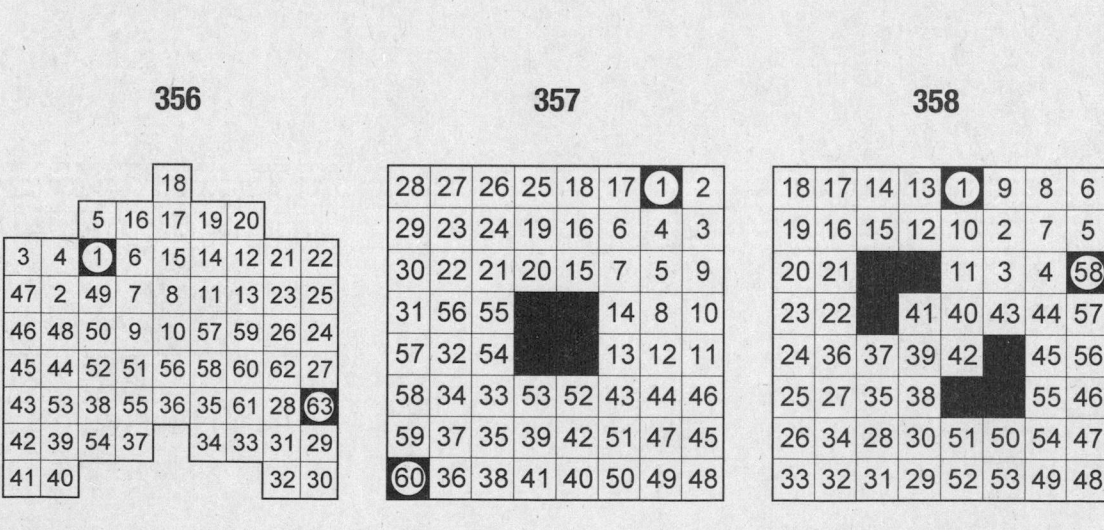

359

3	5	7	8	9
2	4	6	11	10
(1)	13	12	25	26
14	16	24	23	27

15	17	20	22	36	28	29	32	31	47
18	19	21	37	38	35	33	30	46	48

39	34	44	45	49
40	43	56	55	50
42	41	57	51	54
(60)	59	58	52	53

360

	3	(1)		13		36		
5	4	2	11	12	33	14	35	37
	6	9	10	32	15	34	38	
7	8	30	31	19	17	16	41	39
	28	29	20	21	18	42	40	
(65)	27	26	23	22	43	44	45	46
	64	24	25	57	53	52	47	
63	61	60	58	56	54	50	51	48
	62		59		55		49	

361

(60)	59	58	56	54	52		
5	6	3	(1)	57	55	53	51
7	4	19	2	33	34	35	50
8	20	18	16	47	32	49	36
21	9	15	17	46	48	31	37
22	10	14	12	45	30	39	38
23	25	11	13	44	29	42	40
	24	26	27	28	43	41	

362

12	13	14	58	16	18	20	21	
11	10	59	15	57	17	19	■	22
63	62	9	60	56	55	■	50	23
64	8	61	6	54	■	51	24	49
65	67	7	5	■	53	52	25	48
68	66	4	■	44	45	32	47	26
69	70	■	3	43	33	46	31	27
71	■	2	42	34	35	36	30	28
(72)	(1)	41	40	39	38	37	29	

363

	56	55	54	53	2	(1)	
58	57	7	5	3	52	44	43
59	8	6	4	51	45	40	42
(60)	9	10	50	46	39	41	36
12	11	17	47	49	38	37	35
13	19	18	16	48	27	28	34
20	14	15	24	26	29	32	33
21	22	23	25	30	31		

364

	33		27		25		17	
35	34	32	28	26	24	20	16	18
	36	31	29	23	21	15	19	
37	38	55	30	22	52	51	14	13
	56	39	54	53	49	50	12	
57	40	41	42	47	48	11	7	6
	58	44	43	46	10	8	5	
60	59	62	45	64	9	(1)	2	4
	61		63		(65)		3	

365

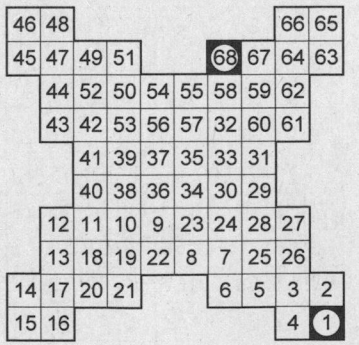

46	48					66	65
45	47	49	51		(68)	67	64	63
	44	52	50	54	55	58	59	62
	43	42	53	56	57	32	60	61
		41	39	37	35	33	31	
		40	38	36	34	30	29	
	12	11	10	9	23	24	28	27
	13	18	19	22	8	7	25	26
14	17	20	21		6	5	3	2
15	16					4	(1)	

366

	62	61	58	59	24	23	21	
(65)	63	■	60	57	25	■	22	20
64	■		56	26	27	■		19
37	36	55	33	32	31	28	18	17
38	54	35	34	9	8	30	29	16
39	53	52	51	7	10	12	13	15
40	■		50	6	11	■		14
41	43	■	49	46	5	■	3	2
	42	44	45	48	47	4	(1)	

367

(60)	42	41	40	39					
59	43	44	37	38					
58	57	46	45	36					
56	48	47	35	33					
55	52	49	34	30	32	21	19	17	16
53	54	51	50	29	31	20	22	18	15
					28	24	23	14	13
					27	25	7	8	12
					26	6	3	9	11
					5	4	2	(1)	10

368

	52		50		45		41	
53	54	51	49	46	44	43	42	40
	56	55	47	48	17	20	39	
59	58	57	14	16	18	19	21	38
	60	12	13	15	23	22	37	
61	11	10	9	24	26	36	35	34
	62	6	8	25	27	28	33	
64	63	5	7	3	(1)	29	31	32
(65)		4		2			30	

369

43	42	38	37	55	56	57	59
44	41	39	54	36	35	58	60
47	45	40	53	13	34	61	(62)
46	48	50	12	52	14	33	
	49	11	51	18	16	15	32
9	10	5	20	19	17	30	31
8	6	4	21	22	24	29	27
7	(1)	2	3	23	25	26	28

370

	53		57		60		62	
51	52	54	56	58	59	61	64	63
	50	55	22	23	25	27	(65)	
48	49	46	21	24	26	28	31	30
	47	45	20	19	33	32	29	
13	14	15	44	17	18	34	35	36
	12	8	16	43	3	2	37	
11	9	7	6	4	42	40	(1)	38
	10		5		41		39	

371

47	45	44	10	9	7	5	(1)
48	46	11	43	8	6	4	2
49	51	42	12	14	16	18	3
50	52	41	13	15	17	19	
	53	40	39	24	23	22	20
57	54	55	38	25	27	28	21
58	56	61	37	26	33	32	29
59	60	(62)	36	35	34	31	30

372

28	27	26	25	43	42	41	40	39	38
	29	30	44	24	22	21	36	37	
		45	31	23	20	34	35		
			46	32	33	19			
			47	18					
			17	48					
		16	49	51	53				
	4	15	6	50	52	54			
3	14	5	7	10	9	55	58		
2	(1)	13	12	11	8	56	57	59	(60)

373

				5	6	10	11			
				4	7	9	12			
				61	3	8	13			
55	57	58	60	62	2	(1)	14	15	23	
54	56	59	47	46	63	(64)	16	24	22	
53	49	48	41	40	45	17	18	25	21	
52	51	50	39	42	43	44	26	19	20	
				38	32	33	27			
				37	34	31	28			
				36	35	30	29			

374

			32	30	29	28			
			33	31	27	26			
			34	19	20	25			
40	36	35	49	18	17	21	24	5	4
41	39	37	50	48	16	22	23	6	3
42	38	51	46	47	12	15	9	7	2
43	44	45	52	13	14	11	10	8	(1)
			53	58	61	60			
			57	54	59	62			
			56	55	(64)	63			

375

34	35	36	29	38	39	44	43
33	31	30	37	28	40	42	45
32	22	23	25	26	27	41	46
21	20	24	50	49	48	47	
	16	19	5	51	53	61	(62)
15	17	18	4	6	52	54	60
14	12	10	7	3	56	55	59
13	11	9	8	(1)	2	57	58

376

80	(81)	35	34	33	32	31	28	27
79	78	36	6	8	30	29	25	26
77	37	5	7	9	11	24	23	22
76	74	38	4	10	(1)	12	21	20
75	73	39	40	3	2	13	15	19
67	69	72	71	41	42	14	16	18
68	66	70	58	56	43	51	50	17
63	65	59	57	55	44	52	49	48
64	62	61	60	54	53	45	46	47

377

```
    78  12  11   9  20  21
76  77  14  13  10   8  19  27  22  23
75 (1)  2  15  16  18   7  28  26  24
74  73  72   3  17   6  32  29  30  25
        71   4   5  33  34  31
        70  69  ██  35  36
63  62  65  68  ██  38  37  41  42
61  64  67  66  ██  39  40  46  43
60  59  57  55  53  52  49  47  45  44
        58  56  54  51  50  48
```

378

```
73  75  76  77  15  79 (80)  7   6   5
74  72  70  14  78  16   8   2   3   4
        71  69  13  10   9  17  18 (1)
        65  66  68  12  11  22  19  20
            64  67  ██  ██  23  21
            62  63  ██  ██  43  24
        61  48  47  46  44  42  25  26
        60  52  49  45  40  41  29  27
55  53  59  51  50  38  39  28  30  31
54  56  57  58  37  36  35  34  33  32
```

379

```
69  71  72  73  74  75  31  28 (84) 83
68  70  36  35  76  32  30  29  27  82
67  38  37  34  33  77  78  79  81  26
66  64  39  ██████████████  80  23  25
65  63  40  ██████████████  22  21  24
43  41  62  ██████████████  20   6   5
44  42  61  ██████████████  19   7   4
45  50  60  59  58  57   9   8  18   3
46  49  51  53  56  11  10  16  17   2
47  48  52  54  55  12  13  14  15 (1)
```

380

```
12  13  14  15  16  18  19  20  23
11   9   8   2   3  17  21  22  24
10  49   7  (1)  5   4  30  27  25
46  48  50   6  ██      31  29  28  26
47  45  51  ██  ██  ██  32  74 (76)
44  43  52  63  ██  37  73  33  75
54  53  42  62  64  38  36  72  34
55  58  61  41  39  65  68  35  71
57  56  59  60  40  66  67  69  70
```

381

```
    43  42 (77) 75  74  73  67
40  41  44  76  64  65  66  72  68
39  37  45  47  51  63  62  69  71
38  36  46  48  50  52  56  61  70
27  26  35  49  53  55  57  58  60
28  25  34  23   6  54   8   9  59
29  33  24  22   5   7  10  11  13
30  32   3   4  21  19  17  14  12
31   2  (1) 20  18  16  15
```

382

```
 7   9  10  11          58  60  63  62
 6   8  12  14          57  59  61  64
 5   4  13  15          56  54  67  65
(1)  3  17  16          55  68  53  66
 2  23  22  18  42  44  45  69  70  52
25  24  21  41  19  43  46  47  51  71
26  39  40  20          48  50  75  72
27  29  38  31          49  76  73  74
28  37  30  32          82 (84) 77  79
36  35  34  33          83  81  80  78
```

383

```
11   7   6  76  75  74  73  72  71
12  10   8   5  77  78  79  69  70
13   9   2   3   4  80  27  67  68
14  16  (1) 21 (81) 26  66  28  30
15  17  20  22  25  65  64  31  29
52  18  19  23  24  63  36  32  33
53  51  48  47  46  62  37  35  34
54  50  49  59  45  61  38  42  41
55  56  57  58  60  44  43  39  40
```

384

```
    21  20  18  15  16   2
28  22  23  24  19  17  14 (1)  3   4
29  27  26  25  39  38  12  13   5   6
30  31  32  40  34  37  11   9   8   7
        41  33  35  36  10  59
        44  42  ██████  58  60
47  48  45  43  ██████  57  55  61  62
(78)46  49  72  ██████  56  54  64  63
77  76  73  50  71  52  53  67  66  65
        75  74  51  70  69  68
```

385

```
    34  33  38  39  42  43
29  31  32  35  37  41  40  44  46  48
28  30  25  68  36  55  54  45  47  49
27  26  24  69  67  56  53  52  51  50
        70  23  66  65  57  58
        22  71  ██████  64  59
(78)21  73  72  ██████  63  61  60  11
77  74  20   2  ██████  62  13  12  10
75  76  (1) 19   3   4  14   6   8   9
        18  17  16  15   5   7
```

386

					36	35			
74	72		38	37	34	1	2	3	
73	75	71	70	40	39	33	9	8	4
76	67	68	69	41	32	10	13	7	5
77	66	65	64	31	42	11	12	14	6
78	62	63	44	43	30	29	23	22	15
79	61	45	59	57	28	27	24	21	16
80	46	60	58	56	55	26	25	20	17
47	48	49	52	53	54			19	18
	50	51							

387

61	59	58	57				84	83	82	81
62	60	56	68				45	44	75	80
63	66	67	55	69	46	43	74	79	76	
65	64	54	52	47	70	73	42	77	78	
		53	51	48	71	72	41			
		50	49	19	38	39	40			
9	10	12	13	18	20	37	36	30	29	
8	11	14	15	17	21	22	35	28	31	
6	7	1	16			23	27	34	32	
5	4	3	2			24	25	26	33	

388

70	69	74	75	76	77	60	79	81
71	73	68	63	62	61	78	59	80
72	67	1	65	64	57	58	35	36
5	4	66	2	55	56	34	33	37
6	8	3	54	52	50	31	32	38
7	10	9	53	51	49	30	39	40
12	11	19	21	22	48	29	46	41
14	13	18	20	23	28	47	45	42
15	16	17	24	25	26	27	44	43

389

66	65	70	71	72	4	6	77	78	79
67	69	64	73	3	5	76	7	82	80
68	63	62	2	74	75	84	83	8	81
60	61	1	■	■	■	■	9	12	13
56	59	58	■	■	■	■	10	11	14
55	57	45	■	■	■	■	18	17	15
54	46	44	■	■	■	■	19	22	16
53	47	43	41	40	25	24	23	20	21
52	48	42	39	36	26	27	28	32	31
51	50	49	38	37	35	34	33	29	30

390

						80	78		
52	53			74	75	79	77	10	9
51	54	55	56	73	1	76	7	8	11
50	49	57	72	71	2	4	5	6	12
44	43	48	58	61	70	3	68	14	13
45	47	42	60	59	62	69	67	15	16
46	40	41	30	63	64	24	66	17	18
38	39	31	29	28	25	65	23	22	19
37	36	34	32	27	26			21	20
		35	33						

391

	36	63	64	65	69	70	4	
35	37	62	66	68	71	3	2	5
34	32	38	61	67	72	58	6	1
33	31	39	40	60	59	73	57	7
28	29	30	41	75	74	9	8	56
27	22	23	76	42	10	44	55	54
26	24	21	77	11	43	45	53	52
25	20	18	12	13	14	46	49	51
	19	17	16	15	47	48	50	

392

	49	74	75	76	77	3			
	48	50	52	73	1	2	78	4	
47	43	51	■	53	72		7	9	5
46	44	42	■	71	54		8	6	10
45	41	63	70	69	68	55	57	12	11
39	40	64	62	61	67	58	56	13	14
38	34	■	65	66	60	59	■	16	15
37	33	35	■	■	■		17	18	19
	36	32	30	27	26	23	22	20	
	31	29	28	24	25	21			

393

	11	69	68	67	66	65			
8	9	10	12	70	71	72	64	63	62
7	5	13	2	1	74	73	55	61	60
6	14	4	3	75	53	54	56	58	59
		15	76	77	78	52	57		
		16	17	■		51	50		
22	21	18	19	■		41	43	49	48
23	26	20	31	■		42	40	44	47
25	24	27	30	32	34	38	39	45	46
	29	28	33	35	36	37			

394

30	29	28	18	17	16	1	2	3	4
31	27	19	20	15	13	11	10	5	6
32	34	26	22	21	14	12	9	8	7
33	35	25	23	78					
39	40	36	24	79	77	74	73	72	71
38	37	41	42	43	80	76	75	68	70
				44	81	67	69	90	
54	53	52	51	45	46	82	83	66	89
55	57	59	50	49	48	47	65	84	88
56	58	60	61	62	63	64	85	86	87

395

11	12	16	17	20	21	23	27	28	29
10	13	15	18	19	22	24	25	26	30
9	14							31	32
(1)	8	(82)	80	78	77			33	35
2	7	81	70	79	76			34	36
3	6	71	68	69	75			37	38
4	5	67	72	73	74			40	39
59	58		66	53				41	42
60	63	57	65	54	50	52	47	46	43
61	62	64	56	55	51	49	48	45	44

396

60	62	64	65	66	121	122	123	125	126	128	129
59	61	63	49	67	69	120	124	118	127	131	130
58	56	50	48	68	71	70	119	136	117	134	132
57	55	51	47	72	73	75	137	108	135	116	133
54	52	45	46	77	76	74	138	109	107	(1)	115
53	44	43	42	78			139	106	110	2	114
83	82	81	41	79		(140)	105	111	113	3	
84	85	40	80	89	90	98	97	104	112	4	5
38	39	86	87	88	99	91	103	96	95	8	6
36	37	30	28	100	101	102	92	94	15	9	7
35	31	29	27	25	23	21	93	16	10	14	13
34	33	32	26	24	22	20	19	18	17	11	12

397

	119	120	121	122	98	97	95	87			
	118	104	103	102	99	123	96	86	94	88	
117	116	106	105	100	101	124	85	83	93	92	89
115	108	107		(126)	125	84	82	80	91	90	
109	114	113		27	26	22	21	81	79	78	77
41	110	111	112	28	23	25	20	70	72	74	76
42	40	39	29	30	32	24	69	19	71	73	75
43	45	38	37	35	31	33	68		18	13	14
46	44	53	52	36	34	67		12	17	15	
47	54	55	56	51	66	65	3	2	9	11	16
	48	57	50	60	61	64	4	8	(1)	10	
	49	58	59	63	62	5	6	7			

398

67	69	71	75	76		84	86	87	96	97	
66	68	70	72	74	77	83	85	89	88	95	98
65	63	61	73	78	80	81	82	90	91	99	94
64	62	60	59	79	12	11	102	101	100	92	93
51	52	53	55	58	13	10	103	108	109	110	111
	50	54	56	57	9	14	104	107	114	112	
	49	46	19	17	15	8	105	106	113	115	
48	47	20	45	18	16	123	7	6	5	118	116
25	23	21	44	42	40	122	124	120	119	4	117
26	24	22	43	41	39	38	121	125	126	(1)	3
27	29	31	34	35	37	129	130	127	132	2	(136)
28	30	32	33	36		128	131	133	134	135	

399

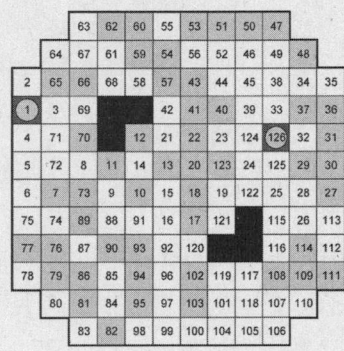

400

Andrews McMeel Publishing
a division of Andrews McMeel Universal
1130 Walnut Street, Kansas City, Missouri 64106

www.andrewsmcmeel.com
puzzles.usatoday.com

22 23 24 25 26 PAH 10 9 8 7 6 5 4 3 2 1

ISBN: 978-1-5248-6995-3

Editor: Patty Rice
Art Director/Designer: Spencer Williams
Production Editor: Meg Daniels
Production Manager: Julie Skalla

Attention: Schools and Businesses
Andrews McMeel books are available at quantity discounts with bulk purchase for educational, business, or sales promotional use. For information, please e-mail the Andrews McMeel Publishing Special Sales Department: specialsales@amuniversal.com.